Newcastle United

Day by Day

1892 - 2015

Bumper book of historical facts and trivia for every day of the year.

Kenneth H Scott

Published by KayLynM Publishing
Newcastle upon Tyne, England

ISBN: 978-0-9934201-0-8

DEDICATION

This book is dedicated to every Newcastle United Fan wherever you may be...

Together we have experienced the highs and lows of following our beloved Newcastle United and despite the rollercoaster of emotions that is associated with our allegiance we remain proud members of the Toon Army!

Special thanks has to go to my wife and daughters without whose tolerance and support this book would not have been possible. So to Lynn (my wife), Kayleigh, Lynsey and Megan (our daughters) a very special thank you.

Howay the Lads - *and Lasses*!

Table of Contents

ACKNOWLEDGEMENTS

During the course of authoring this book I have had the opportunity to collect and read many fantastic books by other authors on both the subject of football in general and Newcastle United in particular. Add to this an expansive collection of match day programmes, and other officially produced paraphernalia, never forgetting the huge amount of information available on the Internet and many, many hours spent in various libraries the research has been long but invariably interesting and enjoyable.

So I would like to thank each and every one of those people - far too numerous to mention by name, and some of whom I unfortunately never got to know their name - but without each and every one of them there would have been no motivation for this book. Also to anyone who has written an article in newspapers, or books or who has taken the time to populate some excellent websites my thanks go to you too. This is acknowledgement of your very valued contribution.

Special mentions go to **Matt Steel** and **PinkTeaVanity**.

Matt is a keen photographer and provided the cover image of the Tyne Bridge. To me the Tyne Bridge epitomises what Newcastle is and arriving back from 'away days' its sight was a one that meant you were 'home'. Whether you were elated with a win, comfortable with a draw or despondent with a loss the Tyne Bridge could almost capture your mood in its magnificence and sometimes stark coldness. Matt captures this perfectly I think in his photograph. Thanks Matt.

PinkTeaVanity is a local artist, a lady of many talents. She provided the sketches used within these pages. Again the imagery PinkTeaVanity provides captures the at times energetic, yet other times drabness, of being an always proud member of the Toon Army.

Thank you all.

INTRODUCTION

There is no doubt that Newcastle United have been involved in some absolutely brilliant games over the years. There's been the truly memorable games such as the thrilling 4-3 defeat to Liverpool (03/04/1996) that even though Newcastle lost, the game stays in the memory as an exceptional advert for football. There was the thrilling fight-back in the 4-4 draw with Arsenal where after being 4-0 down after only 26 minutes, Newcastle clawed their way back into the game to score 4 themselves in the last 22 minutes. The great 5-1 win over Sunderland (31/10/2010) and 5-0 win over Manchester United (20/10/1996) and of course the two-legged final win over Ujpesti Dozsa to win the Inter-Cities Fairs Cup, *unfortunately the last major trophy I have had the pleasure of seeing Newcastle win.*

We don't want to mention the succession of 'derby' defeats to Sunderland over the last few seasons, or the time they beat us 9-1 at St James's Park! Nor do we want to remember the heartbreak of losing in six FA Cup finals and the League Cup final. However, they did unfortunately happen so they are included in this book.

They have also had some fantastic players, Hughie Gallacher, Jackie Milburn, Bobby Mitchell, Len White, Colin Veitch, Alan Shearer, Kevin Keegan, Malcolm Macdonald, the list goes on and on. This book also remembers those who for whatever reason only appeared on a single occasion, their contribution is equally valued.

Presented in a diary, or almanac, fashion this book plots its way through the history of Newcastle United on a day-by-day basis and highlights interesting facts, figures and trivia. It includes every debut by every player, every first meeting with every opposition team faced, each scoring debut and much, much more...

JANUARY

January-01

Happy New Year!

It was for Newcastle fans in **1980** and **1985** as they recorded two 3-1 victories over arch rivals Sunderland. Also in **1921** when they enjoyed a 6-3 victory over Manchester United but perhaps the best may have been in **1934** when they would have seen 11 goals at St James's Park in a 9-2 demolition of Liverpool. Lincoln City would have been sick of the sight of St James's Park on a New Year's Day as in **1894** and **1895** they were the visitors and lost both games with Newcastle being the victors by 5-1 and 4-2 respectively. New Years Day of **1930** saw the appointment of Andy Cunningham as manager at Newcastle which made him their first "recognised" manager following the sterling stewardship of Frank Watt.

1904: Tyne-Wear Derby No. 13

Newcastle travelled to Roker Park for a League Division 1 fixture with Sunderland, the 13th Tyne-Wear Derby. The first half was goalless but each side scored in the second half making the final result 1-1. Ron Orr scored for Newcastle and the Sunderland scorer was Andrew McCombie - and therein lies a tale...

1904: Newcastle Break World Transfer Record

Within days of the Tyne-Wear Derby mentioned above Newcastle broke the world transfer record to bring Andrew McCombie to St James's Park from Sunderland - the then absolutely huge sum of £700!

1921: Newcastle Win 9 Goal Encounter

Manchester United came to St James's Park for a League Division 1 fixture and were soundly beaten in this high scoring game. It has to be admitted that at half-time, with the scores being 2-2 it did not look like either team would run away with the result but Newcastle certainly did. Scoring another four in the second half, to a single goal from Manchester, the game ended 6-3 to Newcastle. Their scorers were Stan Seymour and Neil Harris both getting two each and Andy Smailes and Tom Phillipson netting the other two.

1934: Newcastle Score 9 in 11 Goal Encounter

This League Division 1 fixture where Liverpool came to St James's Park was probably the best New Years Day seen on Tyneside for many a year.

A rampant Newcastle put 9 past Liverpool in a 9-2 demolition of the Merseysiders. Even one of their two goals was an Alec Betton own-goal. Newcastle's goals came from hat-tricks for Jimmy Richardson and Sammy Weaver and a goal each for Ron Williams, Tommy Lang and Jimmy Boyd.

1935: Hat-Trick Debut

An excellent debut indeed for Outside-Right Wilfred Bott, not only did he score - but he scored a hat-trick on his debut today in the League Division 2 fixture with Bury. Further goals from Tommy Pearson and Jock Smith ensured an emphatic 5-1 victory for Newcastle at St James's Park.

1980: Tyne-Wear Derby No. 116

Newcastle played hosts to Sunderland for a League Division 1 fixture, the 116th Tyne-Wear Derby. Goals from Peter Cartwright, Alan Shoulder and Tommy Cassidy giving Newcastle a 3-1 victory. Stan Cummins was the scorer for Sunderland.

1985: Tyne-Wear Derby No. 118

Newcastle played hosts to Sunderland for a League Division 1 fixture, the 118th Tyne-Wear Derby. A hat-trick from Peter Beardsley giving Newcastle the same 3-1 victory as the corresponding fixture the previous season. Colin West was the scorer for Sunderland.

First Meeting on January-01:

Year	V	F	A	R	Opposition	Competition
1969	A	2	3	L	Real Zaragoza	Inter Cities Fairs Cup

KEY:

V= Venue; **F** = For (goals scored); **A** = Against (goals conceded); R = Result

Debut on January-01:

Year	Player	Opposition
1896	John McDonald (Inside Left) John Warburton (Left Back)	Leicester Fosse
1913	James Wilson (Goalkeeper)	Liverpool
1934	William McPhillips (Goalkeeper)	Liverpool
1935	Wilfred Bott (Outside Right) Billy Cairns (Inside Forward)	Bury
1947	Robert Fraser (Centre Half)	Nottingham Forest
1955	John Harold Taylor (Outside Right)	Sheffield United

Born on January-01:

Year	Player	Position	Years
1889	Angus Douglas	Outside-Right	1913-1918
1995	Adam Campbell	Forward	2005- *current*

January-02

No 'hangovers' for Newcastle in **1894** when they beat Middlesbrough Ironopolis 7-2 at St James's Park, with two goals apiece from Bobby Willis and C. Quinn, the others being from John Law, Willie Thompson and William Graham. Nor in **1960** when they beat Manchester United 7-3 with Len White scoring a hat-trick, George Eastham scoring a penalty and goals from Ivor Allchurch, John Bell and Andy Anderson.

Poor Lincoln City were again the recipients of a heavy defeat when they were beaten 5-0 in **1896**, the goals coming from Andy Aitken, Jimmy Stott, James Collins and two for Malcolm Lennox.

A winning score of 5-1 was recorded by Newcastle in **1911** at Goodison Park when they faced Everton in a League Division 2 fixture. It was the same 5-1 score-line in **1926** against Bolton Wanderers at St James's Park in a League Division 1 fixture - this included four goals from Hughie Gallacher, the other being scored by Tom Urwin.

Bolton's 'consolation' goal being scored by Ted Vizard.

1993 saw Newcastle dispose of Port Vale in their FA Cup Third Round tie at St James's Park. Gavin Peacock scored twice and further goals from Rob Lee and Kevin Sheedy ensured a comprehensive 4-0 victory.

First Meeting on January-02:

Year	V	F	A	R	Opposition	Competition
1969	A	2	3	L	Real Zaragoza	Inter Cities Fairs Cup

Debut on January-02:

Year	Player	Opposition
1978	David Barton (Central Defence) Mark McGhee (Forward)	Leeds United

Born on January-02:

Year	Player	Position	Years
1968	Paul Stephenson	Midfield	1984-1988
1987	Loic Remy	Forward	2013-2014
1991	Davide Santon	Right Back	2011 - 2015

January-03

In **1910** Albert Shepherd scored four goals in the League Division 1 fixture with Preston North End at St James's Park, two in either half. With Preston scoring an 'own goal' that made it five for Newcastle. Preston did manage to score twice in the second half making the eventual score 5-2, but this was still an easy victory for Newcastle. Unfortunately though, in **1903** Newcastle were on the wrong side of five goals. This when they were soundly beaten 5-0 in a League Division 1 fixture by Stoke City at the Victoria Ground.

Five was also the total number of goals scored in a League Division 1 fixture when Aston Villa were the visitors in **1925**. A Willie Cowan hat-trick and a goal from Tom McDonald ensured the 4-1 win. Also, in a League Division 2 fixture with Luton Town in **1948** Newcastle were the better in a five goal game. A Jackie Milburn hat-trick and a George Stobbart goal, Newcastle were the winners by 4-1 at St James's Park in front of a huge crowd of 64,931.

1966: Tyne-Wear Derby No. 98

Newcastle travelled to Roker Park for a League Division 1 fixture against Sunderland, the 98th Tyne-Wear Derby. Goals from Herd and O'Hare gave Sunderland a 2-0 victory.

Debut on January-03:

Year	Player	Opposition
1910	Henry Thompson (Left Back)	Preston North End
2015	Callum Roberts (Midfield) Lubomir Satka (Defence)	Leicester City

Born on January-03:

Year	Player	Position	Years
1961	Bruce Halliday	Central Defence	1977 - 1982
1962	Albert Craig	Midfield	1987-1989

Born on January-03:

Year	Player	Position	Years
1977	Lee David Bowyer	Midfield	2003-2006

January-04

1958: Six of the Best

A Len White hat-trick, two goals from George Eastham and a goal from Bobby Mitchell saw Newcastle easily outclass Plymouth Argyle 6-1 in this FA Cup Third Round tie at Home Park.

1964: FA Cup Humbling

In what was one of the biggest shocks in the FA Cup, Bedford Town pulled off a huge 'giant killing' act by coming to St James's Park and knocking Newcastle out of the cup.

2-0 up at half-time with a goal from Fahy and a deflected 'own goal' by McKinney, (though this is credited to Fahy in some reports) Bedford looked to be surprisingly in control. Newcastle piled on the pressure in the second half and it would be fair to say that Bedford were 'hanging on' a bit. Their defence stayed resolute and Newcastle were kept at bay right up until only three minutes of the game were left. Stan Anderson scored to really set their nerves jangling and give Newcastle a little bit of hope that they could rescue this tie. Credit to Bedford though, they clung on and took the tie 2-1.

First Meeting on January-04:

Year	V	F	A	R	Opposition	Competition
1896	A	2	5	L	Manchester City	Division 2
1964	H	1	2	L	Bedford	FA Cup

Debut on January-04:

Year	Player	Opposition
1896	O. Reid (Inside Left)	Manchester City

Born on January-04:

Year	Player	Position	Years
1874	Jim Lockey	Right Back	1895-1899
1936	Jimmy Fell	Left Wing	1962-1963
1986	James Philip Milner	Midfield/Wing	2004-2008

Born on January-04:

Year	Player	Position	Years
1987	Daniel Peter Simpson	Right Back	2009-2013

January-05

1946: Scoring Debuts & Beginning of a Legend!

Both Jackie Milburn and George Hair scored on their debuts today in the FA Cup Third Round, First Leg (**see note*) tie against Barnsley at St James's Park.

Milburn getting two goals in this game - the first two in what was to become a long standing record of 200 goals for Newcastle. *This rises to 201 if you take his Charity Shield goal, scored in the 1951 2-1 defeat to Tottenham Hotspur at White Hart Lane into account, which for some reason the official records do not.* It took some 49 years for this record to be equalled and then passed, and it took another 'Geordie' Newcastle legend, Alan Shearer, to break it.

This game actually saw Newcastle handing out debuts to no less than nine players that day. Despite this Newcastle still went on to win the game 4-2 - with the brace from "Wor Jackie", the goal from Hair the other being scored by Albert Stubbins.

Another notable making his debut that day was "Mr Newcastle" Joe Harvey, however it was not so much of a happy one for him as one of Barnsley's two goals was an "own goal" from him. Incidentally the Barnsley team that day contained a certain Jorge Oliver Robledo - who was later of course to become quite a hero at St James's Park.

*The FA Cup of 1946, the season immediately after the cessation of hostilities of the Second World War (WWII), was for the only time in the history of the competition played over two legs - this for all matches from the First Round Proper up to and including the Sixth Round Proper.

Incidentally the FA Cup games of the 1945-46 season are the only games which count in "official" statistics.

This, as even though League football had resumed the leagues themselves had been split into a Football League North and a Football League South as the country was still obviously recovering from involvement in the hostilities.

1974: More FA Cup Drama

Non-League side Hendon were the visitors to St James's Park for a FA Cup Third Round tie and did they give Newcastle a shock!

Newcastle were leading 1-0 at half-time thanks to a goal from Pat Howard but in honesty they never looked comfortable with that lead. It was no more than the non-leaguers deserved when they equalised with a goal from Rod Haider to force a replay.

First Meeting on January-05:

Year	V	F	A	R	Opposition	Competition
1974	H	1	1	D	Hendon	FA Cup

Debut on January-05:

Year	Player	Opposition
1946	George Hair (Outside Left) Charlie Wayman (Centre Forward) Jackie Milburn (Centre Forward) Charlie Crowe (Left Half) Thomas Smith (Centre Half) Joe Harvey (Wing Half) Bobby Cowell (Right-Back) Bobby Corbett (Full Back) Ray King (Goalkeeper)	Barnsley
2013	Paul Dummett (Defence)	Brighton & Hove Albion

Born on January-05:

Year	Player	Position	Years
1923	George King	Centre Forward	1946-1948
1940	William Thompson	Centre Half	1957-1967
1964	Chris Hedworth	Defence	1982-1986

January-06

1962: FA Cup Exit

Going out of the FA Cup to lower league clubs is not, unfortunately, a rare occurrence for Newcastle and in this Third Round tie it was exactly what happened. In what was the first meeting between the two clubs Peterborough United pulled off somewhat of a shock with their 1-0 victory at St James's Park thanks to a second-half strike from Terry Bly.

2008: Return of the King

Having left Newcastle some 11 years previously, under not very happy circumstances, it came as a bit of a surprise and shock to see Kevin Keegan return to take charge as manager of Newcastle for the second time.

Suffice to say that if this was to bring back the style of football played by his "Entertainers" the first time he was here the Newcastle fans were very excited. Unfortunately history tells us something quite different happened...

First Meeting on January-06:

Year	V	F	A	R	Opposition	Competition
1962	H	0	1	L	Peterborough United	FA Cup

Debut on January-06:

Year	Player	Opposition
2008	Kazenga LuaLua (Midfield)	Stoke City

Born on January-06:

Year	Player	Position	Years
1952	Robert Thomas Shinton	Forward	1980-1982
1974	Daniel Cordone	Midfield	2000-2001
1989	Andrew Carroll	Forward	1999-2011

January-07

In total Newcastle have played 19 times on this day, failing to score in only three of those games. Losing 0-3 and 0-2 to Liverpool in **1933** and **1998** respectively and playing a goalless draw with Watford in **1989**. In some of those others games though the goals have went flooding in!

Unfortunately though Newcastle weren't always on the right side of the high scoring games as in **1928** Tottenham Hotspur beat Newcastle 5-2 at White Hart Lane in their League Division 1 fixture.

But here are some where they were...

1922: Six of the Best

This FA Cup First Round tie at St James's Park seemed evenly balanced when Newcastle went in 1-0 at half-time but epitomising the "game of two halves" cliché, Newcastle were rampant in the second-half scoring a further five times to record a 6-0 victory over Newport County. The goals coming from Tom McDonald and Eddie Dixon, both getting two apiece, and Neil Harris and Edward Mooney getting the other two.

1950: Seven of Nine

This FA Cup Third Round tie at Boundary Park saw nine goals in total with Newcastle bagging seven of them as they were 7-2 winners over Oldham Athletic. A hat-trick from Jackie Milburn, a brace from Tommy Walker a goal from Bobby Mitchell and an 'own goal' secured an emphatic victory.

1961: Five Star Performance

This FA Cup Third Round tie at St James's Park saw a hat-trick from Duncan Neale and goals from Ivor Allchurch and Charlie Wood to wrap up a 5-0 victory over Fulham.

2006: Shearer Equals Milburn's Record

Alan Shearer equals Jackie Milburn's "official" goal scoring record (for some reason Newcastle do not count Milburn's goal in the 1951 Charity Shield in his record) with his 200th goal for Newcastle in the FA Cup Third Round tie with Mansfield at St James's Park. Being the only goal of the game it also gave Newcastle the win and progression to the next round.

2006: Alf McMichael, R.I.P.

McMichael was described as being a "most magnificent full back" and he captained Newcastle for the vast majority of the 14 (1949 - 1963) seasons he was at St. James's Park.

In total he made 433 appearances for Newcastle and was their most 'capped' player right up until 2003 when Shay Given exceeded his total of 40 senior appearances for Northern Ireland.

First Meeting on January-07:

Year	V	F	A	R	Opposition	Competition
1922	H	6	0	W	Newport County	FA Cup

Debut on January-07:

Year	Player	Opposition
1933	William Gallantree (Outside Right)	Liverpool
1939	Willie Scott (Centre Forward)	Brentford
2006	Alan O'Brien (Midfield)	Mansfield Town

Born on January-07:

Year	Player	Position	Years
1862	John Auld	Centre Half	1896-1997
1901	Jimmy Nelson	Right Back	1930-1935
1950	Malcolm Ian Macdonald	Centre Forward	1971-1976
1895	Wayne Routledge	Midfield	2010-2011

January-08

1927: Two Hat-Tricks Help Newcastle to Eight

A hat-trick from Hughie Gallacher and another from Tom McDonald, goals from Stan Seymour and Tom Urwin, this was a devastating 8-1 win for Newcastle in this FA Cup Third Round tie at St James's Park.

The opponents that day, Notts County, must have been sick of the sight of Newcastle as in the last two encounters they had scored nine goals, winning 3-1 in 1927 and 6-3 in 1925.

1997: Keegan Quits

Kevin Keegan's first stint in charge at Newcastle sensationally ended as he resigned as manager today.

Having brought some excellent players to Newcastle, and a style of football that had earned them the nickname of the "Entertainers" it was quite a shock to most. Terry McDermott was appointed caretaker manager.

Debut on January-08:

Year	Player	Opposition
1966	Keith Kettleborough (Midfield)	West Ham United
2011	Philip Airey (Forward)	Stevenage Borough

Born on January-08:

Year	Player	Position	Years
1884	Robert Blanthorne	Inside Right	1908-1910
1938	Robert Ferguson	Full Back	1955-1962
1949	John Cowan	Midfield	1967-1973
1950	Gordon Hindson	Outside Left	1968-1971

January-09

1946: FA Cup Aggregate Exit

As mentioned previously the FA Cup of 1946 was played over two legs for the one and only time in the history of the competition. Today saw the second leg of Newcastle's Third Round tie with Barnsley played at Oakwell Stadium.

Though Newcastle had won the first leg 4-2 with them losing this second leg 3-0, thereby losing 5-4 on aggregate, they exited the FA Cup at the Third Round.

2008: Allardyce Away

Sam Allardyce leaves his position as manager of Newcastle "by mutual agreement". Once again Nigel Pearson is asked to take charge as caretaker manager.

First Meeting on January-09:

Year	V	F	A	R	Opposition	Competition
1926	H	4	1	W	Aberdare Athletic	FA Cup
1954	H	2	2	D	Wigan Athletic	FA Cup
2005	A	2	0	W	Yeading	FA Cup

Debut on January-09:

Year	Player	Opposition
1946	Ernie Taylor (Inside Forward)	Barnsley
1999	Didier Domi (Defence) Louis Laurent Saha (Forward)	Chelsea
2005	Jean Alain Boumsong (Central Defence) Celestine Hycieth Babayaro (Left Back)	Yeading

Born on January-09:

Year	Player	Position	Years
1913	Ralph Birkett	Outside Right	1938 - 1941
1921	George Stobbart	Inside Forward	1946 - 1949
1968	Franck Dumas	Defence	1999 - 2000
1971	Paul Kitson	Forward	1994 - 1997

January-10

Newcastle were on either end of five goals in **1914** and **1976**. In the former they were beaten 5-0 by Sheffield United in a FA Cup First Round tie at St James's Park.

In the latter they beat Everton 5-0 in a League Division 1 fixture, again at St James's Park. Newcastle's scorers that day were Alan Gowling with a hat-trick, Geoff Nulty and Irving Natrass netting the other two.

1953: Abandoned Match

Newcastle played hosts to Swansea Town for a FA Cup Third Round tie at St James's Park. It was reported that there were in excess of 60,000 spectators (63.499 according to one report) in attendance. You can image the disappointment when after only eight minutes of play the referee abandoned the match due to fog! The game was rescheduled and took place on 14th January, with Newcastle the winners by 3-0. Reg Davies, Vic Keeble and Bobby Mitchell with the goals. The gate was 61,064.

First Meeting on January-10:

Year	V	F	A	R	Opposition	Competition
1925	H	4	1	W	Hartlepool United	FA Cup

Debut on January-10:

Year	Player	Opposition
1989	Tommy Wright (Goalkeeper)	Watford

Born on January-10:

Year	Player	Position	Years
1965	Paul Sweeney	Left Back	1989 - 1990
1981	Jamie Coppinger	Forward	1998 - 2002

January-11

1936: Scoring Debut

Inside-Forward Eddie Connelly scored on his debut today in the FA Cup Third Round tie against Walsall at Fellows Park. With Jock Smith also scoring Newcastle were victorious 2-0 at Fellows Park. With both goals being scored in the second half the game was not quite as comfortable as the score-line may suggest.

1947: Newcastle Cruise in Eight Goal Encounter

Newcastle played hosts to Crystal Palace in a FA Cup tie and were emphatically victorious with a 6-1 score line. Len Shackleton scored twice with Roy Bentley, George Stobbart, Tom Pearson and Charlie Wayman getting the others

2009: Tommy Casey R.I.P.

Today sees the sad news of the death of Tommy Casey who passed away at the age of 78 in a Nursing Home in Bristol.

Casey was an excellent wing-half who played 134 games for Newcastle and was also a member of Northern Ireland's 1958 World Cup squad.

First Meeting on January-11:

Year	V	F	A	R	Opposition	Competition
1930	H	1	1	D	York City	FA Cup

Debut on January-11:

Year	Player	Opposition
1936	Eddie Connelly (Inside Forward)	Walsall

Born on January-11:

Year	Player	Position	Years
1925	Jimmy Scoular	Right Half	1953 - 1961
1973	Lee Makel	Midfield	1990 - 1992

January-12

In 18 games played on this day in history Newcastle have lost no fewer than 11 times. The worst of these being in **2008** when it was a miserable journey home from Old Trafford as the travelling Toon Army had seen their side crushed 6-0 by Manchester United. They also suffered a 6-1 defeat at their hands in **1957**, again at Old Trafford.

Newcastle did however come on the right side of six goals when they beat Hull City 5-1 in **1935** at Boothferry Park, Two goals from Wilf Bott, one apiece for Tom Pearson and Billy Cairns and Hull scoring an 'own goal'.

There were also two 4-2 victories, the one at Fratton Park in **1924** being the first time Newcastle and Portsmouth had met. This game saw Stan Seymour, Neil Harris, James Low and William Gibson all on the score-sheet. Whilst in **1952** a Bobby Mitchell brace and goals from Billy Foulkes and Jorge Robledo saw off Aston Villa at St James's Park. All three games were Third Round FA Cup ties.

1991: Scoring Debut

David Mitchell scored on his debut today in the League Division 2 fixture against Blackburn Rovers. With it being the only goal of the game it ensured the points stayed at St James's Park.

First Meeting on January-12:

Year	V	F	A	R	Opposition	Competition
1907	H	0	3	L	Crystal Palace	FA Cup
1924	A	4	2	W	Portsmouth	FA Cup

Debut on January-12:

Year	Player	Opposition
1957	Malcolm Scott (Centre Half)	Manchester United
1991	David Mitchell (Forward)	Blackburn Rovers
2013	Mathieu Debuchy (Right Back)	Norwich City

January-13

1906: Six of the Best

Newcastle travelled to Blundell Park for this FA Cup First Round tie against Grimsby Town. With two goals each from Ron Orr and Bill Appleyard, together with goals from Albert Gosnell and Jock Rutherford, Newcastle were easy 6-0 winners.

1990: Nine Goal Thriller

St James's Park saw nine goals scored today with Newcastle just edging this League Division 2 fixture with Leicester City 5-4. Evenly poised at 2-2 at the break this game could have went either way. Luckily for us it went our way, thanks to two goals each for Mark McGhee and Micky Quinn and a goal from John Gallacher.

Debut on January-13:

Year	Player	Opposition
1894	J Laverick (Full Back)	Northwich Victoria
1968	John Sinclair (Winger)	Nottingham Forest

Debut on January-13:

Year	Player	Opposition
1990	Robert Sime Aitken (Defence)	Leicester City
2001	Wayne Quinn (Defence/Left Back)	Coventry City

January-14

1911: Six of the Best

Bury visited St James's Park for a FA Cup First Round tie and they found Newcastle, and Albert Shepherd in particular, in fine form. In what was a 'rampant' display from Newcastle, Shepherd scored a hat-trick. With further goals from Jimmy Stewart, Scott Duncan and Peter McWilliam a 6-1 score line made it an 'easy day at the office'.

1992: Game Abandoned After 17 Minutes

The FA Cup Third Round Replay at Dean Court with Bournemouth was abandoned after only 17 minutes due to a thick swirling fog.

The re-arranged fixture (22/01/1992) was to go down in the history books...

1997: Dalglish Takes Over

With the departure of Kevin Keegan, Newcastle turned to another Liverpool legend, Kenny Dalglish, to be their manager.

So once again he found himself replacing Keegan, just as he had done as a player at Liverpool. Just like before Keegan was going to be a hard act to follow, and just like before Dalglish seemed more than up for the task.

Debut on January-14:

Year	Player	Opposition
1933	John Dryden (Outside Left)	Leeds United
1961	Ken Hodgson (Forward)	Nottingham Forest
1970	David Young (Wing-Half)	Southampton
1989	Frank Pingel (Forward)	Aston Villa

Born on January-14:

Year	Player	Position	Years
1944	Colin Clish	Left Back	1961 - 1963
1968	Ruel Adrian Fox	Midfield	1994 - 1995

Born on January-14:

Year	Player	Position	Years
1986	Yohan Cabaye	Midfield	2011 - 2014

January-15

A winning score line of 2-1 has been the result on no fewer than five occasions on this day. These were in **1927** against Aston Villa in Division 1, **1930** against York City in a FA Cup Third Round Replay, the game mentioned below in the Fairs Cup in **1969**, another FA Cup Third Round Replay in **1997** this time against Charlton Athletic and a Premiership victory in **2005** against Southampton.

Also Newcastle have been on both sides of a 4-0 score line, with a defeat at the hands of Sheffield United in a League Division 2 fixture in **1938** and recording a victory in **1921** in a League Division 1 fixture over Bradford City. Newcastle's scorers being Andy Smailes with two and one each for Neil Harris and Billy Aitken.

1898: One and Only Appearance

Today saw the one and only appearance for Newcastle of defender John Allen, this when he deputised for the injured Jock Peddie in the home game against Darwen in United's first promotion campaign in 1897-98.

Newcastle won the game 1-0 without scoring, it was an 'own goal' from a Darwen player but the records available currently don't indicate which one, unfortunately.

1969: Fairs Cup Progression on 'Away Goals'

The 'away goals rule' kept Newcastle's dreams of winning the Inter Cities Fairs Cup alive. With today's Round 3, Second Leg, finishing 2-1 to Newcastle the aggregate score was 4-4.

However, as Newcastle had scored two goals over in Spain (in their 3-2 defeat) they progressed to the next round on the 'away goals' rule.

Debut on January-15:

Year	Player	Opposition
1898	John Allen (Centre Forward)	Darwen

Born on January-15:

Year	Player	Position	Years
1897	Albert Chandler	Right Back	1925 - 1926
1983	Hugo Miguel Ferreira Viana	Midfield	2002 - 2006

January-16

With a 5-0 victory over Clapton Orient in **1909** and another over Southampton in the Premiership in **2000**, five is a recurring number on this day.

Starting in **1897** Newcastle won 4-1 against Blackpool at St James's Park, as mentioned the **1909** victory 5-0 over Clapton Orient.

This was followed by a 3-2 victory over West Ham United in **1915**, a 3-2 victory over Watford in **1982** and the 5-0 victory over Southampton in **2000**. Unfortunately the other 'five' is not a happy one...

1898: One and Only Appearance

Joe Ford, Centre Forward, made his one and only appearance today for Newcastle as they welcomed Grimsby Town to St James's Park for a League Division 1 fixture.

Though Newcastle won the game, 2-0, with both goals being scored by Jackie Cape, Ford never made another appearance for Newcastle.

1909: Five Star Performance

In what was the first meeting between these clubs, Newcastle United and Clapton Orient faced each other in a FA First Round tie. Played at St James's Park, a hat-trick from George Wilson, together with goals from Andy Anderson and Albert Shepherd gave Newcastle an easy 5-0 victory and progression to the next round.

1965: Newcastle Edged in Nine Goal Thriller

Newcastle travelled to Highfield Road for this League Division 2 fixture with Coventry City. With the score 4-1 at half-time in Coventry's favour the game looked dead and buried.

However Newcastle put up a spirited fight in the second half but it was to no avail, Coventry ran out 5-4 winners. Newcastle's scorers were Ron McGarry and David Hilley, both scoring twice.

2011: Tyne-Wear Derby No. 145

Newcastle travelled to the Stadium of Light for a League Division 1 fixture against Sunderland, the 145th Tyne-Wear Derby. After a goalless first-half Kevin Nolan put Newcastle ahead on 52 minutes. However, four minutes into stoppage time Gyan scored a Sunderland equaliser.

First Meeting on January-16:

Year	V	F	A	R	Opposition	Competition
1909	H	5	0	W	Clapton Orient	FA Cup
1979	H	3	1	W	Torquay United	FA Cup

Debut on January-16:

Year	Player	Opposition
1932	Joe Ford (Centre Forward)	Grimsby Town
2011	Daniel Gosling (Midfield)	Sunderland

Born on January-16:

Year	Player	Position	Years
1951	Alex Cropley	Midfield	1980
1959	Stuart Robinson	Left Wing	1975 - 1980

January-17

Won four, drew six and lost nine, not the happiest of days in Newcastle's history. Of the meagre four wins ..

1921: Capital Victory

Any win in the capital is a good win and Newcastle travelled to London, and Highbury, in **1921** to face Arsenal in a League Division 1 fixture. Goals from Neil Harris and Stan Seymour ensured a happy journey home as Newcastle won the game 2-0.

1931: Newcastle Edge Seven Goal Encounter

Manchester United were the visitors to St James's Park in this League Division 1 fixture. Newcastle were leading 3-1 at half-time but Manchester fought back though couldn't do enough with the game ending at 4-3 to Newcastle. It was a brace from Harry Bedford and goals from Jimmy Boyd and Duncan Hutchison that ensured the victory. It was also in this game that James Robinson made his one and only appearance for Newcastle.

In **1981 a** second-half goal from Sunderland born Mick Harford, being the only goal of the game, secured the points for Newcastle at Kenilworth Road in their League Division 2 fixture against Luton Town.

1998 saw goals from John Barnes and Temuri Ketsbaia secure the Premiership points stayed at St James's Park in a narrow 2-1 victory over Bolton Wanderers.

Debut on January-17:

Year	Player	Opposition
1914	William Mellor (Goalkeeper) James Spink (Right Half)	West Bromwich Albion
1931	James Robinson (Centre Half)	Manchester United
1948	Willie McCall (Outside Left)	Brentford
1996	Darren Huckerby (Forward)	Chelsea

January-18

A 6-1 defeat to Leicester City in **1930** and a 5-1 defeat to Manchester City in **1975** are certainly the 'lows' concerning this day in history, but to that you could easily add the 4-3 defeat to Charlton Athletic in **1992** and the 3-1 defeat to Queens Park Rangers in **1986.**

Being knocked out of the FA Cup in a Third Round Replay against Watford in **1989**, where it was a Glenn Roeder 'own goal' that did the damage, could be seen as equally galling.

But let's look on the bright side - a 3-1 victory over Woolwich Arsenal in **1897** and a 2-1 win in **1969** over their 'successors' - Arsenal, both at St James's Park, are always worth mentioning. The pick of the bunch for today in Newcastle's history though goes to the following two games...

1964: Two Plus Two Equals Four

Grimsby Town were the visitors to St James Park in this League Division 2 fixture. Two goals each from Barrie Thomas and Stan Anderson ensured they left empty handed as Newcastle were easy winners 4-0.

1982: Newcastle Edge Seven Goal Encounter

Having drawn 1-1 with Colchester United at St James's Park this FA Cup Third Round Replay had all the hallmarks of being a huge banana skin for Newcastle at Layer Road.

At the close of the first half Newcastle had a narrow one goal margin in holding a 2-1 lead. With four goals being scored in the second half, each side netting twice, Newcastle maintained that narrow margin to win 4-3 - but it could have went either way.

Debut on January-18:

Year	Player	Opposition
1930	Jackie Cape (Outside Right)	Leicester City

Born on January-18:

Year	Player	Position	Years
1954	Jeff Clarke	Central Defence	1982 - 1987
1961	Peter Andrew Beardsley	Forward	1983 - 1997

January-19

The winter of **1959** was a particularly bad one in terms of disruption to the sporting calendar. Well before the days of 'under soil' heating and with the pitch being both ice bound and several inches deep in snow the FA Cup Third Round tie with Chelsea at St James's Park had been postponed twice before finally going ahead today.

Probably better if they had postponed it again as Newcastle lost 4-1 on a thoroughly miserable winters day.

Newcastle's consolation goal being scored by George Eastham in the second half.

Debut on January-19:

Year	Player	Opposition
1929	George Mathison (Right Half)	Bury
1935	Stanley Docking (Inside Left)	Fulham

Born on January-19:

Year	Player	Position	Years
1942	Ken Hodgson	Forward	1959 - 1961
1945	Robert Moncur	Central Defence	1960 - 1974
1976	Wayne Quinn	Left Back	2000 - 2003

January-20

1979: William McCracken, R.I.P.

William "Bill" McCracken is arguably one of the best full-backs ever to have played the game. He will go down in history as the man who was so clever at 'abusing' the offside law that the FA actually changed the rules.

His tactical awareness and understanding with Frank Hudspeth saw them perfect the 'offside trap' to such an extent thus forcing the aforementioned change in the rules. If not always appreciated elsewhere, the Newcastle captain was adored on Tyneside during his 19-year career at St James's Park.

In a peculiar turn of events Bill scored eight times for Newcastle and all were from the penalty spot.

First Meeting on January-20:

Year	V	F	A	R	Opposition	Competition
1894	A	1	2	L	Rotherham Town*	Division 2

*Rotherham Town became Rotherham United, first meeting on 11/11/1961.

Debut on January-20:

Year	Player	Opposition
1962	Barrie Ernest Thomas (Centre Forward)	Huddersfield Town

Born on January-20:

Year	Player	Position	Years
1947	Jimmy Smith	Midfield	1969 - 1976
1948	Graham Winstanley	Centre Back	1964 - 1969
1971	Peter Garland	Midfield	1992 - 1992

January-21

1949: Newcastle put 11 Players on Transfer List

Newcastle placed 11 players on the transfer list today. These included Andy Donaldson, George Hair, Albert Sibley and Colin Gibson whom they had just paid £15,000 to Cardiff for in the summer.

1950: One and Only Appearance

Today saw the one and only appearance for Newcastle of Centre Forward Andy Graver. Whilst Newcastle earned a draw, 1-1, at Maine Road in their

League Division 1 fixture against Manchester City it was not meant to be for Andy at Newcastle - though he later went on to become quite a goal-scoring machine. Indeed ending up as Lincoln City's highest ever goalscorer with 144 goals.

1976: Through to League Cup Final

Following a 3-1 win over Tottenham Hotspur at St James's Park, this following a 1-0 defeat at White Hart Lane, Newcastle finally reach the League Cup Final with a 3-2 aggregate score line.

2012: Second-Half Slump at Craven Cottage

When Newcastle travelled to Craven Cottage to face Fulham in this Premier League fixture few would have guessed the spectacular change in fortunes that was about unfurl between the teams.

Leading 1-0 at half-time with a goal from Danny Guthrie just before the break (43 minutes) Newcastle dramatically slumped in the second half.

Conceding five goals, of which three are a Dempsey hat-trick, and the other two are penalties! Newcastle managed to be masters of their own downfall and Fulham took the points with a 5-2 victory.

Debut on January-21:

Year	Player	Opposition
1928	William Gillespie (Right Back)	Manchester United
1939	Clarence Alfred Theaker (Goalkeeper)	Cardiff City
1950	Andy Graver (Centre Forward)	Manchester City
1995	Keith Robert Gillespie (Right Winger)	Sheffield Wednesday

Born on January-21:

Year	Player	Position	Years
1901	Henry Wake	Right Half	1919 - 1923
1975	Nicky Butt	Midfield	2004 - 2010

January-22

1966: First Trip to Sealand Road

Newcastle met Chester City for the first time today so it was a new trip for the travelling Toon Army to Sealand Road for this FA Cup Third Round tie. It turned out to be a happy one for them as well with Pop Robson, Ron

McGarry and David Craig all scoring so Newcastle progressed to the next round with a 3-1 victory.

1992: First Live Televised FA Cup Penalty Shoot-Out

Another entry in the history books for Newcastle, but one the fans may wish to forget.

After the original, replay on 14/01/1992, was abandoned after only 17 minutes, due to a swirling thick fog, this FA Cup Third Round Replay against Bournemouth, played at Dean Court, was the first ever live televised FA Cup penalty shoot-out, arising out of the fact that the game ended scoreless.

Vince Bartram, the Bournemouth 'keeper, became the toast of the Cherries with his save from Kevin Brock's penalty sealing a memorable giant-killing act as Bournemouth won it 4-3.

First Meeting on January-22:

Year	V	F	A	R	Opposition	Competition
1966	A	3	1	W	Chester City	FA Cup

Born on January-22:

Year	Player	Position	Years
1948	Denis Laughton	Midfield	1973 - 1975
1980	Jonathan Woodgate	Defence	2003 - 2004
1982	Fabricio Coloccini	Defence	2008 - current

January-23

1909: Four Goal Shepherd

Newcastle travelled to the County Ground, Meadow Lane to face Notts County in a League Division 1 fixture. With the score being 0-0 at half-time there was little to suggest what was to happen in the second half. Upping their game somewhat Newcastle scored four times in the second half - or should that be Albert Shepherd scored four goals! Newcastle therefore running out 4-0 winners.

2010: Dumped Out The Cup in Six Goal Encounter

Newcastle travelled to The Hawthorns for this FA Cup Fourth Round tie with West Bromwich Albion. Shall we say it was an “interesting” game...

Newcastle picked up four yellow cards, a straight red for Ryan Taylor and gave away two penalties, both scored by Graham Dorrans.

Whilst Andy Carroll managed to score twice it was not good enough as West Bromwich Albion ran out quite comfortable winners at 4-2 over what was quite an 'angry' Newcastle side.

First Meeting on January-23:

Year	V	F	A	R	Opposition	Competition
1932	H	1	1	D	Southport	FA Cup

Debut on January-23:

Year	Player	Opposition
1988	Anthony Lormor (Forward)	Tottenham Hotspur

Born on January-23:

Year	Player	Position	Years
1901	Jeremiah Best	Inside Left	1919 - 1920
1907	Ronald Williams	Centre Forward	1933 - 1935
1917	Robert Fraser	Centre Half	1946 - 1950
1986	Steven Vincent Taylor	Defence	2003 - current
1986	Jose Sanchez Enrique	Left-Back	2007 - 2011

January-24

You cannot mention the FA Cup on this day without mentioning Hereford United...

1972: Minnows Force FA Cup Replay

Taking the lead at St James's Park in the first minute, being levelled three minutes later then behind 20 minutes after that yet still coming back to draw the game 2-2 to force a replay. It is Hereford United who get all the praise - and deservedly so.

1920: One and Only Appearance

Today saw the one and only appearance for Newcastle of Left Half Alex Rainnie. Deputising for the injured Jock Finlay he was part of a heavy defeat at Goodison Park as Newcastle lost 4-0 to Everton in a League Division 1 fixture.

First Meeting on January-24:

Year	V	F	A	R	Opposition	Competition
1972	H	2	2	D	Hereford United	FA Cup

Debut on January-24:

Year	Player	Opposition
1914	William Hampson (Right Back)	Sheffield Wednesday
1920	Alex Rainnie (Left Half) Tom Phillipson (Outside Right)	Everton
1953	Stan Keery (Wing Half)	Preston North End

Born on January-24:

Year	Player	Position	Years
1942	Herbert Garrow	Goalkeeper	1960 - 1963

January-25

1913: One and Only Appearance

Today saw the one and only appearance of goalkeeper John "Jack" Alderson. Newcastle won the League Division 1 fixture against Arsenal 3-1 at St James's Park.

Goals from Jimmy Stewart, Sandy Higgins and a Frank Hudspeth penalty secured the win but Alderson was not to feature again.

First Meeting on January-25:

Year	V	F	A	R	Opposition	Competition
1958	H	1	3	L	Scunthorpe United	FA Cup
1998	D	1	1	A	Stevenage Borough	FA Cup

Debut on January-25:

Year	Player	Opposition
1913	John Alderson (Goalkeeper)	Arsenal

Born on January-25:

Year	Player	Position	Years
1967	David Ginola	Left Wing	1995 - 1997

January-26

1952: Six of the Best

Newcastle played hosts to Charlton Athletic in a League Division 1 fixture. Already leading 3-0 at half-time they scored another three in the second half and were comfortable 6-0 winners. The goals came courtesy of two from Jackie Milburn, two from Jorge Robledo and one each for Billy Foulkes and Tommy Walker.

Debut on January-26:

Year	Player	Opposition
1924	James Hunter (Left Back)	Tottenham Hotspur
1931	Alec Betton (Centre Half)	West Ham United

Born on January-26:

Year	Player	Position	Years
1968	Anthony Nesbit	Midfield	1985 - 1987
1969	John Gallacher	Wing	1989 - 1992
1993	Florian Thauvin	Wing	2015 - current

January-27

1912: One and Only Appearance

Today saw the one and only appearance for Newcastle of Outside Right John "Jack" Thomas. Newcastle secured a creditable 1-1 draw at Hyde Park against Manchester City in their League Division 1 fixture but Thomas was not to make another appearance for Newcastle.

First Meeting on January-27:

Year	V	F	A	R	Opposition	Competition
1900	H	2	1	W	Reading	FA Cup
1968	H	0	1	L	Carlisle United	FA Cup

Debut on January-27:

Year	Player	Opposition
1912	John Thomas (Outside Right)	Manchester City
1923	James Clark (Inside Left)	Chelsea
1934	John Hughes (Left Half)	West Bromwich Albion

Debut on January-27:

Year	Player	Opposition
2010	Wayne Routledge (Midfield) Mike Williamson (Defence)	Crystal Palace

January-28

1956: Newcastle Edge Nine Goal Thriller

Newcastle travelled to Craven Cottage for their FA Cup Fourth Round tie with Fulham. Four goals were scored in the first half, with Newcastle leading 3-1. A further five goals were scored in the second half with Newcastle just edging the victory 5-4. The goals came courtesy of a Vic Keeble brace and goals from Jackie Millburn, Bob Stokoe and Tommy Casey.

First Meeting on January-28:

Year	V	F	A	R	Opposition	Competition
1899	A	1	0	W	Glossop North End	FA Cup
1978	H	2	2	D	Wrexham	FA Cup
2006	A	2	0	W	Cheltenham United	FA Cup

Debut on January-28:

Year	Player	Opposition
2009	Peter Lovenkrands (Forward)	Manchester City
2013	Moussa Sissoko (Midfield) Mapou Yanga-Mbiwa (Defence) Yoan Gouffran (Forward)	Aston Villa

Born on January-28:

Year	Player	Position	Years
1948	Stuart Boam	Centre Half	1979 - 1981
1989	Siem de Jong	Midfield	2014 - current

January-29

In **1997** Newcastle faced Everton in a Premiership fixture at St James's Park and were victorious with a 4-1 score-line. Goals from Les Ferdinand, Rob Lee, Alan Shearer and Robbie Elliott secured the win - but it is a game worth mentioning as the scorer for Everton that day was Gary Speed.

After only three minutes of the game had elapsed it was Speed who opened the scoring and it wasn't until 16 minutes before the end that Newcastle 'woke up' and scored four!

First Meeting on January-29:

Year	V	F	A	R	Opposition	Competition
1898	A	2	1	W	Preston North End	FA Cup

Debut on January-29:

Year	Player	Opposition
2005	Amady Moustapha Faye (Midfield)	Coventry City

Born on January-29:

Year	Player	Position	Years
1883	William McCracken	Full Back	1904 - 1923
1917	Jimmy Woodburn	Left Half	1935 - 1948
1963	Tommy Gaynor	Forward	1990
1980	Peter Rosenkrands Lovenkrands	Forward	2009 - 2012

January-30

Newcastle have been on both the right and wrong side of 5-0 scores on this day. In **1897** they travelled to Villa Park for a FA Cup First Round tie with Aston Villa and were soundly beaten 5-0.

It was much better in **1988** when they played hosts to Swindon Town in a FA Cup Fourth Round tie. With two goals from Paul Gascoigne and others from Darren Jackson, Paul Goddard and Michael O'Neill, they were convincing 5-0 winners.

Five goals was also the losing margin in **1937** when they travelled to Ewood Park for a League Division 2 fixture against Blackburn Rovers, the score being 6-1 to Blackburn with John Park getting Newcastle's 'consolation' goal.

1977: Lee Leaves

Gordon Lee resigns as manager. Lee's track record, *purely from a results perspective*, was very good at Newcastle. He also led them to the League Cup Final in 1976 and when he left Newcastle they were in a position to be able to hold onto a qualification place for European football the following season. However will the majority of the fans from that era remember him for anything else other than being the manager who sold Malcolm 'Supermac' Macdonald?

1991: Scoring Debut

David Mills scored on his debut today in the League Division 2 fixture against Norwich City. With a goal from Imre Varadi to add to Mills's goal Newcastle recorded a 2-1 victory at St James's Park.

First Meeting on January-30:

Year	V	F	A	R	Opposition	Competition
1915	H	1	1	D	Swansea Town*	FA Cup

*Swansea Town became Swansea City, first meeting on 24/11/1979.

Debut on January-30:

Year	Player	Opposition
1932	Wilfred Feeney (Inside Left)	West Ham United
1971	John Tudor (Forward)	Burnley
1982	David Mills (Forward)	Norwich City
2010	Patrick van Aanholt (Defence)	Leicester City

January-31

1935: Cunningham Quits

Andy Cunningham celebrated his 45th birthday in some style as he "left" his role as Newcastle manager.

1959: Eight Goals Shared at Old Trafford

Newcastle travelled to Old Trafford for a League Division 1 fixture against Manchester United and in an eight goal thriller they shared the points with the final score being 4-4.

With Newcastle being 4-1 down at half-time it was not the outcome that many would have expected. The scorers for Newcastle were, Ivor Allchurch, Len White scoring twice and John McGuigan getting the vital equaliser.

First Meeting on January-31:

Year	V	F	A	R	Opposition	Competition
1920	H	0	1	L	Huddersfield Town	FA Cup

Debut on January-31:

Year	Player	Opposition
1903	Arthur Turner (Outside Right)	Notts County
1920	Edward Mooney (Right Half Back)	Huddersfield Town
1948	Frank Calvert Houghton (Inside Forward)	Leicester City

Born on January-31:

Year	Player	Position	Years
1890	Andrew Cunningham	Inside Right	1923 - 1930
1903	John Allen	Centre Forward	1931 - 1934
1934	Ron Greener	Centre Half	1951 - 1955

FEBRUARY

February-01

1935: Mather Moves In

Tom Mather appointed as manager.

1936: Nine Goals for Newcastle!

In what was a quite remarkable score-line Newcastle beat Southport 9-0 in a FA Cup 4th Round tie. Not only was it remarkable because of the nine goals scored, but that this was the second replay. The original tie, at St James's Park had ended 1-1, the first replay at Haig Avenue also ended 1-1 so it was expected that this second replay, played at Hillsborough as a 'neutral' venue, would be equally as tight a game. Newcastle obviously had different ideas!

Newcastle's scorers were, Jimmy Richardson with a hat-trick, Jackie Cape with a brace and a goal each for Jimmy Boyd, Tommy Lang, Harry McMenemy and Sammy Weaver.

1958: Tyne-Wear Derby No. 91

Newcastle played hosts to Sunderland for a League Division 1 fixture, the 91st Tyne-Wear Derby.

With Bill Curry and Alex Tait each scoring in the first half and no reply from Sunderland, it looked like this was going to be a stroll in park for Newcastle. Unfortunately though Sunderland scored two themselves in the second half, through Billie Elliott and Alan O'Neill, so the game ended all-square at 2-2.

2004: Bob Stokoe R.I.P.

Sunday, 01/02/2004 was a sombre day across the North East as it saw the sad news of the death of Bob Stokoe who passed away at the age of 73. A true Newcastle Legend, *as well as a Sunderland one*!

2009: Tyne-Wear Derby No. 143

Newcastle played hosts to Sunderland for a Premiership fixture, the 143rd Tyne-Wear Derby. Sunderland took a first half lead with a goal from Djibril Cisse but Newcastle equalised in the second half with a Shola Ameobi penalty, so the game ended all-square at 1-1 In an interesting turn of events Sunderland's scorer was substituted in the second half by one Michael Chopra!

2014: Tyne-Wear Derby No. 151

Newcastle played hosts to Sunderland for a Premiership fixture, the 151st Tyne-Wear Derby and lost for the third Derby in row. Sunderland easily outclassed a very lack-lustre Newcastle and one of their scorers on the day was Jack Colback. The others being Fabio Borini and Adam Johnson.

First Meeting on February-01:

Year	V	F	A	R	Opposition	Competition
1896	A	4	0	W	Chesterfield	FA Cup
1908	H	2	0	W	West Ham United	FA Cup

Debut on February-01:

Year	Player	Opposition
1930	David Davidson (Centre Half) Joeseph Devine (Inside Right)	Huddersfield Town
1992	Terry Wilson (Midfield)	Oxford United
1998	Andreas Andersson (Forward)	Aston Villa
2009	Kevin Anthony Jance Nolan (Midfield)	Sunderland
2014	Luuk de Jong (Striker)	Sunderland

Born on February-01:

Year	Player	Position	Years
1900	Samuel Russell	Left Back	1920 - 1925
1927	Hugh Cameron	Left Wing	1951 - 1952
1947	Terry Hibbitt	Midfield	1971 - 1981
1966	Robert Martin Lee	Midfield	1992 - 2002
1987	Giuseppe Rossi	Forward	2006

February-02

1977: Dinnis Takes Over

Richard Dinnis appointed as manager. Upon Gordon Lee's resignation, the players demanded that Dinnis, who had been Lee's First Team coach and had came with him from Blackburn Rovers, be given the manager's job, even threatening to go on strike otherwise. Dinnis was duly appointed. History will show that this was not one of the better decisions made by the Newcastle board and perhaps they would have been better off telling the players to stick to their own jobs of playing football, which they did not do very well under their chosen leader...

2005: 250 Premiership Goals for Shearer

Alan Shearer reaches the staggering landmark of scoring 250 Premiership goals when he scored against a Kevin Keegan managed Manchester City in the 1-1 draw at the City of Manchester Stadium.

2006: Souness Sacked

Arriving at St James's Park in 2004 the odds were stacked against Souness from the start. There was no way he was the fans choice to replace Sir Bobby Robson - perhaps not even in their top ten. He quickly fell out with a number of players. Craig Bellamy, Laurent Robert, Olivier Bernard and Jermaine Jenas all left the club on bad terms.

A 14th place finish was hugely disappointing after the reign of Sir Bobby, and despite making it to the semi-final stage of both the FA Cup and UEFA Cup he was under mounting pressure from the supporters. Despite splashing out a club record fee of £16 million for Michael Owen his other signings were a disaster in particular £10 million for Albert Luque and £8 million for Jean-Alain Boumsong, whom Rangers had got on a free transfer only six months prior! This deal was at the centre of Newcastle's involvement in the Steven's Inquiry into football corruption. He became deeply unpopular with the Newcastle fans and rightly or wrongly most celebrated when his contract was terminated.

Glenn Roeder and Alan Shearer were appointed as caretakers until the end of the season.

First Meeting on February-02:

Year	V	F	A	R	Opposition	Competition
1895	H	2	1	W	Burnley	FA Cup

Debut on February-02:

Year	Player	Opposition
1929	Andrew Cunningham (Inside Right)	Leicester City

Born on February-02:

Year	Player	Position	Years
1894	William Aitken	Inside Forward	1920 - 1924
1903	Hugh Kilpatrick Gallacher	Forward	1925 - 1930
1923	Thomas Smith	Centre Half	1941 - 1952
1951	Martin Burleigh	Goalkeeper	1968 - 1974

Born on February-02:

Year	Player	Position	Years
1990	Daniel Gosling	Midfield	2010 - 2014

February-03

One of only three Americans to have played for Newcastle made their debut today, Oguchialu Chilioke Onyewu, quite a mouthful so thankfully commonly known as 'Gooch'.

At 6'5" (1.95m) he was quite an imposing player and was expected to add some 'steel' to what had been a rather 'flaky' Newcastle defence. History will show that this was unfortunately not to happen.

Debut on February-03:

Year	Player	Opposition
2007	Oguchialu Chilioke Onyewu (Defence)	Fulham

Born on February-03:

Year	Player	Position	Years
1968	Darren Peacock	Centre-Half	1994 - 1998
1974	Stephen Alan Harper	Goalkeeper	1997 - 2013

February-04

1939: One and Only Appearance

Today saw the one and only appearance for Newcastle of Centre Half Dominic Kelly. Newcastle were soundly beaten 4-0 at St James's Park by Coventry City in their League Division 2 fixture.

1990: Tyne-Wear Derby No. 121

Newcastle played hosts to Sunderland in the 121st Tyne-Wear Derby. With both teams scoring a single goal in the second half honours were even, 1-1.

Newcastle's scorer was Mark McGhee with Marco Gabbiadini scoring for Sunderland.

2006: Shearer Breaks Milburn's Record

Alan Shearer breaks Jackie Milburn's goal scoring record with his 201st goal for Newcastle in the Premiership clash with Portsmouth.

First Meeting on February-04:

Year	V	F	A	R	Opposition	Competition
1905	H	1	1	D	Plymouth Argyle	FA Cup

Debut on February-04:

Year	Player	Opposition
1921	Thomas Mitchell (Outside Left)	Chelsea
1922	Harry Woods (Inside Right)	Arsenal
1933	William Leighton (Inside Right)	Chelsea
1939	Dominic Kelly (Centre Half)	Coventry City

Born on February-04:

Year	Player	Position	Years
1938	Dave Hollins	Goalkeeper	1961 - 1967
1953	Alan Shoulder	Forward	1978 - 1982

February-05

1972 - Hereford United - this day in Newcastle United's proud FA Cup history belongs to Hereford United. Having secured an excellent draw at St James's Park (2-2) Hereford earned the right to face Newcastle on their own turf, Edgar Street, and boy did they put in a performance that shocked Newcastle to the core. Ronnie Radford's equaliser to make the score 1-1 and take the game into extra-time will forever be etched in the memory, an absolute corker. With Ricky George getting the winner it was a stunned and silent journey home to Tyneside.

1992: Ardiles Out - Keegan In

Osvaldo Ardiles dismissed after barely 12 months in charge at St James's Park. Ardiles's time on Tyneside was not a successful one, with only ten wins in total from his 47 games in charge. Of those there were just eight League wins (out of 41 played) and this saw Newcastle secured to the foot of the Second Division - facing relegation to the third tier of English football for the first time in their history. In a surprise move it was Kevin Keegan who was appointed as manager.

2000: Tyne-Wear Derby No. 131 – First at Stadium of Light

Newcastle travelled to the Stadium of Light for the very first time. This Premiership fixture against Sunderland being the 131st Tyne-Wear Derby. Didier Domi and Cris Helder gave Newcastle a 2-0 lead within 21 minutes, but Kevin Philips pulled one back for Sunderland a minute later. That was the way the first half ended. Philips scored again in the second half to pull Sunderland level and with no further goals scored the game ended 2-2.

2012: Scoring Debut

Papiss Cisse scored on his debut today in the Premier League fixture against Aston Villa. With Demba Ba having already scored on 30 minutes, but Villa levelling it at 1-1 through Robbie Keane on the stroke of half-time this debut goal from Cisse was the decisive one in a slender 2-1 victory for Newcastle at St James's Park.

Debut on February-05:

Year	Player	Opposition
1949	Jorge Oliver Robledo (Inside Forward)	Charlton Athletic
1974	Alex Bruce (Forward)	Southampton
2000	Diego Antonio Zarate Gavilan (Midfield)	Sunderland
2010	Leon Julian Best (Forward) Fitz Benjamin Hall (Defence/Midfield)	Cardiff City
2012	Papiss Demba Cisse (Forward)	Aston Villa

Born on February-05:

Year	Player	Position	Years
1896	Robert Roxburgh	Right Back	1920 - 1924
1896	Tom Urwin	Outside Left	1924 - 1930

February-06

1915: FA Cup Replay Win

A Bill McCracken penalty for Newcastle at St James's Park in the original FA Cup Second Round tie meant the score was 1-1 and Newcastle travelled to Vetch Field for the replay against Swansea Town. Goals from John King and Bob Pailor ensured a 2-0 win for Newcastle and a happy journey home for the travelling Toon Army.

1924: FA Cup Replay Draw

Two goals from Tom McDonald at the Baseball Ground, had cancelled out by two goals from Derby County's Storer, four days previously making the score 2-2, had forced this FA Cup Second Round Replay at St James's Park - which itself ended 2-2 once more. Newcastle's scorers on this occasion were Neil Harris and Willie Cowan.

1978: FA Cup Replay Loss

Having drawn the original FA Cup Fourth Round tie 2-2 at St James's Park against Wrexham (28 January) Newcastle travelled to the Racecourse Ground for this replay and were soundly beaten 4-1. Their 'consolation' goal coming from Mickey Burns.

Born on February-06:

Year	Player	Position	Years
1903	Robert Clark	Inside Right	1923 - 1928

February-07

With two 4-3 victories (see below), a 3-4 loss (Wolves, **1959**), a 4-2 loss (Liverpool, **1931**) and a 4-1 victory Nottingham Forest, 1925) this day in history has presented some high scoring games.

1914: Newcastle Win 4-3

Newcastle played hosts to Bolton Wanderers in a League Division 1 fixture and two goals each from George Wilson and Albert Shepherd saw them victorious 4-3.

1976: Another 4-3 Win for Newcastle

Newcastle played hosts to Derby County in a League Division 1 fixture and goals from Tommy Craig, Malcolm Macdonald, Geoff Nulty and a Colin Todd 'own goal' saw Newcastle take the points with a 4-3 score-line.

Debut on February-07:

Year	Player	Opposition
1987	Albert Craig (Midfield)	Luton Town
1998	Andy Griffin (Defence) Gary Speed (Midfield)	West Ham United
2004	Michael Bridges (Forward)	Leicester City
2009	Ryan Taylor (Defence/Midfield)	West Bromwich Albion

Born on February-07:

Year	Player	Position	Years
1905	Oswald Park	Centre Half	1924 - 1931
1943	Joe Butler	Right-Back	1960 - 1965

February-08

1894: Objection to St James's Park Pitch Rejected

Bolton Wanderers objection to having to play their FA Cup Second Round tie at St James's Park owing to "the slopes" being unfair to visitors was rejected by the Football Association.

St. James's Park had a very bad slope in those days. It was measured at 18 feet from goal to goal - *meaning the goal-line at the Gallowgate end was 18 feet below the goal-line at the Leazes end*!

1936: One and Only Appearance

Today saw the one and only appearance of David Smith, Outside Right.

Newcastle had to came back from being a goal down to earn a draw with a second half equaliser from Bill Imrie at St James's Park against Burnley in their League Division 2 fixture.

Debut on February-08:

Year	Player	Opposition
1913	Thomas Hughes (Inside Left)	Bradford City
1936	David Smith (Outside Right) William Forster (Right Back)	Burnley

Born on February-08:

Year	Player	Position	Years
1909	Sammy Weaver	Midfield	1929 - 1936
1911	James Robert Richardson	Inside Forward	1928 - 1938
1969	Terry Wilson	Midfield	1992 - 1992
1975	Clarence Acuna	Midfield	2000 - 2003

February-09

1929: Five Star Performance

Newcastle played hosts to Manchester United in a League Division 1 fixture and were resounding winners 5-0.

A Hughie Gallacher hat-trick and goals from Tommy Lang and Tom Urwin ensured the victory.

1974: Another Five for Newcastle

Coventry City came to St James's Park for a League Division 1 fixture and probably wish they hadn't!

Conceding two 'own goals', from John Craven and Alan Dugdale, together with goals by John Tudor, Malcolm Macdonald and Alex Bruce they were soundly beaten 5-1.

Debut on February-09:

Year	Player	Opposition
1924	Albert Keating (Inside Right)	Huddersfield Town
1980	Alex Cropley (Midfield)	Wrexham
1985	Anthony Eugene Cunningham (Forward)	Manchester United
2002	Jermaine Anthony Jenas (Midfield)	Southampton

Born on February-09:

Year	Player	Position	Years
1883	Robert Benson	Right Back	1902 - 1904

February-10

1951: March to the FA Cup Final Continues

Newcastle travelled to the Victoria Ground for their FA Cup 5th Round tie against Stoke City and were victorious 4-2.

Two goals from Jorge Robledo and one apiece from Jackie Milburn and Bobby Mitchell kept Newcastle on track for their eighth FA Cup Final.

1962: Scoring Debut

Jimmy Kerray scored on his debut today in the League Division 2 fixture against Southampton. With other goals from Duncan Neale and Barrie Thomas, Newcastle were victors 3-2 at St James's Park.

Incidentally all five goals were scored in the first half.

First Meeting on February-10:

Year	V	F	A	R	Opposition	Competition
1894	H	1	2	L	Bolton Wanderers	FA Cup

Debut on February-10:

Year	Player	Opposition
1962	Jimmy Kerray (Inside Forward)	Southampton
1968	Alan Foggon (Midfield / Wing)	Arsenal
1996	Faustino Hernan Asprilla (Forward)	Middlesbrough

Born on February-10:

Year	Player	Position	Years
1880	Albert Arthur Gosnell	Left Wing	1904 - 1910
1903	Edmund Wood	Centre Half	1928 - 1930
1945	David Elliott	Midfield	1966 - 1971
1950	Keith Dyson,	Forward	1967 - 1971
1964	Michael Dudley Hooper	Goalkeeper	1993 - 1996
1997	Adam Armstrong	Forward	2013 - current

February-11

1924: Another 2-2 Draw Stalls FA Cup Progression

Newcastle and Derby County played out yet another 2-2 draw in what was proving to be an epic FA Cup Second Round tie.

The original tie, at the Baseball Ground, had been drawn 2-2, the replay at St James's Park had been drawn 2-2 and now this second replay at Burnden Park (home of Bolton Wanderers) was also drawn 2-2!

A Frank Hudspeth penalty and a Stan Seymour goal were equalled by goals from Galloway and Thornewell for Derby.

Debut on February-11:

Year	Player	Opposition
1933	Harold Heward (Left Half)	Huddersfield Town
1961	John Thomas McGrath (Centre Half)	Leicester City
1989	Gary Nicholas Brazil (Forward)	Coventry City

Born on February-11:

Year	Player	Position	Years
1996	Alex Gilliead	Forward	2014 - current

February-12

Start as you mean to go on, go to The Dell and lose! The first meeting between Newcastle and Southampton was to start a very unhappy run of visits to The Dell for Newcastle and the travelling Toon Army. In all they went there 40 times and only ever returned with a victory on three occasions.

1902: Tyne-Wear Derby No. 8

Newcastle hosted Sunderland for a FA Cup Round 2 tie, the 8th Tyne-Wear Derby. Ron Orr scored for Newcastle in the second half. With it being the only goal of the game Newcastle took the tie 1-0.

First Meeting on February-12:

Year	V	F	A	R	Opposition	Competition
1898	A	0	1	L	Southampton	FA Cup

Debut on February-12:

Year	Player	Opposition
1994	Ruel Adrian Fox (Midfield)	Wimbledon
2011	Shefki Kuqi (Forward)	Blackburn Rovers

Born on February-12:

Year	Player	Position	Years
1959	Mick Harford	Forward	1980 - 1981

February-13

1904: Impressive Victory

Two goals from Ron Orr and a goal each from Bill Appleyard and Jim Howie gave Newcastle an impressive 4-1 victory over Notts County at St James's Park in their League Division 1 fixture.

1905: FA Cup Progression after Second Replay

After two 1-1 draws Newcastle finally beat Plymouth Argyle in this FA Cup First Round tie. The original tie at St James's Park (February 04) saw Albert Gosnell score Newcastle's goal, it was Gosnell again who scored Newcastle's goal in the first replay at Home Park (February 08). In this second replay at the Manor Field, Plumstead (home of Arsenal) a brace from Ron Orr, a goal in each half, secured the eventual 2-0 victory.

1924: FA Cup Progression after Third Replay

After three 2-2 draws Newcastle finally beat Derby County in this FA Cup Second Round tie. This third replay was at St James's Park and a first half hat-trick from Neil Harris, together with a goal apiece in the second half from Stan Seymour and Willie Cowan gave Newcastle a 5-3 victory though the match had been evenly poised throughout. Derby's goals came from Galloway and Storer.

1991: Forest Force Replay

After being 2-0 down at half-time Nottingham Forest turned it around in the second half to score twice themselves to force a replay in this FA Cup Fourth Round tie. Micky Quinn and Mark McGhee had gave Newcastle the first half lead at St James's Park but Stuart Pearce and Nigel Clough earned the replay in the second half.

Debut on February-13:

Year	Player	Opposition
1904	Andrew McCombie (Full Back)	Notts County

Born on February-13:

Year	Player	Position	Years
1949	Geoff Nulty	Midfield	1974 - 1978

February-14

1890: Protest Withdrawn

At the Northern League Committee meeting, held at the North-Eastern Hotel, Darlington, Newcastle East End's protest against Elswick Rangers that their game on 14/12/1889 was "played in short time" was withdrawn.

1976: Bolton Force FA Cup Fifth Round Replay

Newcastle trailed in this FA Cup Fifth Round tie at Burnden Park after only five minutes - and the Bolton goal was scored by Sam Allardyce of all people! Two goals from Malcolm Macdonald though saw Newcastle go 2-1 up at half-time. Within six minutes of the second half starting Bolton were back on level terms through Gary Jones.

It looked like Alan Gowling had sealed the game when he made it 3-2 to Newcastle on 82 minutes but once again Bolton came back and with only two minutes of the game remaining, Paul Jones scored the equaliser making the score 3-3 and forcing the replay.

First Meeting on February-14:

Year	V	F	A	R	Opposition	Competition
1981	H	1	1	D	Exeter City	FA Cup
2013	H	0	0	D	FC Metalist Kharkiv	Europa League

Born on February-14:

Year	Player	Position	Years
1951	Kevin Keegan	Forward	1982 - 1984

February-15

1936: Fight Back Earns Replay

Arsenal were the visitors to St James's Park for this FA Cup Fifth Round tie. They took the lead through Hulme but this was equalised by Jack Smith. Arsenal again took the lead through Bowden and went in at half-time 2-1 up. The second half saw Smith once again equalise for Newcastle only for Arsenal once again to score through Bowden again. Fortunately for Newcastle up stepped Tom Pearson to equalise for the third time, bringing the score to 3-3 and earning a replay.

1955: Andrew Aitken, R.I.P.

Nicknamed 'Daddler', Aitken signed for Newcastle as a raw, but already very talented, 18 year-old striker from Ayr Parkhouse (*predecessor to Ayr United*). His time with Newcastle coincided with a rise to great prominence within the early 1900s and with them he won the Football League in 1905 and reached two FA Cup Finals, in 1905 and 1906. His skills also did not go unnoticed by his country (Scotland) for whom he gained eight full international caps and was Captain for the England-Scotland game in May 1902 (a 2-2 draw). In total he made 349 appearances for Newcastle.

First Meeting on February-15:

Year	V	F	A	R	Opposition	Competition
1930	H	3	0	W	Brighton & Hove Albion	FA Cup
2007	A	3	1	W	SV Zulte Waregem	UEFA Cup

Debut on February-15:

Year	Player	Opposition
1930	Joseph Richardson (Right Back)	Brighton & Hove Albion
1947	Albert Sibley (Outside Right)	Southampton

Debut on February-15:

Year	Player	Opposition
1969	Arthur Horsfield (Forward) Gordon Hindson (Outside Left)	Southampton

Born on February-15:

Year	Player	Position	Years
1926	Frank Calvert Houghton	Inside Forward	1948 - 1953

February-16

1907: One and Only Appearance

Today saw the one and only appearance for Newcastle of Left Back Ben Nicholson. Newcastle travelled to Hyde Road for a League Division 2 fixture against Manchester City and came away with a creditable 1-1 draw. Newcastle's goal being scored by Harry Brown.

First Meeting on February-16:

Year	V	F	A	R	Opposition	Competition
1895	A	1	7	L	Aston Villa	FA Cup

Debut on February-16:

Year	Player	Opposition
1901	Frederick Heywood (Inside Left)	Derby County
1907	Ben Nicholson (Left Back)	Manchester City
1957	Albert Franks (Wing Half)	Luton Town
1977	Kenny Mitchell (Central Defence)	Manchester City

Born on February-16:

Year	Player	Position	Years
1885	Jimmy Lawrence	Goalkeeper	1904 - 1922
1973	Christian Bassedas	Midfield	2000 - 2004

February-17

The **1894** League Division 2 fixture at St James's Park saw Newcastle score four goals without reply, each from different players, Joseph Wallace, Tom Crate, C. Quinn and William Graham. It represented somewhat of a 'revenge' as Rotherham had beaten Newcastle 2-1 in the 'away' fixture.

1999 and **2010** saw Coventry City visiting St James's Park for League fixtures, the first being a Premiership meeting the other being in the Championship. On both occasions Newcastle were 4-1 winners.

Alan Shearer scored twice with Gary Speed and Louis Saha getting the other two in the Premiership fixture whilst Wayne Routledge, Andy Carroll, Peter Lovenkrands and Ryan Taylor scored in the Championship fixture.

1912: Tyne-Wear Derby No. 31

Newcastle played hosts to Sunderland for a League Division 1 fixture, the 31st Tyne-Wear Derby. Andy Anderson, Tommy Lowes and Jimmy Stewart scored for Newcastle whilst Harry Low replied for Sunderland thus the game ended with Newcastle being the victors 3-1.

First Meeting on February-17:

Year	V	F	A	R	Opposition	Competition
2005	W	2	1	A	SC Heerenveen	UEFA Cup

Born on February-17:

Year	Player	Position	Years
1915	Jack Smith	Centre Forward	1934 - 1938

February-18

Two FA Cup Fifth Round Replays occurred on this day. In **1976** Newcastle and Bolton Wanderers played out a tepid 0-0 draw at St James's Park to force a second replay.

The result being a bit of a surprise as the original tie had been a rather exciting 3-3 draw at Burnden Park. In the other Fifth Round replay, in **1981**, Newcastle were quite hammered by Exeter City 4-0 at St James's Park - but not 'their' St James's Park as Exeter's ground bears the same illustrious name.

First Meeting on February-18:

Year	R	F	A	V	Opposition	Competition
1905	D	1	1	A	Tottenham Hotspur	FA Cup
2003	W	3	1	A	Bayer Leverkusen	European Champions League

Debut on February-18:

Year	Player	Opposition
1928	John McCurley (Inside Left)	Bolton Wanderers
1933	Robert Dennison (Centre Half)	Sheffield United

Born on February-18:

Year	Player	Position	Years
1962	John Ryan	Left Back/Midfield	1983 - 1984
1975	Keith Robert Gillespie	Outside Right	1995 - 1999
1977	Paul Kenneth Dalglish	Forward	1998 - 1999
1983	Jermaine Anthony Jenas	Midfield	2002 - 2005

February-19

Following the fighting 3-3 draw in the FA Cup Fifth Round tie at St James's Park four days ago Newcastle travelled to London and Highbury for the replay in **1936** and basically surrendered! Arsenal were easy 3-0 winners and went on to be the eventual winners, beating Sheffield United 1-0 in the Final at Wembley.

On a slightly better FA Cup note, a goal by Jackie Milburn in the **1955** Fifth Round tie at the City Ground against Nottingham Forest was enough to earn a replay, the game ending in a 1-1 draw. This of course was on Newcastle's way to the final!

Debut on February-19:

Year	Player	Opposition
1898	William Smith (Inside Left)	Luton Town

Born on February-19:

Year	Player	Position	Years
1870	Johnny Campbell	Centre Forward	1897 - 1898
1957	Raymond Blackhall	Right-Back	1974 - 1978
1961	Justin Fashanu	Forward	1991

February-20

A FA Cup Fifth Round Replay win (2-1) against Leicester City at Filbert Street in **1947**, with goals from Roy Bentley and Tom Pearson is worth a mention, however perhaps we can overlook the 2-0 defeat at the hands of Clapton Orient in **1926** and the 3-2 defeat at the hands of West Bromwich Albion in **1954**, both in the Fifth Round also. The pick of this day in Newcastle's history must go to the eight goal game at Upton Park...

1960: Hammers Hammered - Not Quite

Newcastle travelled to the Boleyn Ground, Upton Park for a League Division 1 fixture with West Ham and returned with the points in an impressive 5-3 victory. Two goals from Gordon Hughes, two goals from Len White and a goal from George Eastham secured this win.

Debut on February-20:

Year	Player	Opposition
1965	Tommy Knox (Outside Left)	Leyton Orient

Born on February-20:

Year	Player	Position	Years
1957	Anthony Smith	Central Defence	1975 - 1979
1985	Alan O'Brien	Midfield	2001 - 2007

February-21

Newcastle got their Anglo-Italian Inter-League Clubs Competition (Anglo-Italian Cup for short) campaign off to a flying start in **1973** with a 2-0 win over AS Roma at the Stadio Olimpico. Both goals were scored by John Tudor, one in each half.

A Shola Ameobi penalty against FC Metalist Kharkiv in the Metalist Stadium in **2013** was enough to give Newcastle a win in the Europa League.

1925: Tyne-Wear Derby No. 52

Newcastle hosted Sunderland for a League Division 1 fixture, the 52nd Tyne-Wear Derby. Two first half goals, one apiece for Willie Cowan and Tom Urwin gave Newcastle a 2-0 victory.

First Meeting on February-21:

Year	V	F	A	R	Opposition	Competition
1973	A	2	0	W	AS Roma	Anglo-Italian Cup

Debut on February-21:

Year	Player	Opposition
1948	Tommy Thompson (Inside Forward)	Coventry City
1953	Len White (Wing/Centre Forward)	Liverpool
2013	Massadio Haidara (Left Back)	FC Metalist Kharkiv

Born on February-21:

Year	Player	Position	Years
1914	Norman Tapken	Goalkeeper	1933 - 1942

February-22

1930: Tyne-Wear Derby No. 62

Newcastle played hosts to Sunderland for a League Division 1 fixture, the 62nd Tyne-Wear Derby. Goals from Jimmy Boyd, Duncan Hutchison and Tommy Lang, with no reply from Sunderland saw Newcastle being the victors 3-0.

1956: First League Game Under Floodlights

Newcastle's visit to Fratton Park today became the first Football League game to be played under floodlights, and Newcastle ran out 2-0 winners over Portsmouth. Bill Curry and Vic Keeble getting the goals.

1958: Scoring Debut

Arthur Bottom scored twice on his debut today in the League Division 1 fixture against Everton. Though Everton managed to score themselves in the second half, Bottom's first-half brace ensured it was not only a scoring debut but a winning one too. So Newcastle gained a valuable 2-1 victory at Goodison Park.

Debut on February-22:

Year	Player	Opposition
1958	Arthur Edwin Bottom (Inside Forward)	Everton
1992	Kevin Sheedy (Left Midfield) Brian Kilcline (Central Defence)	Barnsley

Born on February-22:

Year	Player	Position	Years
1969	Neil Shaka Hislop	Goalkeeper	1995 - 1998

February-23

1976: Newcastle Win at Third Time of Asking

Today saw the second replay of Newcastle's FA Cup Fifth Round tie against Bolton Wanderers. This after the original tie at Burden Park ended 3-3 and the replay at St James's Park ended 0-0. Finally, with a score-line of 2-1, the goals coming from Alan Gowling and Mickey Burns, Newcastle were back on track for the Final. The venue for this second replay was Elland Road, home of Leeds United.

1991: One and Only Appearance

Today saw the one and only appearance for Newcastle of Forward Paul Moran. Newcastle played out a goalless draw at St James's Park in a League Division 2 fixture against Wolverhampton Wanderers. Moran, on loan from Spurs missed an absolute sitter during the game and was later substituted. Never appearing again for Newcastle, he was shipped back off to Spurs.

First Meeting on February-23:

Year	V	F	A	R	Opposition	Competition
1924	A	1	0	W	Watford	FA Cup

Debut on February-23:

Year	Player	Opposition
1985	George Reilly (Forward)	Luton Town
1991	Paul Moran (Forward)	Wolverhampton Wanderers

Born on February-23:

Year	Player	Position	Years
1950	Alan Foggon,	Wing	1965 - 1971
1963	Wesley Saunders	Central Defence	1980 - 1985
1968	Brian Tinnion	Defence/Midfield	1984 - 1989

February-24

Newcastle faced FA Cup Replays in **1909** and **1999**, the first being against West Ham United in the Third Round at St James's Park after the original tie had ended 0-0. Newcastle duly won this game 2-1 with a goal from Andy Anderson and an Albert Shepherd penalty. The latter was against Blackburn Rovers in a Fifth Round tie at Ewood Park after the original tie had again ended 0-0. Again Newcastle were the victors this time by a solitary goal -

but it is perhaps worth noting as it was Louis Saha's second, and last, goal for the club.

1997: Tyne-Wear Derby No. 113

Newcastle played hosts to Sunderland for a League Division 2 fixture, the 113th Tyne-Wear Derby. A Gary Rowell hat-trick and a goal from Wayne Entwhistle saw them crush Newcastle 4-1. Newcastle's consolation goal coming courtesy of John Connolly.

2002: Tyne-Wear Derby No. 135

Newcastle travelled to the Stadium of Light for a Premiership fixture against Sunderland, the 135th Tyne-Wear Derby. A single second half goal from Nikos Dabizas settled the game 1-0 in favour of Newcastle.

First Meeting on February-24:

Year	V	F	A	R	Opposition	Competition
1894	H	4	1	W	Grimsby Town	Division 2
1951	H	0	0	D	Bristol Rovers	FA Cup

February-25

Quite a decent day for Newcastle over the years: 11 wins, 5 draws and only 3 defeats - these being by the narrowest margins, 1-0. Of the wins they recorded 3-1 victories over Cardiff City in **1984** in a League Division 2 fixture, Kevin Keegan scoring twice and Chris Waddle netting the other, and Aston Villa in **1995** in a Premiership fixture, this time Peter Beardsley scoring twice and Barry Venison scoring his one and only goal for Newcastle.

They also recorded a 3-2 victory in **1911** over Hull City, the first meeting between the two clubs, in their FA Cup Third Round tie when on their way to the Final against Bradford City. Yes, not a bad day for Newcastle at all.

First Meeting on February-25:

Year	V	F	A	R	Opposition	Competition
1911	H	3	2	W	Hull City	FA Cup

Debut on February-25:

Year	Player	Opposition
2006	Matthew Joseph Pattison (Centre Midfield)	Everton

Born on February-25:

Year	Player	Position	Years
1886	Harold Hardinge	Inside Forward	1905 - 1907
1898	Lawrence Crown	Left Back	1926 - 1927
1930	Bill Paterson	Centre Half	1954 - 1958

February-26

If yesterday was a good day for Newcastle then historically this one is even better!

Playing a total of 17 games they recorded no less than 11 wins, 4 draws and only 2 defeats - but one of those defeats was a painful one as it was against Sunderland...

1955: Tyne-Wear Derby No. 84

Newcastle hosted Sunderland for a League Division 1 fixture, the 84th Tyne-Wear Derby.

Sunderland took a 1-0 lead into the break and though Jackie Milburn scored for Newcastle they scored again themselves in the second half to take the game 2-1. Both Sunderland goals were scored by Charlie Fleming.

First Meeting on February-26:

Year	V	F	A	R	Opposition	Competition
2004	A	1	1	D	Valerenga	UEFA Cup

Debut on February-26:

Year	Player	Opposition
1898	William Lindsay (Full Back)	Lincoln City

Born on February-26:

Year	Player	Position	Years
1870	Jock Sorley, Centr	Forward	1891 - 1893
1978	Abdoulaye Diagne Faye	Defence	2007 - 2008
1989	Gabriel Antoine Obertan	Right Wing	2011 - current

February-27

Whilst Newcastle may have been put out of the FA Cup in **1902** when they lost their Third Round Replay against Sheffield United it was a different story in **1932**. They reached the Semi-Final in emphatic style against Watford in the Sixth Round at St James's Park. Already leading 3-0 at half-time, Newcastle increased their dominance with two second-half goals, running out easy winners 5-0. The goals being a hat-trick for John Allen, and one apiece for Jimmy Murray and Jimmy Richardson.

1926: Tyne-Wear Derby No. 54

Newcastle travelled to Roker Park for a League Division 1 fixture, the 54th Tyne-Wear Derby. At half-time the score was 1-1, at full time it was 2-2, so honours were even throughout. Tom Mordue and Tom Urwin scored for Newcastle. Dave Halliday and Billie Death scoring for Sunderland.

Born on February-27:

Year	Player	Position	Years
1934	Stanley Anderson	Right Half	1963 - 1965
1955	Anthony Bell	Goalkeeper	1973 - 1975

February-28

Two FA Cup Replays took place today, one in **1951** the other in **1955**. Newcastle won the first, a Sixth Round Replay, 3-1 against Bristol Rovers, the goals coming from Charlie Crowe, Jackie Milburn and Ernie Taylor. Whilst they drew the second, a Fifth Round replay, 2-2 against Nottingham Forest, forcing a second replay. The goals this time from Vic Keeble and Bobby Mitchell.

1976: Newcastle Lose League Cup Final

Newcastle faced Manchester City at Wembley in the League Cup Final, their first, and to date only, appearance in the final of this competition. Unfortunately it was not a happy occasion.

Manchester City took the lead on 11 minutes through Peter Barnes but Newcastle equalised on 36 minutes with a goal from Alan Gowling, 1-1 going into the break. However, within a minute of the restart City's Willie Donachie advanced down the left wing and put in a cross to the far post. Tommy Booth headed it down and with his back to goal Dennis Tueart - Newcastle born, and ex-Sunderland player - hit an acrobatic overhead kick that bounced beyond Mahoney into the bottom left corner of the net.

Debut on February-28:

Year	Player	Opposition
1975	Micky Barker (Left Back)	West Ham United

Born on February-28:

Year	Player	Position	Years
1930	Arthur Bottom	Inside Forward	1958 - 1958
1958	Kevin Todd	Forward	1981 - 1983
1960	Jamie Scott	Midfield	1976 - 1980

February-29

Of course today only ever happens once every four years - shame it couldn't happen every year as Newcastle have never lost a match on a "Leap Year" day. In fairness though they've only ever played four times, winning two and drawing two. With the exception of the game mentioned next, Newcastle only ever scored one goal in each of the games. So the 'roll-call' for those Newcastle players who have scored on these 'special' occasions are:

Bill Imrie, **1936**, 1-1 draw with Norwich City at St James's Park
Steve Watson, **1992**, 1-0 victory over Port Vale at Vale Park
Craig Bellamy, **2004**, 1-1 draw with Portsmouth at St James's Park

With the following of course....

1964: Solid Win for Newcastle

Swindon Town were the visitors to St James's Park and in the four previous meetings between the clubs Newcastle had not lost, and were in no mood to lose this one either.

With only a slender 1-0 lead at the break it was not that easy for Newcastle but they added another three in the second half to record a respectable 4-1 victory. Newcastle's goals coming from Alan Suddick, Bobby Cummings, Dave Hilley and Ollie Burton.

Born on February-29:

Year	Player	Position	Years
1876	Willie Stewart	Outside Right	1901 - 1903
1984	Darren Paul Ambrose	Wing	2003 - 2005

Gallowgate Stand
viewed from Barrack Road along Strawberry Place

MARCH

March-01

In **1958** Newcastle were on the wrong end of four goals when they were beaten 4-2 at St James's Park in a League Division 1 fixture against Aston Villa. They were back on the right side of four when in **2014** they beat Hull City 4-1 at the KC Stadium in a Premiership fixture. Moussa Sissoko scoring twice and Loic Remy and Vurnon Anita getting the other two.

1902: Scoring Debut

John "Jock" Rutherford scored on his debut today in the League Division 1 fixture against Bolton Wanderers. With a brace from Richard Roberts and a goal from Bob McColl to add to Rutherford's Newcastle were comfortable 4-1 winners at St James's Park.

1952: Six of the Best

Newcastle hosted Huddersfield Town in a League Division 1 fixture and a hat-trick from Jackie Milburn, a brace from Bobby Mitchell and a goal for Jorge Robledo saw them run out easy 6-2 winners. With the score 3-1 at the break you could say the second was 3-1 also! A good day at the office for Newcastle whichever way you look at it.

Debut on March-01:

Year	Player	Opposition
1902	John Rutherford (Right-Wing)	Bolton Wanderers
2003	Jonathan Woodgate (Defence)	Chelsea

Born on March-01:

Year	Player	Position	Years
1893	William Bradley	Goalkeeper	1914 - 1927
1980	Diego Gavilan	Midfield	2000 - 2004
1990	Ben Tozer	Defence	2008 - 2011

March-02

Newcastle finally got past Nottingham Forest in their Fifth Round tie of **1955**. This was the second replay after the original tie ended 1-1, and the first replay ended 2-2. Two goals from Alan Monkhouse, one in each half, finally decided the tie 2-1 in Newcastle's favour. Another noteworthy game was the 4-1 beating of West Ham United in a League Division 1 fixture in **1970** at St James's Park. With four goals there were four scorers - Keith Dyson, Alan Foggon, Wyn Davies and Pop Robson.

1932: Five Scored in Eight Goal Encounter

Newcastle hosted Blackburn Rovers for a League Division 1 fixture that saw a flurry of goals - eight in total, with Newcastle getting the better of them and winning 5-3. The Newcastle goals coming from John Allen, with two, Jimmy Boyd, Tommy Lang and Jimmy Richardson.

1963: Tyne-Wear Derby No. 95

Newcastle travelled to Roker Park to face Sunderland in League Division 2 fixture, the 95th Tyne-Wear Derby. No goals were scored so it ended honours even, 0-0.

Born on March-02:

Year	Player	Position	Years
1897	John Hill	Centre Half	1928 - 1931
1901	Jimmy Naylor	Left Half	1930 - 1932
1913	John Kelly	Centre-Forward	1933 - 1935
1945	David Ford	Inside Forward	1969 - 1971
1947	Alex Reid	Midfield	1971 - 1973
1979	Damien Anthony Duff	Midfield/Forward	2006 - 2009

March-03

Though it has nothing to do with Newcastle it is worth mentioning that on this day in **1877** at Elswick Rugby Club the first ever recorded game of football on Tyneside was played between two 'scratch' sides, of eight and nine players respectively. The nine men won 2-0. It was perhaps the start of the journey that would eventually lead us to Newcastle United.

1923 saw Newcastle putting five past Blackburn Rovers in a 5-1 victory at St James's Park in a League Division 1 fixture. They also put five past Charlton Athletic in a League Division 2 fixture in **1979**, again at St James's Park. They also put four past Barnsley in the same competition in **1990**, taking the game 4-1. Unfortunately though not every game this day had such a happy ending.

1934: Tyne-Wear Derby No. 70

Newcastle travelled to Roker Park to face Sunderland in League Division 1 fixture, the 70th Tyne-Wear Derby. With a goal in either half from Harry Shaw and Bert Davis, Sunderland took the tie 2-0.

1956: Tyne-Wear Derby No. 87

Newcastle played hosts to Sunderland in a FA Cup Sixth Round tie, the 87th Tyne-Wear Derby. With goals in either half from Bill Holden, Sunderland took the tie 2-0.

Debut on March-03:

Year	Player	Opposition
1906	James Raine (Outside Right)	Middlesbrough
2004	Martin Brittain (Midfield)	Valerenga

Born on March-03:

Year	Player	Position	Years
1903	Duncan Hutchison	Centre Forward	1929 - 1932
1933	Stewart Mitchell	Goalkeeper	1953 - 1963
1990	Emmanuel Riviere	Forward	2014 - current

March-04

Whilst the **1911** game against Bury in the League Division 1 fixture at St James's Park is worth highlighting, as Newcastle won 5-1 with goals from Jimmy Stewart, Arthur Metcalf, Alex Higgins and two for Charles Randall, this day belongs to the Tyne-Wear Derby. Three times the Tyne-Wear Derby has been held on this day with Sunderland winning once and the other two being drawn.

1950: Tyne-Wear Derby No. 74

Roker Park was packed with just over 68,000 spectators for this Tyne-Wear Derby and most would have been very disappointed to see Newcastle take a 2-1 lead into the break. Sunderland equalised in the second-half so the game ended 2-2. Frank Houghton and Ernie Taylor scored for Newcastle whilst Ivor Broadis and Len Shackleton scored for Sunderland - Broadis of course who was to come to Newcastle and Shackleton who had just left!

1967: Tyne-Wear Derby No. 101

Newcastle travelled to Roker Park for the 101st Tyne-Wear Derby. Unfortunately the short journey back from Wearside to Tyneside was a very miserable one - Sunderland running out 3-0 winners.

2012: Tyne-Wear Derby No. 147

This Premiership fixture saw Newcastle playing hosts to Sunderland for the 147th Tyne-Wear Derby but they were not hospitable hosts, nor were Sunderland hospitable visitors! There were eight yellow cards, five for Newcastle and three for Sunderland, two dismissals, one each, and even a third dismissal which came after the final whistle had been blown (Sunderland's Lee Cattermole), certainly not a game for the faint-hearted.

For the record Sunderland opened the scoring with a penalty by Bendtner on 24 minutes and Shola Ameobi scored an injury time equaliser (90+2) so the game ended 1-1.

First Meeting on March-04:

Year	V	F	A	R	Opposition	Competition
1997	H	0	1	L	Monaco	UEFA Cup

Debut on March-04:

Year	Player	Opposition
1996	David Batty (Midfield)	Manchester United

Born on March-04:

Year	Player	Position	Years
1908	William Noble Imrie	Right Half	1934 - 1938
1931	William Wright	Outside Left	1958 - 1959
1944	Leonard Walker	Defence	1963 - 1964
1997	Freddie Woodman	Goalkeeper	2014 - current

March-05

Newcastle's **1930** FA Cup run came to a halt following their Sixth Round Replay defeat to Hull City, 1-0, at Boothferry Park.

On the brighter side though this day produced two Tyne-Wear Derby wins...

1949: Tyne-Wear Derby No. 72

Newcastle hosted Sunderland for the 72nd Tyne-wear Derby, a League Division 1 fixture. Sunderland held a 1-0 lead at half-time but second half goals from Jackie Milburn and Jorge Robledo ensured the points and the 'bragging rights' stayed at St James's Park.

1966: Tyne-Wear Derby No. 99

Two goals from Alan Suddick, one in each half, meant that the 99th Derby was to go in Newcastle's favour. It was a League Division 1 fixture and with both teams hovering around the bottom of the table it was an even sweeter win for Newcastle.

Debut on March-05:

Year	Player	Opposition
1921	Tom McDonald (Inside Left)	Middlesbrough
1949	Robert Carmichael Mitchell (Outside-Left)	Sunderland

Born on March-05:

Year	Player	Position	Years
1952	Keith Kennedy	Left Back	1968 - 1972

March-06

1909: Tyne-Wear Derby No. 23

Newcastle and Sunderland met in the FA Cup Fourth Round at St James's Park, the 23rd Tyne-Wear Derby. Newcastle scored through Jock Rutherford and George Wilson, but Sunderland also scored twice through Arthur Brown and Jackie Mordue - all four goals coming in the first half.

1976: One and Only Appearance

Today saw the one and only appearance for Newcastle by Goalkeeper Eddie Edgar. Newcastle had travelled to the Baseball Ground for a Sixth Round FA Cup tie with Derby County and poor Eddie conceded four in a 4-2 defeat for Newcastle.

1993: Five Star Performance

Brentford were the visitors to St James's Park for a League Division 1 fixture and were soundly beaten 5-1 by a rampant Newcastle. Lee Clark, with two, David Kelly, Paul Bracewell and Rob Lee scored for Newcastle.

2010: Six of the Best

Barnsley visited St James's Park for a Championship fixture and Newcastle ran riot scoring six times to a single reply from Barnsley so they were triumphant 6-1. If you looked at the first half no one would have guessed the game would have turned out as it did. It was on 44 minutes that Peter Lovenkrands opened the scoring for Newcastle, and that was through a penalty. So the first half ended 1-0 to Newcastle. They say it is a game of two halves, and this certainly was - Lovenkrands scored a second within three minutes of the re-start, Danny Guthrie scored two minutes after that, then Jonas Gutierrez scored, Danny Guthrie got his second and then Kevin Nolan scored - five goals and only 16 minutes of the second half had been played! Barnsley got a consolation through their second half substitute Daniel Bogdanovic on 83 minutes.

First Meeting on March-06:

Year	V	F	A	R	Opposition	Competition
1897	H	2	0	W	Walsall	Division 2

Debut on March-06:

Year	Player	Opposition
1897	J Kinsella (Inside Left)	Walsall
1920	Jeremiah Best (Inside Left)	Blackburn Rovers
1926	Lawrence Crown (Left Back)	Huddersfield Town
1976	Eddie Edgar (Goalkeeper)	Derby County

Born on March-06:

Year	Player	Position	Years
1912	Robert Dennison	Centre Half	1931 - 1934

March-07

1903: One and Only Appearance

Today saw the one and only appearance for Newcastle of Right Back Robert Benson. Newcastle travelled to Anfield for a League Division 1 fixture with Liverpool and were soundly beaten 3-0.

1908 saw Newcastle put five past Grimsby Town in a FA Cup Fourth Round tie at St James's Park. A hat-trick from Bill Appleyard, a goal for Alex Gardner and a Grimsby 'own goal'. They went one better in **1963,** again in the FA Cup but this time in a Third Round tie at Valley Parade against Bradford City when they took the tie 6-1. Two for Ron McGarry, two for Gordon Hughes and one apiece from Barrie Thomas and Dave Hilley.

The Sixth Round tie in **1999** against Everton at St James's Park is worth a special mention - as not only did it see Newcastle putting four past the Merseysiders, but it also saw the one and only goal from Giorgos "George"

Georgiadis for Newcastle, their other scorers being Temuri Ketsbaia, with two, and Alan Shearer.

First Meeting on March-07:

Year	V	F	A	R	Opposition	Competition
2013	A	0	0	D	FC Anzhi Makhachkala	Europa League

Debut on March-07:

Year	Player	Opposition
1896	George Adams (Left Half)	Loughborough Town
1903	Robert Templeton (Outside Left) Robert Benson (Right Back)	Liverpool
1962	Jimmy Fell (Left-Wing)	Middlesbrough
1999	Silvio Maric (Forward)	Everton

March-08

Probably the only highlight of this day in history was the fact that of the 12 games played Newcastle won half of them and drew two.

The best of the wins was in **1952** when Newcastle travelled to Fratton Park for a FA Cup Sixth round tie against Portsmouth. A hat-trick from Jackie Milburn and a goal from Jorge Robledo saw them marching on towards the final with a 4-2 victory. They also recorded a 4-2 victory over AZ Alkmaar in their UEFA Cup Round of 16, 1st Leg tie at St James's Park in **2007**, with goals from Kieron Dyer, two from Obafemi Martins and an 'own goal' by Gretar Steinsson.

1913: Tyne-Wear Derby No. 34

Newcastle and Sunderland met in the FA Cup Fourth Round at Roker Park, the 34th Tyne-Wear Derby. With neither team scoring this set up the 35th Derby and everything was still to play for in the cup...

First Meeting on March-08:

Year	V	F	A	R	Opposition	Competition
2007	H	4	2	W	AZ Alkmaar	UEFA Cup

Debut on March-08:

Year	Player	Opposition
1980	Robert Thomas Shinton (Forward)	Cambridge United

Born on March-08:

Year	Player	Position	Years
1884	James Fleming	Centre Forward	1911 - 1913
1897	John Wilson	Wing Half	1919 - 1920
1972	Giorgos Georgiadis	Midfield	1998 - 1999
1979	David Alexander Beharall	Central Defence	1998 - 2002
1990	Remy Cabella	Midfield	2014 - current

March-09

1907: Charity Shield Winners

Newcastle beat Corinthians 5-2 in the Sheriff of London [Dewar] Charity Shield - this being the fore-runner to the FA Charity Shield. Newcastle's scorers were Harry Brown, with two goals, Jock Rutherford and Bill Appleyard with one each and a Corinthian 'own goal'.

1929: Tyne-Wear Derby No. 60

Newcastle played hosts to Sunderland in a League Division 1 fixture, the 60th Tyne-Wear Derby. It was an extremely tight affair, the scores being 2-2 at half-time and Newcastle just edging it in the second to record a 4-3 victory. The goals coming courtesy of Hughie Gallacher, with two, Tom Urwin and a Sunderland 'own goal'. Sunderland's scorers 'at the right end' were, George Robinson, Bobby McKay and Adam McLean.

1974: Annulled Game

Newcastle played hosts to Nottingham Forest in the 6th Round (Quarter-final) of the FA Cup and after being 1-3 down they fought back to win the game 4-3. However this was only after the match had been stopped following a pitch invasion by Newcastle 'fans'.

Forest made an objection to the FA following the game claiming the pitch invasion and 'other' crowd behaviour unsettled their players. The FA upheld Forest's objection and the game was annulled, therefore being removed from all records, the tie was ordered to be played again at a 'neutral' ground, Everton's Goodison Park being selected.

First Meeting on March-09:

Year	V	F	A	R	Opposition	Competition
1907	N	5	2	W	Corinthians	Charity Shield

Debut on March-09:

Year	Player	Opposition
1910	Arthur Metcalf (Inside Left)	Bradford City
1991	Andy Hunt (Forward) Alan Neilson (Defence)	Watford

Born on March-09:

Year	Player	Position	Years
1894	James Low	Outside Right	1921 - 1928

March-10

1909: Tyne-Wear Derby No. 24

Following a 2-2 draw at St James's Park, on March 06, Newcastle and Sunderland met for their FA Cup Fourth Round Replay at Roker Park, the 24th Tyne-Wear Derby. With two goals from Albert Shepherd and a goal from George Wilson, Newcastle were easy 3-0 winners.

1915: One and Only Appearance

Today saw the one and only appearance for Newcastle of Centre Forward John Soulsby. Newcastle hosted Middlesbrough in a League Division 1 fixture and were narrowly beaten 2-1 *after having trailed 2-0 at half-time.* Newcastle's scorer was Tommy Goodwill.

First Meeting on March-10:

Year	V	F	A	R	Opposition	Competition
2005	A	3	1	W	Olympiakos	UEFA Cup

Debut on March-10:

Year	Player	Opposition
1915	Richard McGough (Centre Half) John Soulsby (Centre Forward)	Middlesbrough
1973	Alan Kennedy (Left Back)	Stoke City
1993	Scott Sellars (Midfield) Mark Robinson (Defence)	Charlton Athletic

Born on March-10:

Year	Player	Position	Years
1968	Pavel Srnicek	Goalkeeper	1990 - 2007

March-11

Without doubt the pick of the bunch for today goes to the 5-1 demolition of Portsmouth at Fratton Park in **1959**. A hat-trick from Bill Curry and goals from George Eastham and Harry Taylor saw Newcastle take this League Division 1 fixture quite comfortably.

Another high-scoring game was in **2004** when Newcastle hosted Real Mallorca in the UEFA Cup 4th Round, 1st Leg tie. Goals from Craig Bellamy, Alan Shearer, Laurent Robert and Titus Bramble securing a 4-1 victory.

1908: One and Only Appearance

Today saw the one and only appearance for Newcastle of Centre Forward Alex McCulloch. Newcastle hosted Preston North End in a League Division 1 fixture and played out a goalless draw.

1939: Scoring Debut

Arthur Frost scored on his debut today in the League Division 2 fixture against Sheffield Wednesday. With Newcastle losing 1-0 at half-time Frost's debut goal and a goal from Willie Scott saved the day in the second-half and ensured that Newcastle were the 2-1 winners at St James's Park.

First Meeting on March-11:

Year	V	F	A	R	Opposition	Competition
1970	A	0	2	L	RSC Anderlecht	Inter Cities Fairs Cup
2004	H	4	1	W	Real Mallorca	UEFA Cup

Debut on March-11:

Year	Player	Opposition
1908	Alex McCulloch (Centre Forward)	Preston North End
1922	Charles Spencer (Central Midfield)	Bolton Wanderers
1939	Arthur Douglas Frost (Forward)	Sheffield Wednesday
1978	Andy Parkinson (Forward)	Manchester United

Born on March-11:

Year	Player	Position	Years
1930	Tommy Casey	Wing Half	1952 - 1958
1952	John Brownlie	Right Back	1978 - 1982

Born on March-11:

Year	Player	Position	Years
1978	Albert Luque	Forward	2005 - 2007

March-12

Newcastle recorded 5-1 wins against Vitoria Setubal in **1969** in the Fairs Cup 4th Round, 1st Leg tie at St James's Park and in **1977**, again at St James's Park this time in a League Division 1 fixture against Norwich City. They also recorded two 4-1 wins, the first in **1898** against Luton Town in a League Division 2 fixture, the other against Bolton Wanderers in **1960** in a League Division 1 fixture. The outstanding game though was the **1994** game highlighted below.

1913: Tyne-Wear Derby No. 35

Following the 0-0 draw at Roker Park, Newcastle and Sunderland met in the FA Cup Fourth Round Replay at St James's Park, the 35th Tyne-Wear Derby. Again the two sides couldn't be separated even with the game going into extra-time.

With both sides scoring single goals in either half, the game ended 2-2 and set up a second replay and what would be the 36th Tyne-Wear Derby. Newcastle's scorers were John McTavish and Colin Veitch, Sunderland's were Charlie Buchan and George Holley.

1994: Seven from Eight

Newcastle hosted Swindon Town in a Premiership fixture and easily swept them aside 7-1. Two goals from Peter Beardsley, two from Rob Lee, two from Steve Watson and another by Ruel Fox was just too much for Swindon

First Meeting on March-12:

Year	V	F	A	R	Opposition	Competition
1969	H	5	1	W	Vitoria Setubal	Inter Cities Fairs Cup

Debut on March-12:

Year	Player	Opposition
1952	Vic Keeble (Centre Forward)	Chelsea
1991	Robert James Elliott (Defence)	Middlesbrough

Born on March-12:

Year	Player	Position	Years
1890	Harry Woods	Inside Right	1922 - 1923
1977	Amady Moustapha Faye	Midfield	2005 - 2006

March-13

Four goals, four different scorers, that's what happened in **1897** when Newcastle beat Derby County 4-0 in the FA Cup Fourth Round at St James's Park. The four scorers being Albert Shepherd, Jimmy Stewart, Jock Rutherford and David Willis.

Four is also the number of goals they scored in **1937** in a League Division 2 fixture against Coventry City at St James's Park, in only the second meeting between the two clubs, Coventry though did score two themselves making the score 4-2 to Newcastle. It was two from Jack Smith and one each for Bill Imrie and Tom Pearson on that day.

Unfortunately four is how many Newcastle conceded in **1948** when they visited The Dell for a League Division 2 fixture. This was the start of a losing streak at The Dell that was to stretch to - you've guessed it - four games.

Debut on March-13:

Year	Player	Opposition
1948	George Lowrie (Centre Forward)	Southampton
1976	Roger Jones (Goalkeeper)	West Ham United
1993	Andrew Alexander Cole (Centre Forward)	Swindon Town

March-14

1906 saw Newcastle win their FA Cup Fourth Round Replay against Birmingham City, with two goals from Bill Appleyard and a one from Jim Howie at St James's Park, the 3-0 score-line propelled Newcastle towards their second successive FA Cup Final.

Perhaps much more important was the **1951** Semi-Final Replay victory over Wolverhampton Wanderers at Leeds Road (the home of Huddersfield Town). Goals from Jackie Milburn and Bobby Mitchell ensured a 2-1 victory and put Newcastle in touching distance of FA Cup glory!

1964: Tyne-Wear Derby No. 97

Newcastle played hosts to Sunderland in a League Division 2 fixture, the 97th Tyne-Wear Derby. A solitary goal from Ron McGarry in the first half giving Newcastle a 1-0 victory.

First Meeting on March-14:

Year	R	F	A	V	Opposition	Competition
1900	W	1	0	H	Glossop	Division 1

Debut on March-14:

Year	Player	Opposition
1923	William Scott (Centre Forward)	West Bromwich Albion
1998	Nikos Dabizas (Defence)	Coventry City

Born on March-14:

Year	Player	Position	Years
1949	Graham Oates	Defence/Midfield	1976 - 1978
1990	Tamas Kadar	Defence	2008 - 2012
1991	Ferreyra Facundo	Forward	2014 - current

March-15

Steve Watson, Rob Lee, Peter Beardsley and Rob Elliott all scored for Newcastle in their 4-0 defeat of Coventry City in a Premiership fixture in **1997**. They were however on the wrong end of four goals in **1930** when Sheffield Wednesday won 4-2 in League Division 1 fixture but the pick of the high-scoring games for this day in history goes to the following...

1958: St James's Park See Eight Goals

Newcastle hosted Leicester City for a League Division 1 fixture and were the winners 5-3. Arthur Bottom scored twice and Len White went one better and got a hat-trick. With Leicester scoring three times themselves this was a bit of a goal fest.

1975: Newcastle Edged in Nine Goal Encounter

Newcastle travelled to Portman Road for a League Division 1 fixture against Ipswich Town. Two goals from John Tudor and a further two goals from Malcolm Macdonald were not enough as they were edged out 5-4, this after going into the break 3-2 up.

Debut on March-15:

Year	Player	Opposition
1913	Edward Cooper (Outside Right)	Blackburn Rovers
1975	Aiden McCaffery (Centre Half)	Ipswich Town
1986	David McKellar (Goalkeeper)	Ipswich Town
2014	Adam Armstrong (Forward)	Fulham

March-16

Having already had to play two replays against Nottingham Forest in the FA Cup Fifth Round and drawing the Sixth Round tie 1-1 at Leeds Road against Huddersfield Town getting to the Final was proving a bit difficult for Newcastle in **1955**.

However they overcame Huddersfield 2-0 at St James's Park, with goals from Vic Keeble and Bobby Mitchell and the Semi-Finals beckoned.

2005 saw another good European night for Newcastle as they breezed past Olympiakos 7-1 on aggregate in their UEFA Cup 3rd Round tie. Having already won 3-1 at Olympiakos, with goals from Alan Shearer, Laurent Robert and Patrick Kluivert, the 4-0 score-line at St James's Park was 'icing on the cake'.

The goals this time coming from Alan Shearer, with two, Kieron Dyer and Lee Bowyer.

Debut on March-16:

Year	Player	Opposition
1912	John George Peart (Centre Forward)	Middlesbrough
2005	Peter Iain Ramage (Defence)	Olympiakos

Born on March-16:

Year	Player	Position	Years
1913	Thomas Usher Pearson	Left Wing	1933 - 1948
1922	Bobby Corbett	Full Back	1943 - 1951
1943	Billy Wilson	Right Half	1960 - 1962
1949	Alan Gowling	Forward	1975 - 1978
1996	Ivan Toney	Forward	2015 - current

March-17

1913: Tyne-Wear Derby No. 36

Following the 0-0 draw at Roker Park and the 2-2 draw at St James's Park, this second replay of the FA Cup Fourth Round brought the tie to an end but unfortunately not in Newcastle's favour. A 3-0 defeat at St James's Park saw the 36th Tyne-Wear Derby, and the tie of course, going Sunderland's way. For the record Sunderland's goals came from Jackie Mordue, who scored twice, and George Holley.

1928: Tyne-Wear Derby No. 58

Newcastle travelled to Roker Park for a League Division 1 fixture, the 58th Tyne-Wear Derby. Both teams scored in the first half, Newcastle through Tom McDonald and Sunderland through Dave Halliday. Being the only goals of the game honours were even, 1-1.

1962: Scoring Debut

Billy Day scored on his debut today in the League Division 2 fixture against Scunthorpe United. As it happened it was Billy's one and only goal for Newcastle but it was an important one. It turned out to be the winning goal in a narrow 2-1 victory at St James's Park.

Debut on March-17:

Year	Player	Opposition
1906	Robert Liddell (Right Half)	Wolverhampton Wanderers
1934	William Noble Imrie (Right Half)	Sheffield United
1962	Billy Day (Outside Right)	Scunthorpe United
1973	Terence McDermott (Midfield)	Manchester United

Born on March-17:

Year	Player	Position	Years
1906	John McCurley	Inside Left	1927 - 1930
1960	Pat Heard	Midfield	1984 - 1985
1979	Andy Griffin	Defence	1997 - 2004
1987	Hatem Ben Arfa	Midfield	2010 - 2015
1988	Fraser Forster	Goalkeeper	2006 - 2012
1992	Michael Richardson	Forward	2011 - current

March-18

The FA Cup Sixth Round tie against Nottingham Forest in **1974** was the game that the FA ordered after annulling the original tie at St James's Park which Newcastle had won 4-3 but only after a pitch invasion and several instances of crowd trouble. Played at a 'neutral' ground, Everton's Goodison Park, it was a rather nervy affair with neither side effective, or scoring, so the 0-0 score-line meant the game had to go to a replay.

Debut on March-18:

Year	Player	Opposition
1975	Ray Blackhall (Right-Back)	Arsenal
1978	Jamie Scott (Midfield)	Chelsea

Born on March-18:

Year	Player	Position	Years
1939	Reg Evans	Left Wing	1956 - 1959
1941	Charles Morgan Parkinson Woods	Forward	1959 - 1963
1968	Temuri Ketsbaia	Midfield	1997 - 2000

March-19

1910 saw Newcastle put four past Tottenham Hotspur, with no reply, to secure a 4-0 victory at St James's Park in their League Division 1 fixture. They also put four past West Ham United in a Premiership fixture in **1994** at Upton Park where they won 4-2. Unfortunately they were on the wrong end of four goals in **2011** when Stoke City beat them 4-0 in the Premiership at the Britannia Stadium.

1902: Scoring Debut & Only Appearance

Daniel Pattinson scored on his debut today in the League Division 1 fixture against Nottingham Forest at the City Ground. With Andy Aitken also scoring for Newcastle, and there being no reply from Forest, Newcastle ran out 2-0 winners. As it happened not only was it Pattinson's one and only goal for Newcastle - it was his one and only appearance too.

1927: Tyne-Wear Derby No. 56

Newcastle faced Sunderland at St James's Park in a League Division 1 fixture - the 56th Tyne-Wear Derby. A single goal from Hughie Gallacher in the first half sealed the win for Newcastle.

1998: Jimmy Scoular, R.I.P.

Scoular was an "ultra-competitive" and tough-tackling right-half who was a double Championship winner whilst with Portsmouth (1949 & 1950). Scoular was bought for £22,250 - what was considered to be a considerable fee at the time, to replace Joe Harvey as Newcastle's captain.

He led Newcastle to their third FA Cup Final success in five years, against Manchester City at Wembley in 1955. In all he made 273 appearance for Newcastle.

Debut on March-19:

Year	Player	Opposition
1902	Daniel Pattinson (Forward)	Nottingham Forest

Born on March-19:

Year	Player	Position	Years
1878	James Howie	Inside Right	1903 - 1910
1896	Joseph Harris	Right Half	1925 - 1931
1967	Darren Bradshaw	Right Back/Midfield	1989 - 1992
1969	Warren Barton	Right Back	1995 - 2002

March-20

A 4-0 win against Sheffield Wednesday in **1909**, a 4-0 win against Bury in **1926**, a 4-0 win against Notts County in **1993**, you'd have thought this was a good day for Newcastle, but the **1907** game takes the shine off everything...

1907: Tyne-Wear Derby No. 19

Newcastle faced Sunderland at Roker Park in a League Division 1 fixture - the 19th Tyne-Wear Derby.

Two second half goals, one from Billy Hogg the other from George Holley saw Sunderland take the game 2-0.

Debut on March-20:

Year	Player	Opposition
1907	William Kelsey (Goalkeeper)	Sunderland
1976	Graham Oates (Defence/Midfield)	Manchester United

Born on March-20:

Year	Player	Position	Years
1942	Ronald Wyn Davies	Forward	1966 - 1971
1959	David John Beasant	Goalkeeper	1988 - 1989
1975	Silvio Maric	Forward	1998 - 2000

March-21

1916: John Fleming, R.I.P.

Fleming never realised his potential at Newcastle, making only four appearances and was soon off to Tottenham. He fared slightly better there, making 19 League appearances in his two seasons there, scoring three goals, before the onset of the Great War (WW1). Fleming signed up with the Queen's Own Cameron Highlanders 8th Battalion. Unfortunately, he suffered a bout of pneumonia at Richmond Camp, Yorkshire and died on 21st March 1916.

1974: FA Cup Progression - At Last

The saga of the 1974 FA Cup Sixth Round tie against Nottingham Forest finally came to an end today.

After an annulled game and a draw Newcastle finally drew a line under this tie with a second half Malcolm Macdonald strike. Being the only goal of the game Newcastle progressed to the semi-final.

First Meeting on March-21:

Year	V	F	A	R	Opposition	Competition
1973	H	1	0	W	Bologna	Anglo-Italian Cup

Debut on March-21:

Year	Player	Opposition
1992	Darron Karl McDonough (Defence/Midfield)	Grimsby Town

Born on March-21:

Year	Player	Position	Years
1877	John Hope Peddie	Forward	1897 - 1902
1967	Malcolm Allen	Forward	1993 - 1995
1971	Marino Rodrigues Cristova Helder	Centre Back	1999 - 2000

March-22

5 - 6 - 7, that's 5 draws, 6 losses and 7 wins, the highlight of them being the game against Blackburn Rovers in **2003**.

It was a Premiership fixture at St James's Park and the goals from Nobby Solano, Laurent Robert, Jermaine Jenas and Craig Bellamy were complemented by a Blackburn 'own goal' and Newcastle were easy 5-1 winners. Interestingly enough the goal that Blackburn did score 'at the right end' came from Damien Duff and in their team they also had Keith Gillespie and brought on Andy Cole as a substitute in the second half.

1969: Tyne-Wear Derby No. 105

Newcastle hosted Sunderland in a League Division 1 fixture, the 105th Tyne-Wear Derby. Newcastle took the lead in the first half through John Sinclair but Sunderland equalised in the second with a goal from none other than Colin Suggett!

Debut on March-22:

Year	Player	Opposition
1961	Jimmy Harrower (Inside Forward) Dave Hollins (Goalkeeper)	Tottenham Hotspur
2006	Craig Moore (Centre-Back)	Chelsea

Born on March-22:

Year	Player	Position	Years
1897	Edward Mooney	Right Half Back	1919 - 1927
1925	Andy Donaldson	Centre Forward	1943 - 1949

March-23

Newcastle scored four against Notts County, a 4-1 League Division 1 victory in **1912** at Meadow Lane, four against Manchester City in **1929**, a 4-0 victory in League Division 1 and four against Sheffield United in a another 4-1 victory in League Division 2 in **1935**, both games at St James's Park. However, they did concede four at Anfield in **1907** when Liverpool won 4-0 in a League Division 1 fixture.

1951: Tyne-Wear Derby No. 75

Newcastle faced Sunderland at St James's Park in a League Division 1 fixture, the 75th Tyne-Wear Derby, on this Good Friday.

Goals from Joe Harvey and Jackie Milburn were cancelled out by goals from Tommy Wright and Trevor Ford for Sunderland. The first half was all-square at 1-1, the game ended all-square at 2-2.

Has there ever been a more even Tyne-Wear Derby than that? Rare indeed if there has.

Debut on March-23:

Year	Player	Opposition
1909	Charles Randall (Inside Forward)	Bradford City
1994	Chris Holland (Midfield)	Ipswich Town

Born on March-23:

Year	Player	Position	Years
1884	George Alexander Thompson	Outside Right	1903 - 1905
1930	Len White	Wing/Forward	1953 - 1962
1993	Curtis Good	Centre Back	2012 - current

March-24

Funnily enough only four of the 14 games played on this day in history have been away from St James's Park. One of those however was a heavy defeat, 5-0, to West Ham United in a League Division 2 fixture in **1979**.

The undoubted highlight of this day has to be in **1894** when Burton Swifts were the visitors to St James's Park for a League Division 2 fixture. With Bobby Willis scoring twice, John Low and Joseph Wallace also scoring, Newcastle were 4-1 winners.

Wallace incidentally is one of a very select group of players who played for Newcastle West End, Newcastle East End and Newcastle United - a very rare 'hat-trick' indeed.

Debut on March-24:

Year	Player	Opposition
1906	James Kirkcaldy (Half Back) Alexander Higgins (Centre Forward)	Aston Villa
1973	Keith Robson (Forward)	Chelsea
1979	Kenny Wharton (Left Back/Midfield)	West Ham United
1990	Billy Askew (Left Midfield)	Blackburn Rovers

Born on March-24:

Year	Player	Position	Years
1953	Jim Pearson	Forward	1978 - 1980
1955	Ray Hudson	Midfield	1973 - 1978

March-25

1899: Scoring Debut

William "Billy" Reid scored on his debut today in the League Division 1 fixture with Derby County. This also represented his one and only goal for Newcastle, but in fairness it has to be said that he did only make four appearances.

James Stevenson also scored that day for Newcastle to record a 2-0 victory at St James's Park. Stevenson was a recent acquisition of Newcastle, and you can guess where they got him from - yes Derby County! There is always something about ex-players coming back to haunt teams!

Debut on March-25:

Year	Player	Opposition
1899	William Reid (Forward)	Derby County
2004	Steven Vincent Taylor (Defence)	Real Mallorca

Born on March-25:

Year	Player	Position	Years
1890	Robert Hewison	Right Half	1908 - 1920

March-26

1951: Tyne-Wear Derby No. 76

Newcastle faced Sunderland at Roker Park in a League Division 1 fixture, the 76th Tyne-Wear Derby, on this Easter Monday. With the Good Friday meeting having ended in a 2-2 draw this game had been eagerly anticipated by both sets of fans. Unfortunately it was the Sunderland fans who were celebrating as a goal from Harry Kirtley and another from Trevor Ford, with only a single reply from Bobby Mitchell meant they took the game 2-1, all three goals coming in the first half.

1991: Smith Resigns

Jim Smith resigns as manager. Initially Smith did well at St James's Park. He took Newcastle to third in the League and therefore the play-offs for promotion to the First Division. However Newcastle lost 2-0 in the play-offs against Sunderland - at St James's Park!

To rub salt in the wound Sunderland were beaten by Swindon in the play-off final who were then subsequently demoted because of "financial irregularities" thus by default Sunderland became the promoted team. Smith lodged an appeal and still firmly believes that as Newcastle finished a long way ahead of Sunderland (who had finished sixth) it should have been Newcastle who took Swindon's place but the appeal was rejected by the FA.

The following season didn't start well for Newcastle and there was clear evidence that all was not well behind the scenes and that there was a rift between Smith and the board. With only 11 wins out of 34 League games, and early exits from both the FA and League Cups, Smith resigned, echoing Charlie Mitten's earlier statement that Newcastle United was "unmanageable".

First Meeting on March-26:

Year	R	F	A	V	Opposition	Competition
1910	W	2	0	N	Swindon Town	FA Cup

Born on March-26:

Year	Player	Position	Years
1912	Harry McMenemy	Inside Left	1931 - 1937

March-27

1897: Scoring Debut & One and Only Appearance

Thomas “Tosh” Blyth scored on his debut today in the League Division 2 fixture with Burton Swifts. This was his only goal for Newcastle and indeed was his one and only appearance. Malcolm Lennox also scored for Newcastle to complete a 2-1 victory at St James’s Park.

1970: Tyne-Wear Derby No. 107

Newcastle faced Sunderland at Roker Park in a League Division 1 fixture, the 107th Tyne-Wear Derby. With the game goalless at half-time it was all to play for in the second half. Both teams scored once each, Jim Smith for Newcastle and Bobby Park for Sunderland so the game ended all-square at 1-1, and honours were even.

Debut on March-27:

Year	Player	Opposition
1897	Thomas Blyth (Centre Forward)	Burton Swifts
1959	Terry Marshall (Outside Right)	West Ham United
1971	Irving Nattrass (Defence/Midfield)	Derby County
1974	Paul Cannell (Forward)	Manchester City

Born on March-27:

Year	Player	Position	Years
1920	Eric Garbutt	Goalkeeper	1939 - 1951

March-28

Newcastle stormed into the **1908** FA Cup Final when they brushed aside Fulham 6-0, in the Semi-Final tie at Anfield. As this was also the first meeting between these clubs Fulham must have wondered what hit them!

Well, what did hit them was Jock Rutherford with two goals, Jim Howie with two goals and goals from Bill Appleyard and Alex Gardner.

1931: Tyne-Wear Derby No. 64

Newcastle hosted Sunderland in a League Division 1 fixture, the 64th Tyne-Wear Derby. The game was goalless at half-time but Harry Bedford scored twice for Newcastle in the second half to give them a 2-0 victory.

First Meeting on March-28:

Year	R	F	A	V	Opposition	Competition
1908	W	6	0	N	Fulham	FA Cup

March-29

Newcastle have played in three FA Cup Semi-Finals on this day, winning one, losing one and drawing the other.

In **1924** two goals from Neil Harris saw them defeat Manchester City at Birmingham's St Andrews, a goal in either half. **1947** was a bit of a disaster when Charlton Athletic won 4-0 at Leeds's Elland Road and in **1952** they played out a goalless draw with Blackburn Rovers at Sheffield Wednesday's Hillsborough.

1992: Tyne-Wear Derby No. 125

Newcastle hosted Sunderland in a League Division 2 fixture - the 125th Tyne-Wear Derby. A first half goal by David Kelly, being the only goal of the game, saw Newcastle take the Derby win 1-0.

2002: Six of the Best

Everton were the visitors today for a Premiership fixture and opened the scoring after only 6 minutes through Duncan Ferguson, whom of course Newcastle had bought from Everton and then duly sold them him back - losing £3m into the bargain! Alan Shearer equalised on 13 minutes and Carl Cort gave Newcastle the lead two minutes later. However it was Everton's turn to equalise on 34 minutes through Niclas Alexandersson, and that's how the half ended, 2-2.

Evenly poised for an entertaining second half - well it was for the Newcastle fans! Andy O'Brien scored on 53, Nobby Solano scored twice in as many minutes, 71 & 73, and Olivier Bernard added a sixth 2 minutes from time - 6-2 to Newcastle!

Debut on March-29:

Year	Player	Opposition
1907	Tom Sinclair (Goalkeeper)	Stoke City
1994	Darren Peacock (Centre-Half)	Norwich City

Born on March-29:

Year	Player	Position	Years
1957	Ian Claude Davies	Left Back	1979 - 1982
1969	Stephen Andrew Guppy	Midfield	1994 - 1998

March-30

Newcastle came through two FA Cup Semi-Finals, one a replay, both with a 2-0 score-line.

1955 saw them beat York City (in the replay), held at Roker Park! It was goals from Vic Keeble and Len White that sealed the victory.

The **1974** Semi-final, against Burnley at Sheffield Wednesday's Hillsborough ground saw a brace from Malcolm Macdonald, one in each half.

2008 saw Newcastle travel to White Hart Lane for a Premiership fixture against Tottenham Hotspur who included in their team Jonathan Woodgate. For whom Newcastle had received a then record receipt of £13.5m from Real Madrid and he had arrived at Tottenham from Middlesbrough. Newcastle had to come back from a goal down but they did this in style taking the game 4-1 with goals from Nicky Butt, Geremi, Michael Owen and Obafemi Martins.

Debut on March-30:

Year	Player	Opposition
1901	Wilfred Innerd (Half Back)	Liverpool
1959	James Gibson (Centre Forward)	West Ham United
1963	Robert Moncur (Defence)	Luton Town

Born on March-30:

Year	Player	Position	Years
1941	John Mitten	Midfield/Wing	1958 - 1961
1949	John Hope	Goalkeeper	1969 - 1971

March-31

1900: Scoring Debut & One and Only Appearance
George Mole scored on his debut today in the League Division 1 fixture against Preston North End. As it happened it was George's one and only goal for Newcastle - and it was his one and only appearance too. Though a scoring debut it wasn't a winning debut as Preston were comfortable 4-1 winners at Deepdale.

1902: Tyne-Wear Derby No. 9
Newcastle travelled to Roker Park to face Sunderland in a League Division 1 fixture, the 9th Tyne-Wear Derby. With no goals being scored honours were even.

1928: One and Only Appearance
Today saw the one and only appearance for Newcastle of Left Half Stanley Barber. Newcastle travelled to Turf Moor for a League Division 1 fixture with Burnley and were soundly beaten 5-1.

1991: Ardiles Appointed
Osvaldo Ardiles appointed as manager. Ardiles, a World Cup winner with Argentina as a player, had moved into football management with Second Division Swindon Town.

Lou Marcari had quit to join West Ham and Ardiles took over in July 1989. His style of management was innovative and his tactics produced attractive attacking football. He led Swindon to their highest ever league position - finishing fourth in the Second Division.

Swindon went on to win promotion to the top flight for the first time in their history - beating Sunderland in the Play-Off Final - only to have the promotion taken from them when the Football League demoted them for irregular payments to players.

Debut on March-31:

Year	Player	Opposition
1900	George Mole (Centre Forward)	Preston North End
1928	Stanley Barber (Left Half)	Burnley
2001	Andrew James O'Brien (Defence)	Bradford City

Born on March-31:

Year	Player	Position	Years
1873	David Richmond Gardner	Left Back	1899 - 1902

APRIL

April-01

1900: Scoring Debut

Edward "Teddy" McIntyre scored on his debut today in the League Division 1 fixture against Everton.

As it happened it was McIntyre's one and only goal for Newcastle but added to a brace from Alex Gardner it ensured an easy 3-0 victory at St James's Park.

2009: Wise Move

Dennis Wise, Executive Director (football) left Newcastle today after just over a year in the job. It's not envisaged there where many Newcastle fans who weren't delighted at this news.

2009: Shearer Appointed until end of season

In a sensational breaking story, that most thought was the biggest April Fool's Day joke of the decade, Alan Shearer was declared as manager until the end of the season. He brought in Ian Dowie as his 'right-hand' man.

First Meeting on April-01:

Year	V	F	A	R	Opposition	Competition
1922	H	0	0	D	Cardiff City	Division 1

Debut on April-01:

Year	Player	Opposition
1903	Edward McIntyre (Forward)	Everton
1911	John Scott (Outside Left)	Arsenal
1914	Edward Stanley Dixon (Inside Forward)	Liverpool
1989	Paul Sweeney (Left Back)	Southampton

Born on April-01:

Year	Player	Position	Years
1957	John Bailey	Left Back	1985 - 1988
1964	Ian Baird	Centre Forward	1984 - 1985
1974	Stephen Craig Watson	Defence	1989 - 1998

April-02

1898 saw Newcastle put five past Gainsborough Trinity, **1983** saw them score four past Grimsby Town, **1988** four past Luton Town and **2011** four past Wolverhampton Wanderers. Some happy times indeed, but perhaps the happiest being the FA Cup Semi-Final Replay victory...

1952: Semi-Final Replay Victory

After the first semi-final saw a 0-0 stalemate at Hillsborough against Blackburn Rovers both teams met again for the replay, this time played at Elland Road, home of Leeds United.

The first half was once again goalless, it seemed like these two teams were never going to be separated, then three goals were scored in the second half, with two going to Newcastle - and it was Newcastle who were heading to Wembley!

The Newcastle goals came courtesy of Bobby Mitchell and Jorge Robledo. Blackburn's goal came from Eddie Quigley.

Debut on April-02:

Year	Player	Opposition
1920	Chris Swan (Inside Right)	Burnley
1969	Preben Arentoft (Midfield)	Tottenham Hotspur

April-03

Newcastle have played 28 times on this day over the years, winning an impressive 17 of them, drawing six and losing only five. In those wins they have scored four goals on four occasions, **1896**, a 4-2 victory over Burslem Port Vale in Division 2, in **1954** a great 4-3 victory over Manchester City in Division 1, another 4-3 victory in **1999** in the Premiership against Derby County and a 4-2 victory over Everton in **2004**, again in the Premiership.

On seven other occasions they've scored three times, **1937**, 3-0 against Burnley, **1963**, 3-2 against Charlton Athletic, **1965**, 3-0 against Derby County, **1990**, 3-0 against Plymouth Argyle, all games in League Division 2. **1993** saw a 3-1 win in League Division 1 against Cambridge United, **1996** saw a defeat 3-4 in the Premiership against Liverpool and **2010** was a return to winning ways with a 3-2 victory over Peterborough United in the Championship.

1963: Scoring Debut

Willie Penman scored on his debut today in the League Division 2 fixture against Charlton Athletic. Along with goals from David Hilley and Alan Suddick it was crucial in ensuring Newcastle a very slender 3-2 victory at St James's Park.

1996: Greatest Game in Premiership History

That is the opinion of others much more knowledgeable about the game than I. It couldn't be the greatest, as Newcastle lost, but it was truly an unbelievably exciting and entertaining advert for football.

Robbie Fowler put Liverpool ahead on 2 minutes, Les Ferdinand equalised for Newcastle on 9. David Ginola put Newcastle in front on 13 and they went into the break 2-1 up. Fowler equalised for Liverpool on 54 minutes, 2-2, Within 2 minutes Asprilla had put Newcastle back in front, 3-2. Stan Collymore than equalised again for Liverpool on 67 minutes, 3-3. Then heartbreak for Newcastle as Collymore put Liverpool 4-3 up in stoppage time and that's how the game ended.

Debut on April-03:

Year	Player	Opposition
1954	William Hamilton Punton (Outside Left)	Manchester City
1963	William Penman (Midfield)	Charlton Athletic

Born on April-03:

Year	Player	Position	Years
1906	Tommy Lang	Outside Left	1926 - 1934
1927	Tom Paterson	Inside Forward	1950 - 1952
1988	Tim Krul	Goalkeeper	2005 - current

April-04

1908: One and Only Appearance

Today saw the one and only appearance for Newcastle of Centre Half William Hughes. Newcastle travelled to Goodison Park for a League Division 1 fixture with Everton and were beaten 2-0.

It is noted that Hughes was the first Welsh player to be signed by Newcastle. There were of course many others to follow him in his journey to St James's Park.

1914: One and Only Appearance

Today saw the one and only appearance for Newcastle of Centre Half Thomas Grey. Newcastle travelled to Villa Park for a League Division 1 fixture with Aston Villa and came away with a creditable 3-1 victory.

Two goals from Albert Shepherd and a goal from George Wilson secured the win.

First Meeting April-04:

Year	V	F	A	R	Opposition	Competition
1973	A	2	0	W	Como Calcio 1907	Anglo-Italian Cup
2013	A	1	3	L	Sport Lisboa e Benfica	Europa League

Debut on April-04:

Year	Player	Opposition
1908	William Hughes (Centre Forward) Scott Duncan (Outside Right)	Everton
1914	Thomas Grey (Centre Half)	Aston Villa

Born on April-04:

Year	Player	Position	Years
1954	George Hope	Forward	1973 - 1974
1989	Vurnon San Benito Anita	Midfield	2012 - current

April-05

1901: Tyne-Wear Derby Abandoned!

The Tyne-Wear Derby on Good Friday of 1901 was abandoned following a reported 120,000 fans trying to get into St James's Park which at the time had a capacity of 30,00.

The decision to cancel the game saw small scale rioting and a number of fans were reported to be injured. The game was subsequently re-arranged for April 24.

1980: Tyne-Wear Derby No. 117

Newcastle travelled to Roker Park to face Sunderland in a League Division 2 fixture, the 117th Tyne-Wear Derby. A first half goal from Stan Cummins gave Sunderland the victory.

1997: Tyne-Wear Derby No. 129

Newcastle played hosts to Sunderland in a Premiership fixture - the 129th Tyne-Wear Derby. A first half goal from Michael Gray gave Sunderland the lead going into the break however Alan Shearer equalised for Newcastle in the second half and honours were even 1-1 at the final whistle.

2010: Promoted!

Newcastle were promoted back up to the Premiership tonight without even kicking a ball. With Nottingham Forest failing to win at Cardiff promotion for Newcastle was ensured - however just to add icing to the cake they beat Sheffield United to close in on the title as well.

2015: Tyne-Wear Derby No. 153

Newcastle travelled to the Stadium of Light to face Sunderland in a Premiership fixture, the 153rd Tyne-Wear Derby.

A goal from Jermaine Defoe in first half stoppage time, being the only goal of the game, gave Sunderland their fifth successive Derby win! A sad, sad, day indeed on Tyneside.

Debut on April-05:

Year	Player	Opposition
1924	Frank Thompson (Centre Forward)	Birmingham City
1999	Jamie McClen (Midfield)	Tottenham Hotspur
2008	Lamine Diatta (Defence)	Reading

April-06

Newcastle were on the wrong end of five goals on three occasions, beaten 5-1 by Newton Heath in **1895**, beaten 5-0 by Portsmouth in **1949** and beaten 5-0 by West Ham United in **1968**.

There was much better news in **1927** though...

1927: Newcastle Score 6 against Arsenal

Arsenal were the visitors to St James's Park in a League Division 1 fixture and Newcastle out-gunned the Gunners with a 6-1 victory.

Hughie Gallacher scored a hat-trick, Robert McKay scored twice and Tom McDonald netted also.

First Meeting on April-06:

Year	V	F	A	R	Opposition	Competition
1895	A	1	5	L	Newton Heath*	Division 2

*Newton Heath became Manchester United, first meeting on 22/12/1906

Debut on April-06:

Year	Player	Opposition
1901	Jim Littlefair (Outside Left)	Sheffield Wednesday

Born on April-06:

Year	Player	Position	Years
1961	Peter Jackson	Central Defence	1986 - 1988
1965	Andrew Walker	Forward	1991

April-07

1923: Scoring Debut

Robert "Bob" Clark scored on his debut today in the League Division 1 fixture against Huddersfield Town at St James's Park. As it was the only goal of the game it ensured it was a winning debut too.

1928: Scoring Debut & One and Only Appearance

William "Bill" Chalmers scored on his debut today in the League Division 1 fixture against Leicester City.

Unfortunately it may have been a scoring debut but it wasn't a winning one with Newcastle being soundly beaten 5-1 at St James's Park. It was also in this game that Right Back Robert Bradley made his one and only appearance for Newcastle.

1993: Six of the Best

Newcastle hosted Barnsley in a League Division 1 fixture and literally hit them for six. A hat-trick from Andy Cole and goals from Lee Clark, John Beresford and Scott Sellars made it a resounding 6-0 victory for Newcastle.

Debut on April-07:

Year	Player	Opposition
1923	Roderick MacKenzie (Right Half) Robert Clark (Inside Right)	Huddersfield Town

Debut on April-07:

Year	Player	Opposition
1928	Robert Bradley (Right Back) William Chalmers (Inside Right)	Leicester City
1956	Robert Ferguson (Full Back)	Manchester City
1980	Brian Ferguson (Midfield)	Burnley

Born on April-07:

Year	Player	Position	Years
1878	Samuel Graham	Outside Right	1902 - 1905
1903	Thomas Evans	Left Back	1927 - 1929
1959	Nigel Walker	Midfield	1977 - 1982

April-08

1905: FA Cup Runners-Up

Newcastle lose the FA Cup Final 0-2 to Aston Villa at the Crystal Palace.

1908: One and Only Appearance

Today saw the one and only appearance for Newcastle of Outside Right Noel Brown. Newcastle hosted Aston Villa in a League Division 1 fixture and were quite convincingly beaten 5-2.

1933: Tyne-Wear Derby No. 68

Newcastle hosted Sunderland in a League Division 1 fixture, the 68th Tyne-Wear Derby. A second half goal from Bobby Gurney, being the only goal of the game handed the victory to Sunderland.

1966: A truly momentous day!

This was the day I attended my first Newcastle match. A truly uneventful 0-0 draw with Everton at St James's Park - but still a game I will never forget…

1972: One and Only Appearance

Today saw the one and only appearance for Newcastle of Left Back Keith Kennedy - the elder brother of Alan Kennedy who was also a Left Back - and kept Keith out of the team! Keith's one game was a 1-0 defeat at Nottingham Forest in a League Division 1 fixture.

1977: Tyne-Wear Derby No. 111

Newcastle travelled to Roker Park to face Sunderland in a League Division 1 fixture , the 111th Tyne-Wear Derby. Sunderland went into the break a goal to the good and scored again in the second half, however Newcastle scored twice in the second half themselves, through Tommy Craig and Paul Cannell so the match ended honours even at 2-2.

Kevin Arnott and Bob Lee were the scorers for Sunderland.

1985: Tyne-Wear Derby No. 119

Newcastle travelled to Roker Park to face Sunderland in a League Division 1 fixture, the 119th Tyne-Wear Derby. With no goals being scored the match ended honours even.

1993: Bobby Mitchell, R.I.P.

Bobby "Dazzler" or "Twinkle-toes", is undoubtedly one of the greatest left wingers of his generation, if not all time. His name is indelibly written in Tyneside football history along with the likes of Hughie Gallacher, "Wor Jackie" and latterly Alan Shearer.

His amazing dribbles down the left wing, his ability to take players on, beating them on the outside or cutting inside were a joy to behold. His crossing ability ensured a supply of goal opportunities for the likes of Milburn, et al, and he could score sublime goals of his own.

The crowd loved Mitchell, and he loved them. To quote Mitchell himself:

"It is a wonderful thing to emerge from the dressing rooms at St. James's Park to the accompaniment of the acclamations of one's faithful supporters. Even after many years with United I used to tingle with satisfaction and pride to hear the Gallowgate Roar."

He made 433 appearances for Newcastle in total.

Debut on April-08:

Year	Player	Opposition
1908	Noel Brown (Outside Right)	Aston Villa
1972	Gordon Henry Hodgson (Midfield) Keith Kennedy (Left Back)	Nottingham Forest
1989	Bjorn Kristensen (Centre Back)	Aston Villa

Born on April-08:

Year	Player	Position	Years
1889	Arthur Metcalf	Inside Left	1901 - 1912

April-09

1905: One and Only Appearance

Today saw the one and only appearance for Newcastle of Inside Forward R. Rutherford. Newcastle travelled to Anfield for a League Division 1 fixture and were quite comprehensively beaten 3-0 by Liverpool.

1932: Tyne-Wear Derby No. 66

Newcastle hosted Sunderland in a League Division 1 fixture, the 66th Tyne-Wear Derby. Newcastle went into the break a goal to the good, scored by Tommy Lang, but Sunderland scored twice in the second half (Benny Yorston & Patsy Gallacher) to take the game 2-1.

1952: Newcastle Fined 50 Guineas

The Football Association fined Newcastle United 50 Guineas today - for giving their players too much allowance (spending money) whilst playing away from home.

Newcastle gave their players £2, the FA rules stated that £1 was the maximum allowance. I would love to see what they would have thought about today's finances in football...

1955: Five Star Performance

Sheffield Wednesday visited St James's Park for a League Division 1 fixture and two goals from Reg Davies, and one each from George Hannah, Bobby Mitchell and Len White saw them leave empty-handed, Newcastle comfortable 5-0 winners.

Debut on April-09:

Year	Player	Opposition
1904	George Thompson (Outside Right)	Nottingham Forest
1906	R Rutherford (Inside Forward)	Liverpool

April-10

1926 saw Newcastle edged in a seven goal encounter at Bramall Lane in a League Division 1 fixture against Sheffield United. Two goals from Frank

Hudspeth and a one from Tom McDonald weren't enough as Sheffield took the points 4-3.

However, there were two occasions where Newcastle scored four themselves...

1936 saw them beat Hull City 4-1 at St James's Park in a League Division 2 fixture, goals from Tom Pearson, two from Eddie Connelly and a Sammy Weaver penalty ensuring the Newcastle victory. It was the same score-line in **2010** when Newcastle beat Blackpool in a Championship fixture. The goals this time coming from Jonas Gutierrez, Andy Carroll, Kevin Nolan and Wayne Routledge.

1909: Tyne-Wear Derby No. 25

Newcastle travelled to Roker Park to face Sunderland in a League Division 1 fixture, the 25th Tyne-Wear Derby. Newcastle went into the break a goal to the good, scored by Albert Shepherd but Sunderland scored three times in the second half, two from Arthur Brown and one from George Holley, to take the game 3-1.

Born on April-10:

Year	Player	Position	Years
1974	Andreas Andersson	Forward	1997 - 1998

April-11

1999 saw Newcastle reach the FA Cup Final as they disposed of Tottenham Hotspur 2-0 in the Semi-Final tie played at Manchester United's ground, Old Trafford.

The game was goalless after 90 minutes so extra-time was played and within this two goals from Alan Shearer, the first being a penalty, saw Newcastle through.

Debut on April-11:

Year	Player	Opposition
1898	Thomas Bruce Niblo (Forward)	Loughborough Town
1950	Jeremiah Lowery (Goalkeeper)	Huddersfield Town
1952	Ken Prior (Outside Left)	Middlesbrough
1955	Alex Tait (Centre Forward)	Everton

Born on April-11:

Year	Player	Position	Years
1974	Anthony Caig	Goalkeeper	2003 - 2006
1991	Nile Ranger	Forward	2008 - 2013

April-12

A pretty miserable day for Newcastle over the years, in the 25 games they have played on this day they have won only 7 times and lost 12 times. They have also failed to score on no less than 11 occasions.

Of those meagre wins they did have two 3-0 victories. One in **1909** over Everton, two goals from Jimmy Stewart and a goal from Bill McCracken - a penalty of course, as all his eight goals for Newcastle came from the spot. The other in **1988** over Watford, goals from Michael O'Neil, Kenny Wharton and Brian Tinnion.

The best of the meagre bunch though was undoubtedly the victory in **1986** over Birmingham City where the score was 4-1, two from Peter Beardsley and one each for John Anderson and Billy Whitehurst.

All three games being at St James's Park and in League Division 1.

We will of course merrily skip over the 6-2 defeat at the hands of Manchester United in the **2003** Premiership fixture at St James's Park.

Debut on April-12:

Year	Player	Opposition
1975	Mick Mahoney (Goalkeeper)	Everton

Born on April-12:

Year	Player	Position	Years
1982	Gary Caldwell	Central Defence	1999 - 2004

April-13

1907: No Home League Defeats All Season

With Newcastle's last home game of the season against Sheffield United ending in a 0-0 draw it meant that they had went undefeated in the League at home for the whole season.

Out of the 19 games played they had won the other 18 - a phenomenal achievement.

1909: Third Football League Title

The game with Liverpool brings the curtain down on a season where Newcastle are crowned as League Champions for the Third time.

1910: Tyne-Wear Derby No. 27

Newcastle hosted Sunderland in a League Division 1 fixture, the 27th Tyne-Wear Derby. A single goal, scored in the second half by Sandy Higgins, was enough to give Newcastle the victory.

Debut on April-13:

Year	Player	Opposition
1895	Donaldson (Inside Right)	Newton Heath
1936	Harry Johnson (Left Back)	Hull City
1985	Paul Gascoigne (Midfield)	Queens Park Rangers

Born on April-13:

Year	Player	Position	Years
1876	Robert Smyth McColl	Centre Forward	1901 - 1904
1929	Tommy Mulgrew	Inside Forward	1952 - 1954
1936	Albert Franks	Wing Half	1953 - 1960

April-14

A score-line of 4-1 has occurred on no fewer than five times on this day, twice it being a winning score for Newcastle and therefore three times it being the losing score.

In **1926** it was 4-1 to Newcastle against Manchester United, in **1932** and **1934** it was Chelsea and Huddersfield respectively who were the winners. Back to winning 4-1 in **1958** this time against Manchester City and the final game that produced this score-line was unfortunately another defeat this time to Sporting Lisbon in **2005**.

The worst of the defeats was yet to come...

2013: Tyne-Wear Derby No. 149

Newcastle hosted Sunderland in a Premiership fixture, the 149th Tyne-Wear Derby. Stephane Sessegnon scored in the first half, then Adam Johnson and David Vaughan scored in the second, handing a 3-0 victory to Sunderland and starting a run of Derby victories for them that stands at five-in-a-row. At the time of going to print Newcastle have still not recorded a Derby victory - or even a draw - to break this run.

Debut on April-14:

Year	Player	Opposition
1900	James Lindsay (Right Back)	Glossop
1906	Tony Whitson (Left-Back) Sid Blake (Goalkeeper)	Notts County

Born on April-14:

Year	Player	Position	Years
1885	Jimmy Soye	Forward	1906 - 1909
1926	Jorge Oliver Robledo	Inside Forward	1949 - 1953
1944	George Watkin	Centre Forward	1962 - 1963
1974	John Watson	Right Back/Wing	1990 - 1993
1997	Callum Roberts	Midfield	2014 - current

April-15

Newcastle suffered their worst defeat in history today in **1895**. Travelling to Derby Turn, the home of Burton Wanderers, for a League Division 2 fixture they were soundly thrashed 9-0.

1905 also saw Newcastle losing in the FA Cup Final, their first appearance in a final, at The Crystal Palace to Aston Villa. Harry Hampton scoring both of Villa's goals, one in either half.

1939: One and Only Goal on 100th Appearance

On his 100th appearance for Newcastle Robert Ancell scored his one and only goal - but what an important goal! Trailing 1-0 to Bury at Gigg Lane in a League Division 2 fixture he scored a second half equaliser and the game ended 1-1. Happy 100 games Robert!

Debut on April-15:

Year	Player	Opposition
1939	Billy Pears (Right Half)	Bury
1989	David Roche (Midfield)	Arsenal

Born on April-15:

Year	Player	Position	Years
1986	Sylvain Marveaux	Midfield	2011 - current

April-16

1932: One and Only Appearance

Today saw the one and only appearance for Newcastle of Centre Forward Tom McBain.

Newcastle travelled to Fratton Park for a League Division 1 fixture and were quite comprehensively beaten 6-0 by Portsmouth.

Debut on April-16:

Year	Player	Opposition
1906	John Dodds (Forward)	Arsenal
1932	Tom McBain (Centre Forward)	Portsmouth

Born on April-16:

Year	Player	Position	Years
1972	Matty Appleby	Centre Back	1990 - 1994

April-17

1948 saw Newcastle win 4-2 over Sheffield Wednesday in a League Division 2 fixture at St James's Park. They went one better in **1954** when they beat Arsenal 5-2 in a League Division 1 fixture, once again at St James's Park. The best though was yet to come!

2006: Tyne-Wear Derby No. 139

Newcastle travelled to the Stadium of Light to face Sunderland in a Premiership fixture, the 139th Tyne-Wear Derby.

Trailing 1-0 at half-time it looked like doom and gloom for Newcastle but a crazy 6 minute period in the second half turned the game on its head.

Michael Chopra scored on 60 minutes to equalise for Newcastle. Barely a minute had passed and Newcastle were awarded a penalty which Alan Shearer scored, 2-1 up. Less than four minutes after that Charles N'Zogbia made it 3-1 to Newcastle.

Shell-shocked, Sunderland offered very little and Albert Luque, just to make sure, made it 4-1 to Newcastle with three minutes to go. A very happy trip home for the Toon Army!

Debut on April-17:

Year	Player	Opposition
1920	Willie Bertram (Inside Left) Henry Wake (Right Half)	Manchester City
1991	Pavel Srnicek (Goalkeeper)	Sheffield Wednesday
1999	David Beharall (Central Defence)	Everton

April-18

Newcastle have played 25 times on this day, winning only five and losing no fewer than 16 times. Whilst the highest losing margin was that to Portsmouth at Fratton Park in **1953**, Portsmouth winning 5-1, the worst undoubtedly being in 1908.

1908: Tyne-Wear Derby No. 21

Newcastle hosted Sunderland in a League Division 1 fixture, the 21st Tyne-Wear Derby. Trailing 1-0 at half-time and ultimately losing 3-1. Their consolation goal coming from Jim Howie. (Sunderland's scorers were Harry Low, George Holley and Arthur Bridgett.)

Debut on April-18:

Year	Player	Opposition
1903	Bill Appleyard (Centre Forward)	Blackburn Rovers
1953	Arnold James Woollard (Right Back)	Portsmouth
1964	Frank Albert Clark (Left Back)	Scunthorpe United
1992	Peter Garland (Midfield)	Millwall

Born on April-18:

Year	Player	Position	Years
1987	Daniel Sean Guthrie	Midfield	2008 - 2012

April-19

1947: One and Only Appearance

Today saw the one and only appearance for Newcastle of Goalkeeper William "Ron" Anderson.

Newcastle played hosts to Leicester City in a League Division 2 fixture and a goal from Charlie Wayman was enough to ensure the game was drawn 1-1.

2010: Champions!

Newcastle were crowned Champions of the Coca-Cola Championship tonight. Needing only one point to secure the title they took all three in the 2-0 defeat of Plymouth at Home Park.

The defeat also meant that Plymouth were relegated, remembering last season and our own relegation we had every sympathy, but well done Newcastle. Andy Carroll and Wayne Routledge being Newcastle's scorers.

Debut on April-19:

Year	Player	Opposition
1947	Ron Anderson (Goalkeeper) Andy Donaldson (Centre Forward)	Leicester City
1976	David McLean (Midfield)	Sheffield United
2011	Stephen James Ireland (Midfield)	Manchester United

Born on April-19:

Year	Player	Position	Years
1944	Ronald George Guthrie	Left Back	1963 - 1973
1995	Kevin Mbabu	Central Defence	2013 - current

April-20

1907: Second Football League Title

The game with Bolton Wanderers at Burnden Park brought the curtain down on a season where Newcastle are crowned as League Champions for the Second time.

Despite losing the game 4-2, Newcastle could not have been caught by second placed Bristol City anyway so the title was already 'sewn up' before kick-off.

2008: Tyne-Wear Derby No. 141

Newcastle hosted Sunderland in a Premiership fixture, the 141st Tyne-Wear Derby. Two first half goals from Michael Owen sealed the victory for Newcastle. As an incidental note, Sunderland brought on Michael Chopra as a late second half substitute.

First Meeting on April-20:

Year	V	F	A	R	Opposition	Competition
1898	H	2	1	W	Stoke City	Test Matches

Debut on April-20:

Year	Player	Opposition
1907	George Jobey (Half Back)	Bolton Wanderers
1987	Brian Tinnion (Defence/Midfield)	Everton

Born on April-20:

Year	Player	Position	Years
1890	Francis Hudspeth	Left Back	1910 - 1929
1942	James Wilson	Outside Left	1959 - 1962
1976	Seamus John James Given	Goalkeeper	1997 - 2009

April-21

1906: FA Cup Runners-Up

Newcastle lose the FA Cup Final 0-1 to Everton at The Crystal Palace. It was their second successive appearance in the final, and unfortunately their second successive defeat.

1934: Five Star Performance

Newcastle put five past Wolverhampton Wanderers in a League Division 1 fixture at St James's Park. The goals coming courtesy of a Bill Imrie hat-trick, and one apiece for Ron Williams and Jimmy Richardson.

1962: Tyne-Wear Derby No. 93

Newcastle travelled to Roker Park to face Sunderland in a League Division 2 fixture, the 93rd Tyne-Wear Derby. Sunderland won the game 3-0 with two goals from George Herd and the other from Willy McPheat.

1986: Newcastle Hammered

Newcastle travelled to Upton Park to face West Ham United in a League Division 1 and were literally hammered 8-1. However this game has to have a special mention if for no other reason than West Ham captain Alvin Martin scored a hat-trick against three different goalkeepers!.

His first, on three minutes was against Martin Thomas, playing despite carrying a shoulder injury. That injury was to force him off at half-time and with Newcastle having no other fit goalkeeper, Chris Hedworth, a defender, took the goalkeeping responsibility for the start of the second half. So it was against Hedworth that Martin scored his second on 62 minutes. Things went from bad to worse for Newcastle, as less than two minutes later Hedworth was carried off with a broken collar bone!.

Newcastle then put their England forward - Peter Beardsley - in goal. It was against Beardsley that Martin scored his third. Also on the score sheet for West Ham was Paul Goddard for whom Newcastle were to smash their transfer record for in the November of 1986.

2001: Tyne-Wear Derby No. 133

Newcastle travelled to the Stadium of Light to face Sunderland in a Premiership fixture, the 133rd Tyne-Wear Derby. After a goalless first half both scored once in the second. Sunderland taking the lead through Patrice Carteron, Newcastle equalising through Andy O'Brien.

Born on April-21:

Year	Player	Position	Years
1981	Titus Malachi Bramble	Defence	2002 - 2007

April-22

The **1911** FA Cup Final between Newcastle and Bradford produced a goalless draw at The Crystal Palace. The replay would be in four days time.

1936 saw Newcastle thrashed 6-0 by Blackpool at Bloomfield Road in a League Division 2 fixture and in **1957** they were beaten 6-2 by Chelsea at Stamford Bridge in a League Division 1 fixture.

It wasn't all doom and gloom however, as this day did produce a 4-1 victory over Bolton Wanderers at St James's Park in a League Division 1 fixture in **1961**, the goals coming from William Tuohy, John McGuigan, Dick Keith and William McKinney.

They also had a 3-0 win over West Bromwich Albion in a Premiership fixture at St James's Park in **2006** with Shola Ameobi scoring twice and Nobby Solano getting a goal too.

Unfortunately though it is the following two games which sum up today in history for Newcastle...

1899: Tyne-Wear Derby No. 2

Newcastle hosted Sunderland in a League Division 1 fixture, the 2nd Tyne-Wear Derby. With Newcastle having edged the first Derby in December at Roker Park, 3-2, it was a return fixture eagerly awaited by both sets of fans. Unfortunately it was the Sunderland fans who were the happier this time as a second half goal from Colin McLatchie, being the only goal of the game, handed Sunderland the win.

1905 Tyne-Wear Derby No. 15

Newcastle hosted Sunderland in a League Division 1 fixture, the 15th Tyne-Wear Derby. To lose at home is bad, to lose at home to your fiercest rivals is excruciating, but Newcastle lost again. Sunderland went into the break with a 2-1 lead and extended it in the second half to make it 3-1 at the final whistle. Newcastle's consolation goal was scored by Colin Veitch and it was George Holley, scoring twice, and Harold Buckle who wrapped it up for Sunderland.

First Meeting on April-22:

Year	V	F	A	R	Opposition	Competition
2004	H	0	0	D	Olympique de Marseille	UEFA Cup

April-23

Newcastle appeared in two FA Cup Finals on this day in history...

1910: Drawn FA Cup Final

This was Newcastle's fourth appearance in a FA Cup Final at The Crystal Palace, a ground they were destined never to win at. Barnsley had taken a 1-0 lead into the break, courtesy of a goal by Harry Tufnell on 38 minutes. However, with only seven minutes left on the clock Jock Rutherford equalised for Newcastle to force a replay.

1932: Third FA Cup Victory (*the "Over the line" final...*)

Newcastle win the FA Cup for the Third time when they beat Arsenal 2-1 in the Final at Wembley

Having went behind on 15 minutes to a goal by Bob John, two goals from John Allen, (38 & 72 minutes) sealed the victory. However the first of these, the equaliser on 38 minutes has been a source of controversy, and much heated debate, over the years. Arsenal were convinced that the ball had crossed the byline prior to Jimmy Richardson putting in the cross from which Allen scored. Without 'instant replays' and the myriad of cameras that appear in any game nowadays, let alone how many in a FA Cup Final, which side of the argument you believed obviously depended upon which team you supported. Analysis using 'modern' technologies does suggest that the ball was indeed over the line - but then I'm a Newcastle fan, we won, and that's all that matters!

1984 produced a game in League Division 2 that had no such controversy - a 5-1 win over Carlisle United at St James's Park. A game that is notable as not only was Bob Stokoe the Carlisle manager that day, but they also included Alan Shoulder in their side. The game was also notable as it saw two goals each for Kevin Keegan and Peter Beardsley and a one for Chris Waddle.

First Meeting on April-23:

Year	V	F	A	R	Opposition	Competition
1910	N	1	1	D	Barnsley	FA Cup

Debut on April-23:

Year	Player	Opposition
1898	Jim Lockey (Right Back)	Stoke City
1960	Brian Wright (Wing Half)	Nottingham Forest

Born on April-23:

Year	Player	Position	Years
1901	Albert McInroy	Goalkeeper	1929 - 1934
1924	Frank Brennan	Centre Half	1946 - 1956
1976	Darren Huckerby	Forward	1995 - 1996

April-24

1901: Tyne-Wear Derby No. 6

The 6th Tyne-Wear Derby eventually took place today after the abandoned Good Friday fixture. Perhaps Newcastle would have preferred it not to have taken place at all as they went down 2-0 at St James's Park with a Hogg goal in either half - though they were different players. Sunderland had both a Bobby Hogg and a Billy Hogg playing for them that day. Reports are quite 'sketchy', and contradictory, but consensus of opinion is that Bobby scored in the first half and Billy scored in the second.

1965: Newcastle Win League Division 2 Title

Perhaps never before has a goalless draw meant so much, but this draw against Manchester City at St James's Park was enough to ensure that Newcastle were not only promoted to the top-flight (League Division 1), but that they were promoted as Champions!

1974: Newcastle Win the Texaco Cup

Burnley and Newcastle faced each other in the Texaco Cup Final at St James's Park. Goals from Malcolm Macdonald and Bobby Moncur hand the cup to Newcastle in a 2-1 victory.

Debut on April-24:

Year	Player	Opposition
1937	Arnold Grundy (Left Half)	Bradford City

Born on April-24:

Year	Player	Position	Years
1962	Stuart Pearce	Defence	1997 - 1999
1967	Lionel Perez	Goalkeeper	1998 - 2000

April-25

1903: Tyne-Wear Derby No. 11

Newcastle hosted Sunderland in a League Division 1 fixture, the 11th Tyne-Wear Derby. A solitary goal in the second half from Bob McColl gave Newcastle the victory.

1908: Newcastle Lose FA Cup Final

Newcastle's third FA Cup at The Crystal Palace, and their third defeat. Wolverhampton Wanderers were the victors on this occasion with a 3-1 score-line. Newcastle's 'consolation' goal coming from Jim Howie in the second half.

1993: Tyne-Wear Derby No. 127

Newcastle hosted Sunderland in a League Division 1 fixture, the 127th Tyne-Wear Derby. A solitary goal in the second half from Scott Sellars gave Newcastle the victory.

Debut on April-25:

Year	Player	Opposition
1936	Ernest Hall (Centre Half)	Blackpool
1964	Geoffrey Barry Allen (Outside Left)	Norwich City

Born on April-25:

Year	Player	Position	Years
1907	Wilfred Bott,	Outside Right	1934 -1936

April-26

1911: FA Cup Runners-Up
After a draw at The Crystal Palace, Newcastle lose the Final replay at Old Trafford 0-1 to Bradford City.

1924: Second FA Cup Victory
Newcastle win the FA Cup for the Second time when they beat Aston Villa 2-0 in the Final at Wembley. Both goals coming in the last eight minutes of the game, Neil Harris on 82 and Stan Seymour three minutes later on 85.

1952: Six of the Best
Newcastle put six past Aston Villa in a League Division 1 fixture at St James's Park. Newcastle led 4-0 at half-time and increased their lead in the second, though Villa did get a consolation goal, the final score being 6-1. Newcastle's scorers were Frank Brennan, Reg Davies, who scored twice, George Hannah, Jackie Milburn and Bobby Mitchell.

2003: Tyne-Wear Derby No. 137
Newcastle travelled to the Stadium of Light to face Sunderland in a Premiership fixture, the 137th Tyne-Wear Derby. A penalty, two minutes before the break from Nobby Solano gave Newcastle the victory 1-0.

Debut on April-26:

Year	Player	Opposition
1905	Robert Crumley (Goalkeeper)	Sheffield Wednesday

Born on April-26:

Year	Player	Position	Years
1906	Alexander Hall	Centre Forward	1907 - 1908

April-27

In **1910** Newcastle faced Aston Villa in a League Division 1 fixture at Villa Park and were soundly beaten 4-0. *We will not mention in any detail the 6-0 thrashing that Liverpool handed out to Newcastle in 2013 - at St James's Park either!*

However it was much better news in 1994.

1994: Five Star Performance

Aston Villa were the visitors to St James's Park in this Premiership fixture and took the lead after 10 minutes through Stefan Beinlich. Five minutes later though Newcastle were level with a goal from Paul Bracewell. Newcastle then took the lead on 23 minutes when Peter Beardsley scored from the penalty spot and Andy Cole made it 3-1 going into the break with a goal on 41 minutes. Beardsley scored again on 66 minutes to extended Newcastle's lead and Scott Sellars wrapped it all up on 79 minutes. A comfortable 5-1 victory to Newcastle.

Debut on April-27:

Year	Player	Opposition
1912	John McTavish (Forward)	Blackburn Rovers
1929	David Fairhurst (Left Back)	Derby County
1935	Jimmy Gordon (Wing Half)	Oldham Athletic

Born on April-27:

Year	Player	Position	Years
1877	Andrew Aitken	Centre Half	1895 - 1906
1933	William Tuohy	Outside Left	1960 - 1963

April-28

1900: Tyne-Wear Derby No. 4

Newcastle travelled to Roker Park to face Sunderland in a League Division 1 fixture, the 4th Tyne-Wear Derby. Any win against Sunderland is always a good one of course, made all the better if you beat them on their 'own turf', and that's exactly what Newcastle did with a 2-1 victory.

John Fraser and Andy Gardner scored for Newcastle and William Fulton scored for Sunderland. All the goals being scored in the first half.

1909: Charity Shield Winners

Newcastle won the Charity Shield when they beat Northampton Town 2-0 at Stamford Bridge. The only time they have won this despite having contested it seven in total times over the years. Though they did win its predecessor the Sheriff of London Charity Shield in 1907. The goals came from Stan Allen and Jock Rutherford.

1910: First FA Cup Victory
After a 1-1 draw against Barnsley at The Crystal Palace, Newcastle win the replay at Goodison Park with two second-half goals from Albert Shepherd, the second being a penalty.

1951: Fourth FA Cup Victory
Newcastle win the FA Cup for the Fourth time when they beat Blackpool in the Final at Wembley. Two second half goals from Jackie Milburn ensuring the cup was on its way back to Tyneside.

1958: One and Only Appearance
Today saw the one and only appearance for Newcastle of Goalkeeper Chris Harker. Newcastle played hosts to Burnley in a League Division 1 fixture and Harker was beaten three times as Burnley were 3-1 victors on the day.

1915: One and Only Appearance
Today saw the one and only appearance for Newcastle of Inside Left, Thomas Cairns. Newcastle played hosts to Aston Villa in a League Division 1 fixture and goals from Tommy Goodwill, Billy Hibbert and Edward Cooper, one of only two goals he scored for Newcastle, saw Newcastle win 3-0 quite comfortably.

2001: Speed Sets Record
Gary Speed set a new Premiership appearance record today. Overtaking Peter Atherton, Speed moved to the top of the Premiership's appearances record by playing in his 318th game in the match against Leicester City.

2009: Gutierrez Settlement
It was revealed today that the three clubs involved in the Jonas Gutierrez move to St James's Park had come to an "out of court" settlement with the result being that Newcastle now hold his registration.

First Meeting on April-28:

Year	R	F	A	V	Opposition	Competition
1898	L	3	4	A	Blackburn Rovers	Test Matches
1909	W	2	0	N	Northampton Town	Charity Shield

Debut on April-28:

Year	Player	Opposition
1915	Thomas Cairns (Inside Left)	Aston Villa
1958	Chris Harker (Goalkeeper)	Burnley

Debut on April-28:

Year	Player	Opposition
1962	David Turner (Midfield)	Leeds United

Born on April-28:

Year	Player	Position	Years
1925	George Hair	Outside Left	1943 - 1949

April-29

1905: First Football League Title

A comprehensive 3-0 victory over Middlesbrough at Ayresome Park brought the curtain down on a season where Newcastle are crowned as League Champions for the First time. Ron Orr, Bill Appleyard and Jock Rutherford supplying the goals.

1922: One and Only Appearance

Today saw the one and only appearance for Newcastle of Goalkeeper John "Jack" Archibald. Newcastle played hosts to Manchester City in a League Division 1 fixture and though Archibald was beaten once, a hat-trick from Tom McDonald and a brace from Alfred Hagan saw Newcastle 5-1 victors on the day.

1932: John Auld R.I.P.

It was sadly noted that John Auld died today. A Centre-Half who upon retiring from playing at Newcastle was appointed to the Board of directors played only 15 games for Newcastle, scoring three times. Auld has the distinction of being the first ever player to transfer from Sunderland to Newcastle.

Debut on April-29:

Year	Player	Opposition
1922	John Archibald (Goalkeeper)	Manchester City

Born on April-29:

Year	Player	Position	Years
1907	James Murray Boyd	Outside Right	1925 - 1935
1917	John Douglas Wright	Wing Half	1938 - 1948
1955	Ralph Callachan	Midfield	1977 - 1978

April-30

1898 saw Newcastle playing Blackburn Rovers in the Test Matches, the forerunner of the Play-Offs for promotion to League Division 1. Having lost the first Test Match 4-3 at Ewood Park, Newcastle took this second match with a resounding 4-0 victory at St James's Park. The goals coming from Johnny Campbell, John Harvey, Tommy Ghee and James Jackson. The win though still wasn't enough to earn them promotion - for now! If you can't wait to find out what happened skip ahead to May-20...

1933: Wilfred Low, R.I.P.

Low came to Newcastle in a deal that saw Jimmy Soye go the other way and he became an absolute institution at St James's Park. In total he was at Newcastle for almost 40 years, as player, trainer and groundsman. As a player he was a 'fearsome' competitor, using his strong build to tremendous effect, which all belied his nickname of the "Laughing Cavalier". Absolutely magnificent at centre-half it was no surprise when he was made team captain then gained international honours with Scotland. Low made 367 appearances for Newcastle.

1969: Five Star Performance

Stoke City were the visitors to St James's Park in this League Division 1 fixture. Newcastle took a slender 1-0 lead into the break but were quite rampant in the second half scoring four more. With no reply from Stoke the result was 5-0 to Newcastle. Their scorers being Benny Arentoft, Wyn Davies, Pop Robson and two for Jim Scott.

Debut on April-30:

Year	Player	Opposition
1921	Robert Roxburgh (Right Back)	Arsenal

Born on April-30:

Year	Player	Position	Years
1963	Glyn Hodges	Midfield	1987 - 1987
1986	Robert Elliot	Goalkeeper	2011 - current

May

May-01

In **2010** Newcastle played the last game of the 2009-10 season at Loftus Road against Queens Park Rangers.

Having already won promotion back to the Premiership and of being promoted as Champions, you may be forgiven to think that there was little to play for - but being on 99 points Newcastle were desperate to get a least a draw to reach the magic 100, and they did so - and better. With a 1-0 win, courtesy of a second half goal from Peter Lovenkrands they finished on 102 points, this with a goal difference of +55 as well.

Debut on May-01:

Year	Player	Opposition
1982	Derek Bell (Midfield) Paul Ferris (Midfield / Wing)	Blackburn Rovers

Born on May-01:

Year	Player	Position	Years
1905	John Dowsey	Inside Right	1924 - 1926
1943	Trevor Hockey	Midfield	1963 - 1965
1973	Jimmy Crawford	Midfield	1995 - 1998
1991	Ryan Donaldson	Forward	2008 - current
1992	Sammuel Ameobi	Forward	2008 - current

May-02

1979 - Goals from Peter Withe, Alan Shoulder and John Bird gave Newcastle a comfortable 3-0 victory over Bristol Rovers in a League Division 2 fixture a St James Park.

A bit of a 'nothing' game as neither had anything to play for really, both were pretty safe from relegation, neither had any chance of getting into the promotion places and only 9, 627 fans bothered to turn up to watch it. Pretty much sums it up!

1998 and **2012** saw Newcastle beating Chelsea, 3-1 and 2-0 respectively, the pick of the bunch today though is the following...

1973: Five Star Performance

Torino Calcio were the visitors to St James's Park in this Anglo-Italian Cup tie. The one and only meeting between the two clubs and will they be thankful of that - Newcastle simply outclassed them with a fine display winning 5-1. The ease of the victory was not apparent in the first half as a single goal from John Tudor was all that separated them.

As they say - "football is a game of two halves" - and this one proved the point with Newcastle running in four goals, they being from Malcolm Macdonald, Jim Smith, Terry Hibbitt and a Torini 'own goal' conceded by Masiello.

First Meeting on May-02:

Year	V	F	A	R	Opposition	Competition
1973	H	5	1	W	Torino Calcio	Anglo-Italian Cup

Debut on May-02:

Year	Player	Opposition
1921	Samuel Russell (Left Back)	Manchester City
1979	Peter Manners (Midfield)	Bristol Rovers

Born on May-02:

Year	Player	Position	Years
1944	Alan Suddick	Midfield/Forward	1961 - 1966
1959	Gary Megson	Midfield	1984 - 1986
1962	Micky Quinn	Centre Forward	1989 - 1992
1978	Didier Domi	Defence	1998 - 2000
1980	Fabrice Pancrate	Wing	2009 - 2010

May-03

1952: Fifth FA Cup Victory

Newcastle win the FA Cup for the Fifth time - and the second time in succession - when they beat Arsenal in the Final at Wembley.

They left it late as it was on 84 minutes when they scored the only goal of the game, but Jorge Robledo delivered the goods - and the cup was on its way back to Tyneside.

1972: Four in Six Goal Encounter

West Bromwich Albion came to St James's Park for a League Division 1 fixture that saw six goals being scored - four by Newcastle. Their goals coming from an Albion 'own goal' by John Wile, two goals from Malcolm Macdonald and one (the second) of only three goals ever scored from perhaps one of the most talented and gifted midfielders Newcastle have had, (*personal opinion only*) Tony Green.

For the record Bobby Gould scored both goals for West Bromwich Albion.

1995: Six Goals Shared at St James's Park

St James's Park saw another six goal encounter when Tottenham Hotspur were the visitors in Premiership fixture. Newcastle were 2-0 to the good after only ten minutes thanks to goals from Keith Gillespie (7 minutes) and Darren Peacock (10 minutes).

If scoring twice in three minutes was good - Spurs went better when they scored three times in four minutes! Nick Barmby pulling one back on 22 minutes, Jurgen Klinsman equalising on 24 minutes and Darren Anderton giving them the lead on 26 minutes. That is how the half ended, 3-2 to Spurs.

Peter Beardsley was Newcastle saviour on 70 minutes when he equalised for Newcastle and with no more goals being scored the game ended honours even at 3-3 - a crazy game!

May-04

1930: Relegation Avoided

Going into the last game of the 1929-30 season Newcastle were still staring at possible relegation. Hosting West Ham United made for nervy St James's Park to say the least. With no goals scored in the first Newcastle had 45 minutes to save their season. It was therefore a divine goal - scored by Joe Devine - that gave Newcastle the vital points and First Division survival.

1974: FA Cup Runners-Up

A dismal display at Wembley! Liverpool outclass Newcastle and win 3-0 - with Kevin Keegan scoring two of their goals!

1968 saw Newcastle being thrashed 6-0 by Manchester United at Old Trafford in a League Division 1 fixture. However it wasn't all bad news on this day, there was one highlight.

1983: Five Star Performance

Newcastle travelled to Oakwell Stadium for a League Division 2 fixture with Barnsley and duly ran out 5-0 winners. Two goals from Imrie Varadi, two goals from Neil McDonald and a goal from Kevin Keegan sealed the victory. Also noteworthy are two of Barnsley's players that day - Stewart Barrowclough and Tony Cunningham. The former an ex-Newcastle favourite and the latter to become the first black player to sign for Newcastle, though not the first to play, that honour and distinction belongs to Howard Gayle who Newcastle had 'on loan' from Liverpool earlier in the season.

Debut on May-04:

Year	Player	Opposition
1983	Martin Richard Thomas (Goalkeeper)	Barnsley
1991	Lee Makel (Midfield)	West Bromwich Albion

Born on May-04:

Year	Player	Position	Years
1922	Len Shackleton	Inside Forward	1946 - 1948

May-05

1947: Martin Moves In

George Martin was appointed as Newcastle's manager after the end of World War II. He replaced the Stan Seymour led Directors Committee which had been in control since the start of hostilities.

When one of his first actions was to sell fans favourite Len Shackleton to Sunderland there were many a raised eyebrow! Martin however turned out to be quite a successful manager, guiding Newcastle to promotion back to the top-flight (League Division 1) in his first season. He actually ended his time with Newcastle with a win percentage of 49.7%, from 149 games, a record that was to stand until the first period of managership from Kevin Keegan.

1969: One and Only Appearance

Today saw the one and only appearance for Newcastle of Goalkeeper John Hope. Newcastle travelled to Maine Road to face Manchester City in a League Division 1 fixture. Hope was beaten by the only goal of the game as Newcastle went down 1-0.

2009: Newcastle Suspend Barton

Newcastle suspended Joey Barton "until further notice", this after his red card at Liverpool and what was said to be a furious bust-up with Alan Shearer in the dressing room after the game.

Debut on May-05:

Year	Player	Opposition
1969	John Hope (Goalkeeper)	Manchester City

Born on May-05:

Year	Player	Position	Years
1959	Andy Parkinson	Forward	1978 - 1979

May-06

2007: Roeder Resigns

Glenn Roeder resigned as manager with one game of the season remaining. There are huge rumours that it was a 'walk or be pushed' situation. Roeder had not only been Newcastle's manager but he had also been a player, indeed captain, as well. It was a somewhat strange decision and had a mixed reaction from the Newcastle fans.

Nigel Pearson was appointed as 'caretaker' manager for the remaining game of the season.

2013: Steve Carney R.I.P.

We were all saddened and stunned by the news of the death of Steve Carney. A versatile and dependable defender. Steve was one of the stars of the Blyth Spartans side that did so well in the FA Cup in 1978, and was consequently snapped up by Newcastle for a mere £1,000. Going on to give 6 seasons of solid and workmanlike service - surely one of Newcastle's greatest ever bargains.

May-07

1955: Sixth FA Cup Victory

Newcastle win the FA Cup for the sixth time when they beat Manchester City 3-1 in the Final at Wembley.

This final produced the then fastest ever goal scored in a FA Cup Final when Jackie Milburn scored with a header after only 45 seconds. Newcastle's other goals coming from Bobby Mitchell and George Hannah.

Though Newcastle won the cup this was the beginning of the end for manager Doug Livingstone who had sensationally left Jackie Milburn out of the team but had been 'ordered' by Stan Seymour and other directors to play him.

Debut on May-07:

Year	Player	Opposition
1938	Albert Stubbins (Centre Forward)	Luton Town

Born on May-07:

Year	Player	Position	Years
1962	Brian Kilcline	Central Defence	1992 - 1994

May-08

Newcastle have played seven times on this day, and failed to score in five of them! The two games in which they did score they won both, and both funnily enough both were against Wrexham in League Division 2 fixtures at St James Park.

The first, in **1979**, they won 2-0 with goals from Jim Pearson and Alan Shoulder. The second game in **1982** ended 4-2 to Newcastle with their goals coming from Chris Waddle, Imrie Varadi, John Trewick and John Brownlie.

Born on May-08:

Year	Player	Position	Years
1936	Malcolm Scott	Centre Half	1955 - 1961
1940	Carl Wilson	Centre Forward	1958 - 1959
1973	Laurent Charvet	Full Back	1998 - 2000

May-09

1993: Seven Heaven

Already Champions of League Division 1, already promoted to the Premiership, you'd have forgiven everyone for thinking that this was nothing more than a stroll out in park in front of your fans to celebrate the end of season. That's exactly what it was - but what a celebration! Going into the break already 6-0 up Newcastle were flying, the crowd was buzzing - well at least the home sections were, and poor Leicester must not have wanted to come out for the second half.

Newcastle though really took their foot off the pedal and enjoyed the occasion, even letting Leicester get a consolation goal, but scoring one themselves also. 7-1 being the final result, a great day for the Toon Army.

Newcastle's goals by the way coming courtesy of hat-tricks from Andy Cole and David Kelly and a one for Rob Lee.

Born on May-09:

Year	Player	Position	Years
1934	William Hamilton Punton	Outside Left	1954 - 1958
1946	Ian Mitchell	Outside Left	1970 - 1971
1959	David Barton	Central Defence	1975 - 1983
1964	Frank Pingel	Forward	1989 - 1989

May-10

1947: Five Star Performance

A hat-trick from Roy Bentley and goals from Tommy Walker and Charlie Wayman secured a 5-0 victory over Bradford Park Avenue at St James's Park in a League Division 2 fixture.

1998: Poor Finish For Newcastle

A 1-0 defeat to Blackburn Rovers at Ewood Park saw the 1997-98 season coming to a close. Newcastle finished 13th, which may sound credible, but with only 44 points they escaped relegation by a mere four points.

May-11

1997: Premiership Runners Up - *by Goal Difference...*

A convincing 5-0 victory over Nottingham Forest at St James's Park secured a second place finish in the Premiership, only seven points behind champions Manchester United. Liverpool and Arsenal were tied with Newcastle on 68 points but the five goals, a brace from Les Ferdinand and others from Tino Asprilla, Alan Shearer and Robbie Elliott meant Newcastle had a goal difference of 33 whilst Arsenal who had also won that day (3-1 at Derby County) had a goal difference of 30. Liverpool were somewhat behind with a goal difference of 25.

2012: Premiership Manager of the Year

Newcastle may not be the best team in the Premiership, but they had the best manager - and that's official. Alan Pardew is awarded the Premier League Manager of the Year Award for the 2011-12 season.

Debut on May-11:

Year	Player	Opposition
1991	John Watson (Right Back/Wing)	Hull City
2003	Darren Paul Ambrose (Winger)	West Bromwich Albion

Born on May-11:

Year	Player	Position	Years
1924	John Edward Thompson Milburn	Centre Forward	1943 - 1957

May-12

1984: Third Place and Promotion Consolidated

Whilst their third place finish, and hence their promotion to the First Division, was never in any danger (as they had a final 10 point cushion over fourth placed Manchester City), the 3-1 win over Brighton & Hove Albion was 'icing on the cake' and only ensured everyone one was in a fine mood on Tyneside and all were eagerly awaiting the return to the top-flight.

Chris Waddle, Peter Beardsley and Kevin Keegan supplying the goals.

2004: Six Goal Thriller at St Mary's

Newcastle took the lead on 7 minutes through Shola Ameobi, Southampton equalised through Kevin Beattie on 19 minutes.

Newcastle led again on 35 minutes through Lee Bowyer, Southampton once again equalised, this time from a Bramble 'own goal' on 39 minutes, the first half ended 2-2. More drama was to come.

With only two minutes of the game remaining Southampton took the lead for the first time in the game. Right 'at the death' up pops Darren Ambrose and his shot takes a massive deflection to wrong-foot the keeper and end up in the back of the net, 3-3! This game was definitely not one for the faint hearted.

Born on May-12:

Year	Player	Position	Years
1948	John Blackley	Central Defence	1977 - 1979

May-13

1892: Entry to League Dismissed

Newcastle East End's bid to enter the Football League Division 1 was refused by the association today. They were instead offered a place in the newly formed League Division 2 but East End in turn refused this offer and remained in the Northern League.

1953: Coronation Cup

Newcastle were invited to participate in the Coronation Cup, a celebration of the coronation of Queen Elizabeth II and faced Aberdeen at Ibrox, coming out easy victors, 4-0, with goals from Jackie Milburn, Len White and George Hannah. The other goal being an own goal scored by Aberdeen's Young.

1967: Heavy Defeat Ends Forgettable Season

Being beaten 6-1 by West Bromwich Albion at The Hawthorns ended a disastrous season for Newcastle where they finished third bottom of division narrowly avoiding relegation. With a goal difference of minus 42 (-42), by far the worst in the division, they were lucky to escape with their top-flight status intact.

1990: Tyne-Wear Derby No. 122

With Newcastle finishing third and Sunderland finishing sixth they were paired together in the Play-Off games for promotion, the 122nd Tyne-Wear Derby. This first leg, away at Roker Park, was drawn 0-0 so honours were even and everything was still to play for in the second leg at St James's Park - but that doesn't tell the full story of a pretty feisty, but perhaps dreary, game that ended in uproar!

It is fair to say that over the years there have been a some pretty x-rated challenges in Tyne-Wear Derbies, but the one at the end of this game probably tops the lot. Sunderland were awarded a last minute penalty and their full back Paul Hardyman stepped up to take the spot kick. Newcastle goalkeeper John Burridge saved the penalty, however Hardyman followed up and only succeeded in kicking Burridge in the head. There was absolute chaos as a result of this and Hardyman was later sent off as things eventually were calmed down.

First Meeting on May-13:

Year	R	F	A	V	Opposition	Competition
1953	W	4	0	N	Aberdeen	Coronation Cup

Debut on May-13:

Year	Player	Opposition
1989	Stephen Howey (Central Defence)	Manchester United

Born on May-13:

Year	Player	Position	Years
1913	James Denmark	Centre Half	1937 - 1945
1917	John Shiel	Centre Forward	1936 - 1938
1979	Jamie McClen	Midfield	1997 - 2005
1982	Oguchialu Chilioke Onyewu	Defence	2006 - 2007

May-14

1969: Fairs Cup Semi-Final First Leg Drawn

Newcastle faced Glasgow giants Rangers in the first leg of their semi-final tie at Ibrox. In an exciting, but ultimately goalless draw there was all to play for back at St James's Park!

2000: Six Goal Thriller Ends Mediocre Season

A goal apiece from Alan Shearer and Andy Griffin, together with a brace from Gary Speed wrapped up a 4-2 victory over Arsenal at St James's Park which saw Newcastle finishing in a very disappointing 11th place in the Premiership.

First Meeting on May-14:

Year	V	F	A	R	Opposition	Competition
1969	A	0	0	D	Glasgow Rangers	Inter Cities Fairs Cup

Born on May-14:

Year	Player	Position	Years
1982	Ignacio Maria Gonzalez Gatti	Midfield	2008 - 2009

May-15

2007: Allardyce is New Boss

Sam Allardyce appointed as manager on a three year contract. So a short and stormy relationship begins...

2011: Brothers Appear For Newcastle

In bringing on Sammy Ameobi as a second-half substitute Newcastle had a pair of brothers playing in the same side for the first time since 1992 when the Appleby brothers played in the Anglo-Italian Cup. Sammy Ameobi was introduced as an 82nd minute substitute in the game against Chelsea. With his elder brother Shola already being on the pitch this made it the first time that Newcastle had played a pair of brothers in a League game since the Robledo brothers, Jorge (George) and Eduardo (Ted) in the1950's.

However in the 1990's Newcastle did have the brothers Richard and Matty Appleby appearing in the same match, in the Anglo-Italian Cup game on 08/12/1992 versus AS Bari, a game Newcastle lost 3-0. Newcastle have had other brother pairings on their books at the same time: Peter & Chris Withe, Ron & Chris Guthrie, Stephen & Gary Caldwell, and Lomano & Kazenga LuaLua, but they never appeared in the same side together.

Debut on May-15:

Year	Player	Opposition
2011	Sammuel Ameobi (Forward)	Chelsea

Born on May-15:

Year	Player	Position	Years
1933	Richard Keith	Right Back	1956 - 1964
1989	Mapou Yanga-Mbiwa	Defence	2013 - 2014

May-16

Unfortunately history has shown that May 16th is not a very good day for Newcastle United...

1953: Coronation Cup Defeat

After beating Aberdeen 4-0 at Ibrox, Newcastle were themselves beaten by the same score line by Hibernian thus ending their interest in the Coronation Cup. Which incidentally was won by Celtic who beat Hibs 2-0 in the final.

1990: Tyne-Wear Derby No. 123

This was the second leg of the Play-Off games for promotion and represents the 123rd Tyne-Wear Derby, not a happy one at all for Newcastle fans, not least that it is a St James's Park. With the first leg, away at Roker Park having been a goalless draw, there were high expectations in bringing

Sunderland to St James's Park, but it was not to be. Goals by Eric Gates and Marco Gabbiadini, one in each half, dashing to any hopes of promotion for this season.

1998: FA Cup Final Defeat!

Newcastle were beaten 2-0 by Arsenal in the FA Cup Final at Wembley. Overmars (23) and Anelka (69) ending any dreams of winning a seventh FA Cup.

2015: Another Defeat Means Brink of Relegation!

Defeat today at the hands of Queens Park Rangers (2-1) meant that Newcastle had managed to gain only one point from their last ten games! Only a home game against West Ham United now stood between Newcastle and relegation.

First Meeting on May-16:

Year	V	F	A	R	Opposition	Competition
1953	N	0	4	L	Hibernian	Coronation Cup

Born on May-16:

Year	Player	Position	Years
1893	Stan Seymour	Outside Left	1920 - 1929
1922	Charlie Wayman	Centre Forward	1941 - 1947

May-17

Newcastle have only ever played twice on this day in history, with both games ending in a draw. In **1947** Newcastle drew 2-2 with Bury in League Division 2, goals from Roy Bentley and Charlie Wayman. In **1969** they drew 1-1 with Liverpool in a League Division 1 fixture. The goal coming from Wyn Davies.

1892: No More West End - Official!

The Annual Meeting of the Northern League was held at the Queens Hotel, Stockton. The meeting officially accepted and recorded that both Newcastle West End and Sunderland Albion were now clubs that "ceased to exist".

Born on May-17:

Year	Player	Position	Years
1924	Roy Bentley	Centre Forward	1946 - 1948

Born on May-17:

Year	Player	Position	Years
1970	John Karelse	Goalkeeper	1999 - 2003

May-18

Nothing happening on the domestic scene for Newcastle so we have to look further afield!

Newcastle, on a tour of the Far East in 1983, played series of games and the first being against Malaysia X1, also known as Malaysia Super League All Stars, who represent the Malaysian League in exhibition matches.

The game was played in Stadium Merdeka, Kuala Lumpur, perhaps better known to most in England as the stadium which hosted the second Ali v Bugner bout. However this was no boxing match, had it have been the referee may have stopped it, as Newcastle ran out easy 5-2 winners.

Born on May-18:

Year	Player	Position	Years
1958	Howard Gayle	Wing	1982 - 1983
1968	Jeffrey Joseph Wrightson	Central Defence	1985 - 1987

May-19

Only two games have been played today, both in the Premiership, and both at St James's Park. The second of the two was a 1-0 defeat at the hands of Liverpool. The first, in 2001, perhaps needs a special mention.

2001: Two Dismissals and Five Yellow Cards

In bringing the curtain down on the 2000-01 season Newcastle beat Aston Villa 3-0. Stephen Glass opening the scoring on 9 minutes, Carl Cort doubling Newcastle's advantage on 13 minutes and an 'own goal' by Delaney on 75 minutes wrapping it up for Newcastle.

Being an 'end of season' game and with neither team having anything to play for, both safe from relegation and neither in contention for a European place you would have thought this game would have been a quite sedate affair but with Villa picking up four cautions (Alpay Ozalan, Gareth Southgate, George Boateng and Mark Delaney) and Newcastle one (David Ginola) no one told the players - especially Gary Speed and Ian Taylor who 'got stuck into each other' on 84 minutes and both were sent off.

Born on May-19:

Year	Player	Position	Years
1937	Barrie Ernest Thomas	Centre Forward	1962 - 1964
1987	David Edgar	Centre-Back	2003 - 2009

May-20

1898: Elected to Division One

Newcastle finished third in the Test Match table thus failing to qualify for promotion to Division 1.

However, following protests at the 'staged' goalless draw between Stoke and Burnley which ensured both those teams qualified, the Football League immediately withdrew the Test Match system, (*to return later as the 'Play Offs'*), and the First Division was expanded to 18 teams and the losing teams in the Test Matches, Newcastle and Blackburn Rovers, were elected into the First Division...

2008: Geremi Loses Goal

The Premier Leagues "Dubious Goals Panel" adjudicated that Newcastle's second goal against West Ham on 26/04/2008 was in fact an own goal by McCartney and not scored by Geremi.

Taking his goal tally for Newcastle from three down to two.

Born on May-20:

Year	Player	Position	Years
1957	Mark McGhee	Forward	1977 - 1991

May-21

1969: Newcastle into the Fairs Cup Final

Following the goalless draw at Ibrox on 14th May a 2-0 win over Glasgow Rangers at St James's Park saw Newcastle reach the final of the Inter-Cities Fairs Cup.

Jim Scott and Jackie Sinclair with the all important goals, both scored in the second half.

1973: Newcastle into the Anglo-Italian Final

A comprehensive 5-1 win over Crystal Palace at St James's Park in the second leg English Semi-Final of the Anglo-Italian Inter-League Clubs Competition, which saw a hat-trick from Malcolm Macdonald complemented by goals from Stewart Barrowclough and Tommy Gibb propelled Newcastle into the final against Fiorentina.

Born on May-21:

Year	Player	Position	Years
1896	Andrew Smailes	Inside Right	1919 - 1922
1975	Pierre Laurent Robert	Outside Left	2000 - 2005

May-22

1999: FA Cup Final Heartache

Teddy Sheringham (11) and Paul Scoles (53) broke the hearts of the watching Geordie nation as Newcastle once again failed at the final hurdle in the FA Cup at Wembley.

2007: Hall's bought out by Ashley

Mike Ashley, a billionaire from Buckinghamshire, successfully bought the Hall's 41.6% stake in Newcastle United PLC for £55.3m.

2011: Newcastle Throw Away a 3 Goal Lead

In a season that never really came to life the final game of it against West Bromwich Albion probably summed it up.

With a 3-0 lead going into the last 30 minutes Newcastle threw it away with Somen Tchoyi scoring a hat-trick (62, 71 & 90) to level the scores. Newcastle's goals coming from Taylor (16), Lovenkrands (39) and an Olsson 'own goal' (47).

Born on May-22:

Year	Player	Position	Years
1881	Colin Veitch	Half Back	1899 - 1915
1901	Roderick MacKenzie	Right Half	1922 - 1935
1931	George Lackenby	Defence	1950 - 1956
1956	David McKellar	Goalkeeper	1986 - 1986
1959	Alan Brown	Forward	1981 - 1982
1968	Paul Moran	Forward	1991 - 1991

May-23

2014: Farewell to Shola (*and others...*)
Though it was already well-known, it was confirmed today as Newcastle announced their 'retained list' that Sola Ameobi would be leaving the club after 14 years service.

Gone also were Loic Remy, who had been on loan from Queens Park Rangers, Luuk De Jong, who had been on loan from Borussia Moenchengladbach, Dan Gosling, who had come from Everton on a free transfer and Connor Newton who had been with the club since he was 9 years old but never managed a senior appearance.

Born on May-23:

Year	Player	Position	Years
1976	Stephen Glass	Midfield	1998 - 2001

May-24

1984: Cox Resigns
It was an absolute bombshell across Tyneside when Arthur Cox announced his departure after 179 games in charge. He had introduced a bit of flair back to a rather lack-lustre Newcastle.

It was under Cox that the emergence of Chris Waddle, the return of Peter Beardsley and the truly inspirational signing of Kevin Keegan had brought some positivity and excitement back to St James's Park. With this came promotion back to the top-flight of the First Division.

2009: Newcastle Relegated
After a 16 year stay in the Premiership, Newcastle are relegated from the top-flight of English football after suffering a 1-0 defeat to Aston Villa at Villa Park. Adding insult to injury the only goal of the game was an 'own goal' by Damien Duff.

2015: Premiership Survival
On the final day of the season Newcastle secure their Premiership status with a 2-0 victory over West Ham United at St James's Park.

Exactly six years to the day when Newcastle were relegated from the Premiership in 2009 they found themselves in the same position on the last day of the season, either they or Hull City would be relegated.

Hull faced a daunting visit from Manchester United whilst Newcastle faced a Sam Allardyce led West Ham United. It all came down to a simple fact - Newcastle had to match, or better, Hull's result. In what was a nervy, but very spirited, performance Newcastle took control of their own destiny beating West Ham 2-0 whilst Hull drew 0-0, a result that no longer mattered of course with Newcastle winning.

May-25

2011 saw the announcement that both Shefi Kuqi and Sol Campbell were 'released' by Newcastle today. Kuqi had came to Newcastle on a only a short-term contract anyway, until the end of the season. This following the sale of Andy Carroll to Liverpool in the final hours of the mid-season transfer window Newcastle did not have the opportunity to sign a replacement - you would have thought they knew they were going to sell Carroll and have a replacement lined up, but this is Newcastle! As a "free agent" Newcastle where allowed to sign Kuqi outside of the window. He ended up only making six senior appearances. The signing of Campbell had always been a strange one in the eyes of the Newcastle fans. Newcastle had the stated policy that they were only interested in signing the "best of the young" - at almost 36 years old upon his arrival Campbell did not really fit the bill. Anyway, after only eight appearances he was gone.

Born on May-25:

Year	Player	Position	Years
1985	Demba Ba	Forward	2011 - 2013
1986	Yoan Gouffran	Forward	2013 - current

May-26

There's only ever been one game played by Newcastle on this day, a narrow 3-2 defeat to West Ham United in **1947**. Even then this was only played so late in the year as a result of a backlog of fixtures that occurred due to very bad weather during the first three months of the year. Played at St James's Park it is probably only worth mentioning for the fact that Jackie Milburn and Len Shackleton were Newcastle's scorers.

Born on May-26:

Year	Player	Position	Years
1894	Edward Stanley Dixon	Inside Forward	1914 - 1923
1957	Kenny Mitchell	Central Defence	1975 - 1981

May-27

Today in **1980** saw the signing of Chris Withe, brother of Peter Withe. They were to join a small select group of brothers who have been on Newcastle's books, but they were never to appear in the same team together. Indeed Chris was only ever destined to appear twice for Newcastle, a 1-0 victory over Shrewsbury Town and a 6-0 humiliation at the hands of Chelsea.

Born on May-27:

Year	Player	Position	Years
1929	Reg Davies	Inside Forward	1951 - 1958
1967	Paul Gascoigne	Midfield	1983 - 1988

May-28

In **1921** Newcastle participated in the "The Tournoi Franco-Britannique de Paris" which was a four-team tournament played over the weekend of 28 and 29 May at the Stade de Colombes. The four competing teams being Newcastle, Celtic, Gallia, and a combined CA Paris / Racing Club de France side. Newcastle's first game was against Gallia. It was a comfortable victory to Newcastle, 4-1, with Billy Aitken scoring a hat-trick and Tom McDonald also netting.

In **2010** Vurnon Anita made his full international debut for the Netherlands today when he was introduced as a substitute in a 2–1 friendly victory over Mexico.

Born on May-28:

Year	Player	Position	Years
1908	Stanley Barber	Left Half	1925 - 1928
1909	William Forster	Right Back	1932 - 1938
1914	Henry Clifton	Inside Forward	1938 - 1946
1986	Charles N'Zogbia	Midfield	2004 - 2008

May-29

1921: The second game for Newcastle in the "The Tournoi Franco-Britannique de Paris" took place today against Celtic and Newcastle were well beaten 3-0.

1969: Halfway There!

With a comfortable 3-0 win over Ujpesti Dozsa in the first leg of the Inter-Cities Fairs Cup Final Newcastle fans are beginning to dream of European silverware arriving in the trophy cabinet at St James's Park. Newcastle's goals coming from Bobby Moncur, who scored two, and Jim Scott.

2015: Gutierrez and Taylor Released

Newcastle United confirmed, via their official website, that both Jonas Gutierrez and Ryan Taylor will be released by the Club when their current deals expire on 30th June, 2015. Issuing the typical rhetoric Managing director Lee Charnley was quoted as saying:

"Ryan and Jonas have both contributed significantly to Newcastle United over a number of years and on behalf of the board, I would like to place on record our sincere thanks to both players for the excellent service they have given the Club.". Adding: "It was a great pleasure to see Ryan and Jonas come back into the team in recent weeks and compete at the highest level after the injury and illness battles they have had to overcome. To come through those difficult periods with such strength and dignity will have given hope and inspiration to many and it is clear that our supporters have a deep connection and affection for both players, as does everyone associated with the Club."

Gutierrez, via social media, had a slightly different opinion of things than Charnley, saying "Two things I learn from my illness: how you can support a player [Newcastle fans] and how you leave a player alone [Newcastle owner]. Thanks to all football fans and Newcastle fans for supporting me and [having] trust in me."

Both players have had a difficult end to their Newcastle careers with Taylor suffering two serious knee injuries and Gutierrez being sent out on loan, seemingly never to return, then suffering testicular cancer and upon recovery being sent back to Newcastle.

First Meeting on May-29:

Year	V	F	A	R	Opposition	Competition
1969	H	3	0	W	Ujpesti Dozsa	Inter-Cities Fairs Cup

Born on May-29:

Year	Player	Position	Years
1926	William Isiah Foulkes	Outside Right	1951 - 1954

Born on May-29:

Year	Player	Position	Years
1976	Claudio Roberto da Silva	Defence	2007 - 2009

May-30

With no domestic, or competitive, action we need to look further afield to follow Newcastle for this day in history.

1906 saw Newcastle touring Europe and they met Celtic in the Czech Republic at the home of SV Slavia Praha. The game ended all-square at 2-2. **1922** saw them in København (Copenhagen) where they faced a København X11 and won 1-0. **1929** saw them in Budapest where they defeated a Hungary X11 with a score-line of 4-1.

2009: Fastest Goal in FA Cup Final History

Ex-Newcastle striker Louis Saha, then with Everton, scored the fastest goal in FA Cup Final history, timed at 25 seconds, in Everton's 2-1 defeat to Chelsea today at Wembley. This beat the record which had previously been held by our own Jackie Milburn of course.

Born on May-30:

Year	Player	Position	Years
1895	Richard Little	Right Back	1912 - 1917

May-31

1956 saw Newcastle were playing in their final three-match tour of Romania when they faced Flacăra Ploieşti at the Ilie Oană Stadium. Ploieşti were probably more famous for changing their name rather than anything else, only formed 32 years earlier, in 1924, they had already changed their name six times! They started out as Juventus Bucureşti, then in 1947 became Distribuţia Bucureşti, a year later they were Petrolul Bucureşti. Move forward a year and they were Competrol Bucureşti, a year later, Partizanul Bucureşti, then another year later they were Flacăra Bucureşti. In 1952 they became Flacăra Ploieşti, which they were when they beat Newcastle 3-2. Len White scoring Newcastle's two goals.

They were to change their name another four times, Energia Ploieşti, Petrolul Ploieşti, FC Ploieşti before reverting to Petrolul Ploieşti in 1993 which they remain to be today.

JUNE

June-01

1958: Mitten Moves In

Charlie Mitten appointed as manager replacing the Stan Seymour led Directors Committee. Mitten began to make wholesale changes at St James's Park, everything from the training regime to the team kit were changed! He however never really felt that he got the "full" backing of the board and his frustrations with their constant interference and internal wrangling was clearly evident. None more so than when he made the now famous "Newcastle is an impossible club to manage" outburst, citing "the Boardroom intrigue" as the reason.

1962: Harvey Heaven

Joe Harvey appointed as manager, replacing Norman Smith who had been "temporary" boss.

Harvey is undoubtedly one of Newcastle's greatest-ever servants, being associated with the club for most of the post-war era up to his dying day - to the fans Joe was "Mr Newcastle" and now their former captain and twice FA Cup winner was their manager - some very happy days were ahead for the Toon Army.

1975: Harvey Hoisted Upstairs

Thirteen years to the day after being appointed as Newcastle's manager Joe Harvey left the position by "mutual" consent with the board and was appointed as "General Manager". Having won the Fairs Cup, the Texaco Cup twice and the Anglo-Italian Cup, plus a League Division 2 title there had been some very good times indeed.

June-02

Nothing happening domestically on the football pitch today so again we look towards 'tour' matches.

1977 and Newcastle were in Malta as part of their pre-season tour. In what was a pretty disappointing tour, having already drawn against Malta's 'second' club Silema Wanderers, they faced their 'first' club, Floriana FC. As current Champions, Floriana had won the Maltese First Division no fewer than 23 times previously, the most successful club in the history of Maltese football. Not to disrespect Maltese football, more to show how well they performed against Newcastle - *though this was a 'tour' match* - at the end of the

2012–13 season, UEFA ranked the Maltese Premier League 44th out of 53 members in their coefficient calculation for UEFA club competitions. So you could say Floriana played very well against Newcastle in earning a 1-1 draw. Alan Gowling scored Newcastle's goal.

Born on June-01:

Year	Player	Position	Years
1908	Hugh Bulloch	Centre Half	1935 - 36

June-03

In **1906** Newcastle were in Germany for a tour match where they faced a Berlin Select X1. In what was an easy win for Newcastle they scored six times with no reply.

1973: Newcastle Win the Anglo-Italian Cup

With a 2-1 win over ACF Florentino at the Stadio Artemio Franchi, Newcastle secured the Anglo-Italian Inter-League Clubs Competition trophy.

An own goal by Superchi on 35 minutes, followed by a David Craig strike on 54 minutes ensured the win despite Florentino getting a goal back on 79 minutes through Clerici, making it a nervy last 11 minutes!

First Meeting on June-03:

Year	V	F	A	R	Opposition	Competition
1973	N	2	1	W	ACF Florentino	Anglo-Italitian Cup

Born on June-03:

Year	Player	Position	Years
1957	John Trewick	Midfield	1980 - 1984
1985	Papiss Demba Cisse	Forward	2012 - current

June-04

1972 and 1983 saw Newcastle in the Far East. It was Hong Kong in **1972** when they faced Brazilian side Santos which included probably the greatest footballer of all time - Pele!

Despite the fact that he was now 31 years of age he did not disappoint the fans, other than the Newcastle ones of course. In rainy and very humid conditions he scored a hat-trick in 15 second-half minutes! This after Newcastle had been 2-1 up at half-time with goals from John Tudor and a 30-yard screamer from Tony Green. The game ended 4-2 to Santos.

In **1983** it was Japan, in the Kirin Cup. This third game in the competition, against Yamaha, Newcastle won 1-0 thanks to a goal from Chris Waddle. Newcastle had already beaten a Japan-X1 4-0, drawn against Syria and would go on to draw against Botafogo Rio de Janerio and thus win the cup, which in fact was a rather large 'vase-like' trophy as opposed to being a cup - but hey, we're Newcastle fans - any trophy is a trophy!

Born on June-04:

Year	Player	Position	Years
1905	David Davidson	Centre Half	1930 - 1937

June-05

The Annual General Meeting of the Northern League was held today in **1891** at the North-Eastern Hotel in Darlington. It was an important one for Newcastle West End as the bottom two clubs were 'retired' from the league but were able to apply for re-election. As it happened Sheffield United, South Bank and Bishop Auckland had all made applications to join the league so West End and Darlington St Augustine, being those bottom two teams, were not assured of league football for the coming season.

A vote was then entered into and the result was that West End were re-elected with Sheffield United and South Bank both being admitted, therefore St Augustine lost out. The league now comprised of two teams from Middlesbrough - Ironopolis and Middlesbrough, two teams from Newcastle - East End and West End, Sunderland Albion, Stockton, Sheffield United and South Bank.

A very interesting argument was put forward by South Bank's spokesman, Mr Tunstall, at the meeting in reasoning for admission - he quoted that the largest expense any of the clubs would face in travelling to a game at his club would be 48s (shillings) in 'today's money' that's less than £2.50! Oh! How things have changed with regards to finance in football.

June-06

In **2007** Newcastle confirmed the rather controversial signing of Joey Barton from Manchester City. The price tag of £5.8m, not the greatest sum of money by the standards of the day, was not the controversy, what was being the fact that Barton was at the time suspended by Manchester City, this arising from an alleged assault on a City teammate, Ousmane Dabo, in a training ground incident. He also had a string of other misdemeanours to his name, with unfortunately more to come. This was a shame really as he was undoubtedly a very talented player.

June-07

Only one game played today.

1947: In a League Division 2 fixture against Newport County at Somerton Park, Newcastle were beaten 4-2. Tom Pearson scored for Newcastle in the first half which saw them going into the break 3-1 down. Len Shackleton scored in the second half but Newport scored again also with the end result being a 4-2 defeat.

2007: Ashley buys out Shepherd

Officially announced on the Stock Exchange that Mike Ashley had bought Newcastle United chairman Freddy Shepherd's 28.06% stake in the club for more than £37.6m.

Born on June-07:

Year	Player	Position	Years
1885	John McTavish	Forward	1912 - 1913
1908	Mick Burns	Goalkeeper	1927 - 1936
1910	William McPhillips	Goalkeeper	1930 - 1938

June-08

Nothing happening competitively on the field of play, so we will delve into the activities on the transfer market...

2005: Midfielder Darren Ambrose departs for Charlton Athletic

Craig Bellamy departs for Blackburn Rovers

There has been much written about Craig Bellamy over the years, a great player, albeit a bit of a firebrand. It would be true to say that the vast majority of Newcastle fans were extremely disappointed at his departure. I'll take this opportunity to talk about Darren Ambrose instead...

Sir Bobby Robson brought Ambrose to Newcastle as one of his "bright young hopes" who were "full of potential". It would be fair to say that whenever Ambrose got the chance he never let the team down, but he never really got many chances. Through no fault of his own he ended up making more substitute appearances than he did starts - 27 starts and 29 substitute appearances. Within those 27 starts he was actually substituted himself on 15 occasions, so in effect he only ever played 12 full games. This was obviously disappointing for him and the many fans he had in the crowd at St James's Park.

With the departure of Sir Bobby as manager and the arrival of Graeme Souness, Ambrose found himself further out of favour and it wasn't long before Charlton Athletic came along with a offer, and at the still young age of 21 he signed a four-year contract at The Valley.

On the international scene..

1996: Euro 96 saw England facing Switzerland at Wembley. The team featured Stuart Pearce, Paul Gascoigne and Alan Shearer. In the 1-1 draw it was Shearer who opened the scoring on 23 minutes. Switzerland equalised with a penalty from Kübilay Türkyilmaz on 83 minutes.

Born on June-08:

Year	Player	Position	Years
1944	David James Craig	Full Back	1960 - 1978

June-09

Nothing happening competitively on the field of play, so we will delve into the activities on the transfer market - but what fantastic signing!

1995: Forward Les Ferdinand arrives from Queens Park Rangers

"Sir Les" - was to become an absolute crowd favourite at St. James's Park, and quite rightly so! Was destined to score on his debut, and just kept on scoring... racking up an incredible 29 goals in his first season.

Ferdinand was an excellent striker all round, brilliant with his head and could produce powerful, accurate shots from just about any range. His ability to read the game, and his team-mates around him was superb. The relationship and understanding he developed with Peter Beardsley during his first season was phenomenal to say the least, the chief performers in a team known nation-wide as "The Entertainers" - and if you thought that was good, better was to come!

2015: Newcastle announce departure of Carver and Stone

Newcastle United today announced that both Head Coach John Carver (actually interim manager since January) and coach Steve Stone have left the club. After the disastrous run of results that saw Newcastle escaping relegation on the final day of the season not many Newcastle fans were too surprised at the news.

Born on June-09:

Year	Player	Position	Years
1948	John Bird	Centre Half	1975 - 1980
1970	Andy Hunt	Forward	1991 - 1993

June-10

2015: McClaren Confirmed Manager

Newcastle United today confirmed the appointment of Steve McClaren as manager. An expected announcement given the recent spate of press speculation, but not an over eagerly accepted one. McClaren had after all just failed to get Derby County promoted, or even into the Play-Offs, when they seemed clearly the best of the sides in the Championship.

Also, in keeping with Newcastle's ridiculous feud with the press there were only "selected" representatives invited to the 'unveiling'!

Born on June-10:

Year	Player	Position	Years
1959	Billy Whitehurst	Forward	1985 - 1986
1969	Ronny Johnsen	Defence	2004 - 2005

June-11

1969: Newcastle Win the Inter-Cities Fairs Cup

What a way for manager Joe Harvey to celebrate his 51st birthday - winning Newcastle's first ever European Trophy!

Goals from Bene (31) and Gorocs (44) for Ujpesti Dozsa had made the aggregate score 3-2 going into the break, still in Newcastle's favour, with them having won the first leg 3-0, so everything was set for an extremely nervy second half.

However, within a minute of the restart Moncur scored for Newcastle and four minutes later Arentoft scored to bring the scores level on the night and 5-2 in favour of Newcastle on aggregate. Just to make sure Foggon popped up with a goal on 75 minutes ensuring a 3-2 win on the night, a 6-42 win on aggregate and that the Inter-Cities Fairs Cup would be coming to St James's Park!

1957: Hughie Gallacher, R.I.P.

Hugh Kilpatrick Gallacher - "Wee Hughie" - at only 5'5" the pocket-sized centre-forward was probably the greatest striker of all time, and certainly the best Newcastle ever had. Even the likes of Jackie Milburn, Malcolm Macdonald and Alan Shearer couldn't beat Hughie's goal-scoring feats.

With 143 goals in only 174 appearances, at strike rate of 82%, he stands top of Newcastle's goal scoring records. Also a Scotland international and in 20 international games he scored an amazing 23 goals. Indeed he was one of the famous "Wembley Wizards" Scotland team that beat England 5-1.

When he retired from football, in September 1939, his career had spanned 624 senior games and he had scored an amazing 463 goals!

Having already returned to his 'adoptive' and 'beloved' Tyneside, Hughie continued to live in Gateshead trying a number of careers, one of them being a sports journalist, a role that led to him being banned from St James's Park for his outspoken remarks about Newcastle!

He continued to be a popular character on Tyneside. Sadly, he lost his wife through illness and began to drink heavily. In 1957 he was charged with ill treatment of his youngest son after throwing an ashtray at him during an argument. Feeling very much trapped, Hughie was summoned to appear before Gateshead Magistrates Court on Wednesday 12 June, 1957, but the veteran of countless sparkling football appearances never made it. The day before, at precisely 12.08, having written a heart-wrenching and genuine letter of apology to the Gateshead Coroner, he jumped in front of the York to Edinburgh express train close to his home. Two small boys witnessed his last desperate moments, and the body of the former goal scoring idol was found close to a spot known as "Dead Man's Crossing".

Tributes flowed in for Hughie, but the headline of the Newcastle Journal said more in their seven words than even the lengthiest of eulogies.

It simply read "HUGHIE OF THE MAGIC FEET IS DEAD".

Born on June-11:

Year	Player	Position	Years
1918	Joe Harvey	Wing Half	1945 - 1953
1941	John McNamee	Central Defence	1966 - 1971

June-12

1975: Lee Appointed

With the 'enforced' resignation of Joe Harvey it was Gordon Lee to whom Newcastle turned. Lee had been a player (full-back) who had a steady, if unspectacular, career with Hednesford Town, Aston Villa and Shrewsbury Town before moving into management. He succeeded Sir Stanley Matthews at Port Vale in 1968, gaining promotion to the Third Division at the first attempt. Leaving Port Vale he moved to Blackburn Rovers in 1974 and led them to promotion to the Second Division.

On the surface this seemed to be a decent selection, history shows though, that whilst delivering on most of the Newcastle Directorship's hopes it was not palatable by the majority of fans.

1988 saw a Jack Charlton managed Republic of Ireland beating an England team that featured Peter Beardsley, Chris Waddle and John Barnes, by the only goal of the game scored on six minutes by Ray Houghton.

Born on June-12:

Year	Player	Position	Years
1960	Ray Ranson	Right Back	1988 - 1993
1991	Shane Ferguson	Midfield	2009 - current

June-13

On the transfer scene...

1991: Midfielder Franz Carr arrives from Nottingham Forest

2011: Defender Andy O'Brien departs for Portsmouth

Early in his career Carr had been considered to be one of English football's brightest prospects. However this promise was never realised, despite well over a 100 appearances for Nottingham Forest. He is notable to Newcastle fans as being one of only two signings made by Ossie Ardiles (the other being David Kelly). Carr joined Newcastle in the Second Division in a move that should have given his career a boost. However, it was a bad time to become a Newcastle player, as they were staring into the abyss of relegation to the third division by Christmas!

Scoring on his debut, and displaying both blistering pace and the ability to dribble past defenders almost at will, things looked well. As he progressed through the season however all too often his pace and dribbling skills yielded little end product, his inconsistent crossing let him down badly. A serious knee injury, picked up in the October basically ruined his season, making only two substitute appearances in the February, then making the last three games of the season. When he returned, things at Newcastle were radically different - Sir John Hall had taken over in the boardroom and Kevin Keegan, had replaced Ardiles as manager. Despite missing the first game of the 1992/93 season, Carr started the next six, however it became obvious with the arrival of Rob Lee that Carr was not in Keegan's long-term plans. This being confirmed when he was allowed to go to Sheffield United on loan - culminating in a permanent move there.

O'Brien had a much better time on Tyneside however. He was a tenacious defender, who learnt his central defensive trade with Bradford City where he made 150 senior appearances. He had the ability to give opposing forwards very little room to manoeuvre, earning him the nickname 'Rash' - as he was said to be "all over them". O'Brien has the distinction of playing for both England Under-21s and the Republic of Ireland Under-21s. Being English born himself he played for England against France in 1999 whilst with Bradford, but having an Irish father O'Brien decided to switch allegiance the following year when he appeared for the Republic's Under-21s against Sweden. His full international debut duly arrived during the World Cup qualifying campaign, shortly after completing his move to Newcastle.

Born on June-13:

Year	Player	Position	Years
1902	Jack Wilkinson	Outside Right	1930 - 1932
1950	John Connolly	Left Wing	1978 - 1980

June-14

On the transfer scene...

2005: Wing-wizard Laurent Robert departs for Portsmouth, temporarily - we thought!

2014: Midfielder Roman Amalfitano departs for Dijion FCO

Robert could be a thrilling match-winner, but was equally capable of being a passenger during a game. He was so frustratingly inconsistent that it drove the fans, if not the management, crazy!

He revived memories of Ginola's French flair on the left wing, could cross the ball with pinpoint accuracy, or easily cut inside his man and deliver a lethal combination of shots, added to that his dead-ball delivery was sublime. But... you never knew which Robert was going to turn up to a game. Robert also had a penchant for mischief, he had several public 'fallings out' with managers Bobby Robson and Graeme Souness. Indeed his very public criticism of Souness, with a swipe at the entire Newcastle squad, was most definitely at the heart of Newcastle's desire to offload him.

The move to Portsmouth was "unique" to say the least - it had both press and fans alike bemused! Was it a loan deal, was it permanent? No one seemed to know. It eventually transpired that Robert was signed by Portsmouth on a year-long loan, with two additional years agreed following the completion of the loan. Whatever the nature of the deal, it never worked out for him at Pompey. Yet again his petulant side was foremost and Pompey fans most remember him for his refusal to sit on the bench for their 4-1 demolition of Sunderland, literally storming out of the ground! There was no way Portsmouth would take up their option, so at the end of the 2005-06 season he was heading back to St James's Park.

On the international scene...

1992 saw Alan Shearer and Stuart Pearce featuring in the Euro's at the Malmo Stadion against Sweden. The game was a disappointing 0-0 draw.

June-15

On the transfer scene...

1999: Defender Alain Goma arrives from Paris St Germain

2005: Midfielder Scott Parker arrives from Chelsea

Goma was a big, strong, centre half who had won the French title whilst with Auxerre and a cup whilst with PSG. His time at Newcastle however was not such a happy one. Missing a large part of his first season through injury, he appeared to have recovered for his second season and was beginning to forge a solid partnership with Aaron Hughes in the centre of the defence. Unfortunately he continued to suffer from injury, suffering a broken nose against Charlton and a broken hand against Chelsea.

The injuries, together with the departure of Ruud Gullit and his replacement by Bobby Robson, meant Goma was disheartened and perhaps not unsurprisingly he never displayed much commitment at Newcastle in the eyes of the fans. It was somehow anticipated that at the end of the season Alain would be moving on, the only surprise being that he put in a transfer request rather than Newcastle putting him up for sale.

Somewhat differently to Goma, Parker's first season at Newcastle was excellent! He seemed to have regained the fire and passion he had at Charlton, which he lost at Chelsea, and his displays were such that he was constantly Newcastle's Man of the Match. His second season however was a disaster, dogged by injury and a mystery illness he was a shadow of his former self.

It became quite obvious that his time at Newcastle was 'up' and the introduction of Joey Barton was to herald the departure of Parker.

1980 saw a yet to be Newcastle favourite player and manager - Kevin Keegan - captain England in 1-0 defeat at the hands of hosts Italy in 1980 UEFA European Football Championship in the Stadio Delle Alpi - Turin.

June-16

On the transfer scene...

1989: Defender Mark Stimson arrives from Tottenham Hotspur

1992: Midfielder Paul Bracewell arrives from Sunderland

2011: Midfielder Kevin Nolan departs for West Ham United

Bracewell, shortly after captaining Sunderland to a FA Cup Final defeat at Wembley v Liverpool, (his third FA Cup Final defeat), he became a free agent. Sunderland had offered him a one year deal but he had wanted a two year contract. Keegan, then manager at Newcastle, offered him a three year deal.

The fee had to be set by a tribunal who decided on £250,000, considerably less than the £700,000 that Sunderland had wanted. The signing was a major coup for Newcastle and even to this day remains one of the most controversial Tyne/Wear transfers. Many at Newcastle were concerned as to how Bracewell would be received at St. James's Park. Any fears however were allayed 10 minutes into his debut against Southend, when he launched a thunderbolt shot into the back of the net from the edge of the visitors area.

In his final season at Newcastle Bracewell did not play his first game until the Boxing Day trip to Leeds, due to injury. At the end of the season he was once again a free agent and was allowed to return to Sunderland where they this time gave him his two year deal!

Strange folk are football folk.

Born on June-16:

Year	Player	Position	Years
1896	Edward Ward	Inside Right	1920 - 1922
1911	Robert Francis Dudgeon Ancell	Left Back	1936 - 1944
1963	Wayne Fereday	Wing	1989 - 1990

June-17

1994: Len White, R.I.P.

White was an absolute hero at St James's Park, a true legend, even though he came to Newcastle after being part of the Rotherham side that dashed their hopes of a third successive FA Cup victory!

Playing on the wing and primarily partnering Jackie Milburn up front, White had an impressive goal-scoring record but often found himself in the shadow of 'Wor Jackie'. Despite this he was instrumental during Newcastle's FA Cup winning campaign of 1955. Once Milburn ended his career White took over as the leading striker, and continued to improve his ratio of goals, scoring at least 25 goals in each of the next four seasons.

In the 1960-61 season White already had 28 league goals in the bag before he broke his leg at White Hart Lane and with their top-scorer out Newcastle were relegated. To-date only Jackie Milburn and Alan Shearer have scored more goals for Newcastle.

In trying to find a fitting tribute I think the words of Trevor Porteous, Stockport's manager who signed him from Huddersfield, sum White up perfectly when he said: "*Len was a good, good player. Brave, pacey and a great goalscorer. He was a quiet lad but everything about him was good*".

On the transfer scene...

1988: Winger John Hendrie arrives from Bradford City

2011: Forward Demba Ba arrives from West Ham United

Hendrie was bought as a winger but ended up in a 'holding midfield' position! Although hardworking, and a product of former Newcastle stalwart Frank Clark at Orient, he unfortunately never really settled into the role properly. He has however a real claim to fame - when he left Newcastle he ended up at Middlesbrough (via Leeds United) and whilst there he scored the final goal to be scored at Ayresome Park.

Born on June-17:

Year	Player	Position	Years
1993	Jak Alnwick	Goalkeeper	2012 - 2015

June-18

Nothing happening on the domestic scene, nothing happening on the 'tour' scene, not even anything happening on the transfer scene - so for this day we turn to Newcastle players on international duty.

1986 saw Peter Beardsley scoring for England in their Mexico World Cup "Round of 16" tie with Paraguay. England won the tie 3-0 with Gary Lineker getting the other two. Despite scoring, or perhaps to save him for the Semi-Final, Beardsley was substituted on 81 minutes with Mark Hateley (then at AC Milan) taking his place.

The England team was managed by Sir Bobby Robson at the time and included in his "standby list" was Paul Bracewell, then at Norwich, but was not needed so didn't make the trip.

June-19

On the transfer scene...

1998: Forward Stephane Guivarch arrives from Auxerre

Guivarch was signed by Dalglish just before the 1998 World Cup Finals started, in an effort to beat growing competition for his signature and what could have possibly been a greatly inflated price!

France duly went on to win the World Cup and Guivarch picked up a winners medal, everything seemed well for the start of the Premiership season. Don't forget this is Newcastle though!

Within weeks of the season starting Dalglish was sacked and replaced by Gullit, Guivarch scores on his debut (albeit a consolation goal in a 4-1 defeat by Liverpool) makes 1 more start and 2 substitute appearances and is sent off packing to Rangers. You have to love Newcastle don't you!

Born on June-19:

Year	Player	Position	Years
1931	Neville Black Tommy Cahill	Inside Forward Left Back	1952 - 1952 1951 - 1955
1936	Gordon Hughes	Outside Right	1956 - 1963
1949	Vivian Dennis Busby	Forward	1971 - 1972

June-20

1987: Andy Donaldson, R.I.P.

Donaldson, a local lad, was a big strong striker who Newcastle signed from works team Vickers Armstrong, and he appeared to have it all, but there was one thing in his way - Jackie Milburn!

Indeed early evidence suggested that Andy would beat 'Wor Jackie' to a place in the Newcastle senior front line, history was to however prove otherwise. When Newcastle sold him to Middlesbrough he was their first ever five-figure transfer.

Donaldson certainly turned into the prolific goalscorer everyone knew he could be, this especially in the two spells he had with Peterborough (his first spell being the 1951/52 and 1952/53 seasons with his second spell being 1955/56 to 1958/59). In total he made 160 Midland League appearances for them, scoring 97 goals, and appeared 21 times scoring 10 goals in the FA Cup.

June-21

Nothing happening on the domestic scene, nothing happening on the 'tour' scene, not even anything happening on the transfer scene - so for this day we again turn to Newcastle on international duty.

In the **1990** World Cup in Italy the Republic of Ireland, in Group F along with England, were managed by Jackie Charlton and in their tie against the Netherlands, which was drawn 1-1, they faced a Dutch side that included Ruud Gullit.

England, managed by Sir Bobby Robson meanwhile beat Egypt 1-0. In the England starting line-up was Stuart Pearce, Chris Waddle, Paul Gascoigne and John Barnes. Peter Beardsley came on as a 84th minute substitute and less than a minute after doing so was given a yellow card!

Born on June-21:

Year	Player	Position	Years
1936	Alan Kirkman	Inside Forward	1963 - 1963
1986	Cheick Ismael Tiote	Midfield	2010 - current

June-22

This day has to go to the "Hand of God" unfortunately.

1986 saw a Sir Bobby Robson managed England side, that had Peter Beardsley in the starting line-up and Chris Waddle appearing as a second half substitute, cheated by Diego Maradona.

In the Estadio Azteca, Mexico City, watched by 114,580 fans the referee Ali Bin Nasser of Tunisia was the only person who did not see Maradona blatantly put the ball into the back of the net with his hand rather than his head!

Even Maradona knew he had done it with him later being quoted as saying "*I was waiting for my teammates to embrace me, and no one came...* I told them, *'Come hug me, or the referee isn't going to allow it'.*" His statement at the press conference later was what eventually gave this game its nickname.

In this Maradona rather facetiously commented that the goal was scored "*un poco con la cabeza de Maradona y otro poco con la mano de Dios*" ("*a little with the head of Maradona and a little with the hand of God*").

Born on June-22:

Year	Player	Position	Years
1868	Robert Foyers	Left Back	1895 - 1897
1879	Robert Bryson Templeton	Outside Left	1903 - 1904
1914	Alfred Garnham	Defence	1939 - 1942

June-23

On the transfer scene...

2011: Defender Ben Tozer departs for Northampton Town

Tozer began his career as a defender in Plymouth Argyle's youth system and moved to Swindon Town in the summer of 2007. Making his debut in the Carling Cup (against Charlton) his reputation began to grow and this brought about a trial with Everton in November 2007. Nothing became of this and Newcastle snapped him up in January 2008 where he made good progress in the reserves.

He eventually broke into the first-team squad but only made one start in the League Cup and a further single substitute appearance in the Championship before being sent on loan to Northampton. This loan was to turn into a permanent move on a free transfer in 2011.

Born on June-23:

Year	Player	Position	Years
1917	Dominic Kelly	Centre Half	1938 - 1945
1921	Bobby Robinson	Goalkeeper	1952 - 1954

June-24

On the transfer scene...

1963: Goalkeeper Gordon Marshall arrives from Heart of Midlothian

Prior to coming to Newcastle Marshall had already been a Scottish Championship winner with Hearts, as well as being a triple Scottish League Cup winner, 1959, 1960 and 1963 (he was also a finalist in 1962).

Marshall was a goalkeeper that was noted for his bravery and during the Second Division Championship winning season of 1964-65 he was an ever-present. His strength and heroics in goal did much to help establish Newcastle back in the top flight in the following seasons. It took another goalkeeper of great merit to dislodge him from his position - Willie McFaul. Upon losing his place Marshall moved to Nottingham Forest.

Incidentally, his son, Gordon George Banks Marshall, with a name like that he HAD to become a goalkeeper, went on to play for Scotland and become a goalkeeping coach.

1976: Henry "Harry" Bedford, R.I.P.

Harry was a phenomenal goalscorer, scoring over 150 goals in a little over 200 appearances for Derby County and along with Dean and Gallacher was one of the nation's top goalgetters. Even in his short time with United he scored 18 goals in only 32 matches. His career total was in excess of 300 goals.

Perhaps lacking in 'finesse', this was more than made up for by his dashing, fearless and fierce shooting ability. He was capped twice for England and twice for the Football League in the Twenties, coming to Newcastle in 1930.

It was ex-Newcastle player George Jobey, then manager of high-flying Derby County who sold Harry to Newcastle and during his time here he gave good service to the club. Harry then went to Sunderland, only to return to St James's Park in the October of 1937 as a coach.

Born on June-24:

Year	Player	Position	Years
1870	James Logan	Centre Forward	1895 - 1896
1982	Kevin Anthony Jance Nolan	Midfield	2009 - 2011

June-25

On the transfer scene...

1997: Midfielder Lee Clark departs for Sunderland

Clark was a Geordie through and through - and proud of it, ask the Mackems! As a Sunderland player Clark went to Wembley to support Newcastle and was famously wearing a derogotory t-shirt regarding Sunderland. He was a great player during his career at Newcastle and always wore his shirt with the utmost pride.

Everyone was stunned with his enforced move, not least that he chose to go to Sunderland!

Clark came back to United at the beginning of the 2005-06 season in what was supposed to be a coaching role and ended up back in the team! Definitely a Geordie institution. He did however, eventually, retire from playing and was gladly welcomed into the back-room staff and rose to become reserve team coach (2006-07).

In October 2007, Lee left Newcastle to join ex-Newcastle boss Glenn Roeder, who had taken over as manager at Norwich City, as his assistant. He then became a manager in his own right.

Born on June-25:

Year	Player	Position	Years
1930	Vic Keeble	Centre Forward	1952 - 1957
1946	John Tudor	Forward	1971 - 1976

June-26

On the transfer scene...

1997: Left Back Ian Davies arrives from Norwich City

Davies, being the type of full-back who tried to get foward as much as possible, and at every opportunity, used to provide the overlap for the final touch into the box. With John Brownlie at right-back, and there being great similarities in their styles, the pair were vital attacking links in Newcastle's cavalier "play-it-wide" approach.

Davies also had a passion for cricket, which saw him playing for Backworth in the Northumberland County League, alongside his team mate Steve Hardwick.

On the international scene...

Italia **1990** and an England team managed by Sir Bobby Robson featured ex-Newcastle favourites Chris Waddle and Paul Gascoigne, and future favourite Stuart Pearce, in their tie against Belgium at the Stadio Renato Dall'Ara. The game went into extra-time but England triumphed with the only goal of the game from David Platt, on 119 minutes. Peter Beardsley was in the England squad but did not feature in this game.

In **1996** football had 'come home' as the slogan and song went, this as the 1996 UEFA European Football Championship (Euro 96) was hosted in England. In their Semi-Final against West Germany the side included Stuart Pearce, Paul Gascoigne and Alan Shearer. On the bench, but not used, was Les Ferdinand. Shearer scored on three minutes, but Germany equalised on 16 minutes. The ultimately being decided on penalties with England losing out 6-5.

Born on June-26:

Year	Player	Position	Years
1986	Francisco Jimenez Tejada	Forward	2008 - 2013

June-27

On the transfer scene...

1988: Forward David Robinson departs to Reading

Robinson, a local lad, came through the junior ranks at Newcastle. He was a lively, pacey winger who had to wait patiently for his chance.

With the big push for the promotion and ultimately the Premiership, and the money Keegan was spending to make it happen, being sent on loan to Peterborough was a sign that he was not in Keegan's plans. A free transfer to Reading soon followed.

His spell at Elm Park was a short one indeed, just four months, as the then manager at newly-promoted Blackpool (fellow Geordie Billy Ayre), came in for his services. Staying with the Tangerines for two seasons he made 26 league appearances for them, scoring four goals. In 1994 he returned to his native North East to spend a year with Gateshead before moving back into league football with Cambridge United. After being released by Cambridge in August 1996, David joined Scottish club Berwick Rangers, where he brought his professional career to an end, with four goals in as many games.

His love of the game however saw him move back into amateur, non-League football with local club Whitley Bay.

June-28

On the transfer scene...

2000: Midfielder Daniel Cordone arrives from Racing Club

Cordone was a team mate of Christian Bassedas at Argentinian club Velez Sarsfield before Bassedas came to Newcastle and Cordone went to Racing Club of Argentina. They briefly linked up again when Cordone also came to Newcastle.

Much the same as Bassedas, Cordone seemed to offer plenty, and certainly sparkled in his early games, but he too was soon away back to Argentina.

Back home he went on to have spells with; Argentinos Juniors, San Lorenzo, Argentino de Merlo and Independiente Rivadavia.

On the tour scene...

Newcastle are on tour in South Africa at Kingsmead, Durban. Two goals from Reg Davies and one from Jackie Milburn secure the win.

Born on June-28:

Year	Player	Position	Years
1902	Albert Keating	Inside Right	1923 - 1925
1948	Jimmy Thomson	Midfield	1968 - 1971

June-29

2005: Colin Taylor, R.I.P.

Colin "Cannonball" Taylor, so nicknamed due to the ferocity of his left-footed shots, passed away today at the age of 64. Though he only played 36 times for Newcastle, scoring six goals, he was a legend at Walsall where over three different stints with the Saddlers he topped 500 appearances and scored 184 league goals.

On the transfer scene...

2007: Defender David Rozenhal arrives from Paris St Germain

Rozenhal, was a Czech international, having played in both the European Championships in 2004 and the World cup in 2006. At club level, he has played for Sigma Olomouc and Club Brugge (with whom he won the title in 2005) prior to his move to PSG. He joined Newcastle on a four year deal was anticipated to hopefully shore up a lamentable defence from the previous season.

It wasn't to be at Newcastle though for him, At the close of the January transfer window Rozenhal was sent to Lazio on loan amid rumours of a bust-up between him and Keegan. As was widely anticipated he was not to return, Lazio taking up the option to make the move permanent at the end of the loan period. This was amid speculation that one or two of Lazio's Serie A rivals were preparing to make a bid for Rozenhal. The reported fee was said to be £3m, but we are led to believe that this was inclusive of the £500,000 Lazio paid for the loan agreement.

Born on June-29:

Year	Player	Position	Years
1935	Keith Frank Kettleborough	Inside Forward	1966 - 1966
1937	Chris Harker	Goalkeeper	1955 - 1961
1938	Robert Gilfillan	Forward	1959 - 1961
1969	Archibald Gourlay	Midfield	1988 - 1992
1979	Andrew James O'Brien	Defence	2001 - 2005

June-30

On the transfer scene...

1995: Defender Barry Venison departs for Galatasaray
1998: Goalkeeper Lionel Perez arrives from Sunderland
2009: Forward Mark Viduka departs as contract expires

The Perez signing was a bit bizarre to say the least! Having played 86 games in only two seasons for Sunderland you could have been mistaken for believing that he had found his niche with the Wearsiders.

However, after a disastrous game in the play-off finals against Charlton - where he conceded four goals (*and seven penalties, as it went to a shoot-out*) he was deemed surplus to requirements as Sunderland set about rebuilding for the new season. In what was therefore a complete surprise to everyone he made the short journey from Wearside to Tyneside! It has to be fair to say he was merely at St James's Park as cover for Given and Harper and was never thought of as being any danger to either of those two. Indeed as it worked out he never got to make it into the first team and rarely even got onto the bench. He spent loan terms at Scunthorpe and Cambridge before being granted a free-transfer to Cambridge in 2000.

Born on June-30:

Year	Player	Position	Years
1876	Andrew McCombie	Full Back	1904 - 1910

Galowgate East Corner
viewed from Strawberry Lane

JULY

July-01

1916: Thomas Goodwill, R.I.P.
Goodwill sadly lost his life on the first day of the Battle of the Somme. Serving with the 16th (Service) Battalion of the Northumberland Fusiliers, also known as the Newcastle Commercials, his battalion were tasked with capturing ground to the south of Thiepval. They met fierce resistance as they crossed the exposed slope and sustained heavy casualties.

Among the dead was Pte Goodwill. He died alongside another player who was on Newcastle's books at the time, Dan Dunglinson. Though Dan never had the opportunity to appear for Newcastle.

Goodwill's body was subsequently lost and his name is among the 72,195 recorded on the Thiepval Memorial to the Missing of the Somme in France. The memorial commemorates the missing British and South African men, who died in the Battles of the Somme of the First World War between 1915 and 1918, with no known grave.

On the international scene...

1990: England have Stuart Pearce, Chris Waddle, Paul Gascoigne and John Barnes in their starting line-up at the Stadio San Paolo, Naples for their World Cup Quarter Final tie against Cameroon, which they won 3-2 after extra time.

Peter Beardsley also figured in the game, coming on at the beginning of the second half as a replacement for John Barnes.

Born on July-01:

Year	Player	Position	Years
1940	George Heslop	Centre Half	1959 - 1962
1976	Patrick Stephan Kluivert	Forward	2004 - 2005

July-02

Nothing happening competitively on the field of play, so we will delve into the activities on the transfer market...

1992: Defender John Beresford arrives from Portsmouth

2001: Defender Robbie Elliott arrives from Bolton (his 2nd stint at Newcastle)

2004: Midfielder James Milner arrives from Leeds United

2008: Midfielder Jonas Gutierrez departs, temporarily, to Real Mallorca

20012: Forward Leon Best departs for Blackburn Rovers

On the international scene...

1950: In their World Cup Finals Pool 2 Game 3 fixture at the Estádio do Maracanã, Rio de Janeiro, England have Jackie Milburn in their line-up. Unfortunately both he and England draw a blank as they lose 1-0 to Spain.

Born on July-02:

Year	Player	Position	Years
1939	Gordon Marshall	Goalkeeper	1963 - 1968
1959	Francisco da Silva [Mirandinha]	Forward	1987 - 1990
1975	Lamine Diatta	Defencer	2007 - 2009

July-03

Nothing happening competitively on the field of play, so once again we will delve into the activities on the transfer market...

2001: Defender Viv Hamilton departs to Cardiff City

2007: Defender Geremi arrives from Chelsea

2008: Forward Michael Owen, Newcastle's most expensive signing, departs for Manchester United

2016: Defender James Perch departs for Wigan Athletic

On the international scene...

1966: In a 'friendly' match against Denmark at the Parken Stadium (Idrætsparken), Copenhagen, England have both Jackie Charlton and George Eastham in their line-up. Not only did both appear, they both scored!

England won 2-0 with Charlton scoring the first of the goals, on 41 minutes, and Eastham getting the second on 61 minutes.

Born on July-03:

Year	Player	Position	Years
1988	James Troisi	Midfield	2007 - 2008

July-04

1990: This day has to belong to Paul Gascoigne. The images of him with tears streaming down his face as he realises that upon receiving a yellow card in the World Cup Semi-Final against West Germany, this being his second of the tournament, he would not be eligible to play in the final.

As it happened England lost on penalties to West Germany so didn't reach the final anyway, but those images will forever remain in the memory of most England fans, and certainly all Geordies throughout the world.

With him in the England team were Peter Beardsley and Chris Waddle. Of course the England team were managed at the time by Sir Bobby Robson.

Born on July-04:

Year	Player	Position	Years
1932	John Thompson	Goalkeeper	1950 - 1957

July-05

1987: Robert Francis Dudgeon Ancell, R.I.P.

Ancell, who was a very skilful defender, had a host of other English clubs vying for his signature whilst at St. Mirren and Newcastle narrowly beat Carlisle United to sign him in 1936.

Whilst with Newcastle Ancell gained his two full Scotland International caps, 3-1 win over Northern Ireland (31/10/1936) and a 2-1 defeat against Wales (02/12/1936). Ancell went on to make 105 appearances for Newcastle.

On the transfer scene...

1993: Goalkeeper Steve Harper arrives from Seaham Red Star

2010: Defender James Perch arrives from Nottingham Forest

2012: Goalkeeper Fraser Forster, who whilst never making a competitive start for Newcastle, as both Shay Given and Steve Harper were always blocking his way, departs for Celtic

On the international scene...

1966: In a 'friendly' match against Poland at the Stadion Slaski, Chorzow, England have Jackie Charlton in their line-up. England win 1-0 with Roger Hunt getting the only goal of the game on 14 minutes..

1982: Kevin Keegan make a second half substitution appearance for England in their 0-0 draw against Spain at the Estadio Santiago Bernabeu, Madrid in the World Cup Finals 2nd Round Group 2 Game 2 fixture.

Born on July-05:

Year	Player	Position	Years
1898	James Hunter	Left Back	1919 - 1925
1946	Arthur Horsfield	Forward	1969 - 1969
1969	Michael O'Neill	Midfield	1987 - 1989
1980	David Sebastian Rozehnal	Defence	2007 - 2008
1983	Jonas Manuel Gutierrez	Midfield	2008 - 2015

July-06

2013 saw a fan protest as Newcastle played a pre-season game at Fir Park against Motherwell. A banner proclaiming "Support the Team Not the Regime" was one of many "anti-Ashley" slogans on display. On a more 'united' front though Newcastle did win the game comfortably 4-2, with goals from Haris Vukic, Yoan Gouffran, Moussa Sissoko and Sylvain Marveaux.

On the transfer scene...

2000: Midfielder Christian Bassedas arrives from Velez Sarsfield
2012: Midfielder Gael Bigirimana arrives from Coventry City

July-07

On the transfer scene...

2012: Midfielder Danny Guthrie departs for Reading

Guthrie graduated from Liverpool's Youth Academy to become a member of the first-team squad but only made three senior appearances, two as a substitute and one start - a Champions League appearance away to Galatasary. Towards the end of the 2006-07 season Danny went to

Southampton on loan. It was initially only to be for the month but he ended up staying until the season ended. The start of the 2007-08 saw Sammy Lee, ex-Liverpool player and coach, then manager at Bolton take Danny on a season long loan to the Reebok. However when Sammy left Bolton "by mutual consent" in the October of 2007 this appeared to jeopardise the loan deal. Ex-Newcastle player Gary Megson took over at Bolton and saw enough in Danny to ensure he saw the whole season out at the Reebok. Indeed Megson wanted to make the deal permanent during the close season but Newcastle stepped in with an "undisclosed" bid (rumoured to be around £2.5m) and Danny decided to come to St James's Park on a four-year deal. With 104 Newcastle appearances under his belt Guthrie had been a good and solid player.

On the international scene...

1990: In what was to be Sir Bobby Robson's last game as manager of England the starting line-up in the third place play-off match against Italy at the Stadio San Nicola, Bari featured Peter Beardsley. Also making an appearance as a 73rd minute substitute was Chris Waddle.

Born on July-07:

Year	Player	Position	Years
1897	Bob Pailor	Centre Forward	1914 - 1915
1911	Jesse Carver	Centre Half	1936 - 1939

July-08

A rather 'blank' day for Newcastle, no friendly/tour matches, no transfer, so we'll go for some 'hot gossip'.

2013: Whilst manager Alan Pardew had been on holiday owner Mike Ashley had dropped a bit of a bombshell bringing Joe Kinnear back to St James's Park and handing him responsibility for all football-related matters.

Pardew told BBC Radio Newcastle: "I'm very open-minded to Joe's position. I will take it as I see it. People who work with me will know that I am my own man. I will manage this football club and manage this team to the best of my ability. On the back of last year I am even more motivated to do well this year."

We all know how Kinnear's first few days in the post went - in a series of interviews he muddled up facts, or told outright 'porkies' depending upon which you want to believe, and mispronounced the names of some of the club's senior players.

Pardew said of this: "Some of the things Joe said he has apologised for, especially getting the names wrong of our players. That needs to be corrected because there is a certain respect needed there. I spoke to one or two players and my staff here and made them very aware of where the position lies."

Yes, this can only be Newcastle!

Pardew concluded: "Joe's experience of what he's had as a manager, Mike feels that he probably knows the scene slightly better than Derek [Llambias], in Mike's opinion. As far as I am concerned, the most important factor for Joe is transfers. Between myself, Lee and Joe we hope to get some transfers over the line - and some out, by the way, because the squad is little thin in areas."

A bit contradictory statement there, 'thin squad' - move players out! Really! So what did happen in the summer 2013 transfer market?

Danny Simpson - out, contract expired
James Perch –out, sold to Wigan
Mehdi Abeid - out, loaned to Panathinaikos
Shane Ferguson - out, loaned to Birmingham City
Adam Campbell - out, loaned to Carlisle United
Bradden Inman - out, sold to Crewe Alexandra

Not a single 'in'! Yes, that's how you strengthen a 'thin squad' ala Messer's Kinnear, Pardew & Charnley.

Oh, and did I mention that with Pardew returning from holiday, Kinnear was away on a pre-arranged break. Is it any wonder we got no one in, is it any wonder why the frustrations of the fans was so high? It could really only be Newcastle!

Born on July-08:

Year	Player	Position	Years
1959	Imre Varadi	Forward	1981 - 1983

July-09

On the transfer scene...

1998: Defender Carl Serrant arrives from Oldham Athletic

Serrant was a player who had a big reputation and was tipped for full England honours. Unfortunately for him things could not have been worse for him than when he came to Newcastle! Having just been signed by Dalglish, who was subsequently sacked, he was making his debut with the 'manager-in-waiting' Ruud Gullit watching from the stands.

Serrant was having an absolute nightmare of a time, and even though he was not officially in charge, Gullit came down from the stands to substitute him with Barton. Needless to say Serrant was never given a proper chance after that and he was loaned out to both Bury and Sheffield United. Sadly Serrant picked up a serious knee injury and he was released by Newcastle and his professional career was over at the age of 25.

Born on July-09:

Year	Player	Position	Years
1951	Mick Martin	Midfield	1978 - 1983
1986	Sebastien Bassong	Defence	2008 - 2009

July-10

1997: Ivor Allchurch, R.I.P.

"The Welsh Wizard", Ivor was probably the most skilful player produced by Wales. He was two footed, had complete control of the ball with either, and was said to possess a cannonball shot in both feet. Ivor is number 100 of the Football League '100 league legends' which means in the opinion of the football league he was one of the best one hundred players ever to play football.

Even at 30 years of age when he joined Newcastle he was an excellent player, with an almost unparalleled knowledge of the game and a shot that invariably challenged the opponents goal Ivor was a great favourite of the St. James's Park faithful. When Ivor left Newcastle to return to Wales with Cardiff City he continued to thrill the crowds wherever he played.

Until 1986 Ivor held the record for the number of goals scored for Wales, 23, and the number of appearances, 68.

Upon his retirement Ivor had played in well over 700 games and in 1966, he was awarded an MBE in recognition of his services to football and is also a member of the Welsh Hall of Fame. Ivor passed away at his home in Swansea.

Born on July-10:

Year	Player	Position	Years
1965	Paul Ferris	Wing	1981 - 1986

July-11

1966: England face Uruguay at Wembley in their World Cup Final Group 1, Game 1 fixture. The game ends all-square at 0-0 and in their line-up is Jackie Charlton.

2009: In the first match of the Festival of Football being put on by Shamrock Rovers, Newcastle played their first pre-season friendly. Though the final score-line of 3-0 to Newcastle looks at bit one-sided, the game was far closer than it suggests. Rovers definitely gave as good as they got, especially in the scoreless first half where the phrase "an end to end game" was an apt description. Newcastle's goals were scored by Steven Taylor, Shola Ameobi and Nile Ranger.

Born on July-11:

Year	Player	Position	Years
1872	Matt Scott	Left Back	1900 - 1901

July-12

1952: Newcastle are coming to the end of their exhaustive ten-week tour of South Africa and play a Select X1 in the Rand Stadium, Johannesburg. They lose 5-2 and in a rather scathing attack upon them after the game Johannesburg Daily Mail columnist Eric Litchfield, an ex-Newcastle player, intimated that Newcastle were suffering from "delusions of grandeur" and that they should never again be invited back to South Africa. Harsh words indeed. Litchfield had, as indicated, been a Newcastle player but he arrived shortly before the onset of World War II and whilst he played some war-time games for Newcastle he never made an official competitive appearance. As Newcastle were parading the FA Cup on their South Africa tour - the first time the FA had allowed it to leave our shores - perhaps there was a tinge of sour-grapes in his assertions.

July-13

1919: Local lad Albert Stubbins born today, though he was actually brought up in the USA as his family moved to Detroit in 1923, but they returned to his birthplace Wallsend in 1930.

Signing for Newcastle in 1937 it was a tragedy that his best years for them would be during the war years, where he scored a staggering 245 goals in only 199 war-time games, exceeding the 40-goals per season mark on three occasions. However as it was war time one has to question the quality of the opposition. Stubbins also scored 39 goals in the 'Football League North' for Newcastle, this, along with the 'Football League South' being the leagues instigated by the FA as it was considered too late to arrange the resumption of full Football League fixtures in time for the 1945-46 season.

Nevertheless this sort of form was sure to attract the attentions of higher placed clubs and he duly joined Liverpool shortly after normal service was resumed in 1946-47 season.

At Liverpool he earned 'legendary' status, scoring on his debut and going on to record 83 goals in 180 games. Whilst at Liverpool he won the 1st Division in 1947 and was an FA Cup runner-up 1950.

Such was Albert's 'cult' status in Liverpool that he appears on the cover of the Beatles famous LP "Sgt Peppers Lonely Hearts Club Band".

Born on July-13:

Year	Player	Position	Years
1919	Albert Stubbins	Centre Forward	1936 - 1946
1962	David Mitchell	Forward	1991 - 1991
1979	Craig Douglas Bellamy	Forward	2001 - 2005

July-14

2001: Comfortable Win in the Intertoto Cup

Newcastle easily managed what seemed to be a potential 'banana skin' of a game with Lokeren in the first leg of their Round 3 draw at the Daknam Stadion.

Two goals from Shola Ameobi and others from Wayne Quinn and Lomano LuaLua settled the nerves for the home tie to follow.

First Meeting on July-14:

Year	V	F	A	R	Opposition	Competition
2001	A	4	0	W	Lokeren	Intertoto Cup

Debut on July-14:

Year	Player	Opposition
2001	Craig Douglas Bellamy (Forward)	Lokeren

July-15

2006: Luque Earns Draw in the Intertoto Cup

An Albert Luque equaliser on 50 minutes earned Newcastle a draw in their Second Round, First Leg tie against Lillestrom Sportsklubb at St James's Park. Lillestrom having taking the lead in the first half with a 21st minute strike from Robert Koren.

First Meeting on July-15:

Year	V	F	A	R	Opposition	Competition
2006	H	1	1	D	Lillestrom Sportsklubb	Intertoto Cup

Born on July-15:

Year	Player	Position	Years
1908	William Carlton	Right Half	1926-1929
1921	Doug Graham	Full Back	1940-1950
1976	Jose Rodrigues Alves Antunes Fumaca	Midfield	1999-2000

July-16

1966: England face Mexico at Wembley in their World Cup Final Group 1, Game 2 fixture. Jackie Charlton features in the England line-up, as does brother Bobby who scores one of England's goals as they triumph 2-0. England's other goal coming from Roger Hunt.

1997: Newcastle Win a Trophy!

Yes, we won a trophy today, but don't get too excited - it was the Dublin International Trophy, a pre-season tournament in Ireland. After yesterday's 3-0 victory over PSV Eindhoven, two goals from Jon Dahl Tomasson and one from Keith Gillespie, Newcastle beat Derry City in Dublin 2-0. This time the goals coming from Jimmy Crawford and Peter Beardsley.

Born on July-16:

Year	Player	Position	Years
1944	Albert Bennett	Centre Forward	1965-1969

July-17

2005: Comfortable First Leg Victory in the Intertoto Cup

Two goals within two minutes in the very early stages of this first leg tie virtually ended it as a competitive game. Chopra on 4 minutes and N'Zogbia on 6 minutes saw Newcastle relaxing into the game. Tesak pulled one back for Dubnica just before half-time but there was no panic and on 70 minutes Milner restored Newcastle's two goal cushion going into the second leg.

2013: Cisse Quits Tour

Following months of hinting at his displeasure over Newcastle having 'payday lender' Wonga as the shirt sponsor Papiss Cisse pulled out of the preseason tour of Portugal - refusing the wear the shirt on religious grounds.

First Meeting on July-17:

Year	V	F	A	R	Opposition	Competition
2005	H	1	1	D	FK ZTS Dubnica	Intertoto Cup

July-18

On the transfer scene...

1975: Forward George Hope departs for Charlton Athletic
1979: Defender John Blackley departs for Preston North End
1988: Midfielder Paul Gascoigne departs for Tottenham Hotspur

So much has been written about Paul Gascoigne that I'll look instead at Blackley and Hope.

Hope had the misfortune of having the likes of Malcolm "Supermac" Macdonald and John Tudor in front of him for a first team place, hence he only made only six appearances for Newcastle, scoring one goal. His one goal though was an important one however as it ensured Newcastle took all the points against Manchester United.

Blackley was one of the most prominent players in Scotland during the 1970s. He won seven International Caps for Scotland and appeared in several Cup Finals for Hibernian. Newcastle had tried to sign him on numerous occasions. He finally joined Newcastle in 1977, in what could be described as his "veteran" stage, in an unsuccessful effort to help avoid relegation into Division Two. He was a stylish player, very cool on the ball, and under pressure, which sometimes came across as rather arrogant, however, at times, he was a treat to watch.

July-19

2015: Friendly - Really?
No one gets sent off in a pre-season 'friendly' game - well no one except Massadio Haidara that is! Someone must have forgot to tell him the meaning of the word 'friendly'.

The game against Sacramento Republic on their pre-season tour of the USA proved to be a rather trying one for Newcastle and a perplexing one for Haidara. It was his cross on 49 minutes that James Kiffe volleyed past his own keeper, but it was also his sending off for a foul on Danny Barrera that reduced Newcastle to ten men. They did hold on though and the Kiffe 'own goal' turned out to be the only one of the match.

Born on July-19:

Year	Player	Position	Years
1962	Paul Bracewell	Midfield	1992-1995

July-20

1966: England face France at Wembley in their World Cup Final Group 1, Game 3 fixture. Jackie Charlton features in the England line-up and they are triumphant 2-0.

Roger Hunt getting both of England's goals, one in each half.

2013 saw Newcastle at the Estadio do Rio Ave in Portugal for a pre-season tour game against Rio Ave FC. Unfortunately they were to lose 3-1 to the Portugese Primeira Liga side.

Born on July-20:

Year	Player	Position	Years
1906	David Fairhurst	Left Back	1929-1946
1908	Jonathan Wilkinson	Forward	1927-1929

Born on July-20:

Year	Player	Position	Years
1936	William McKinney	Right Back	1956-1965
1990	Ole Soderberg	Goalkeeper	2009-2012
1996	Olivier Kemen	Midfield	2013 - current

July-21

2001: Progression in the Intertoto Cup

Following the 4-0 win at the Daknam Stadion, a goal from Craig Bellamy on the hour at St James's Park made this a very comfortable 5-0 aggregate win against Lokeren. Newcastle therefore progress into the next round of the Intertoto Cup.

Debut on July-21:

Year	Player	Opposition
2001	Olivier Jimmy Wilfrid Bernard (Defence)	Lokeren

Born on July-21:

Year	Player	Position	Years
1898	William Gibson	Left Half	1923-1929
1943	John Sinclair	Wing	1967-1969

July-22

2006: 4-0 Aggregate Win in the Intertoto Cup

A brace from Shola Ameobi (28 & 6) and a goal from Emre (89) built upon the 1-1 draw at home in the first leg to send Newcastle through to the next round of the Intertoto Cup at the expense of Lillestrom.

Born on July-22:

Year	Player	Position	Years
1905	Thomas Mordue	Centre Forward	1925-1926
1989	Daryl Janmaat	Right Back	2014 - current

July-23

1966: England face Argentina at Wembley in their World Cup Final Quarter-Final fixture. Jackie Charlton features in the England line-up and they are triumphant 1-0. Geoff Hurst getting England's goal on 78 minutes.

2005: 5-1 Aggregate Win in the Intertoto Cup

A brace from Shearer (71 & 90) sealed a 5-1 aggregate win over Dubnica at St James's Park. This after the 3-1 win in Slovakia.

2013 and no one told Coloccini it was only a friendly! He received his marching orders in an ugly confrontation with Rui Caetano in a pre-season game at the Estadio da Captital do Movel. Both players were eventually sent off but the images of Coloccinin with his hands around the throat of Caetano were displeasing to say the least. The game itself was drawn 1-1 with Shola Ameobi equalising Caetano's earlier goal.

Born on July-23:

Year	Player	Position	Years
1993	Ayoze Perez	Forward	2014 - current

July-24

On the transfer scene...

1987: Forward Peter Beardsley departs to Liverpool

2006: Defender Robbie Elliott departs for Sunderland
Damien Duff arrives from Chelsea

In Beardsley and Elliott Newcastle let 356 games worth of experience walk out the door! This following a season where they had finished 17th, only five points above the relegation places, this was a bit of a gamble to say the least.

Of course, perhaps realising their mistake, Beardsley was to return to Newcastle some six years later. He has in fact got quite a rare record in that he played for both Merseyside clubs, Liverpool and Everton, and appeared in the Merseyside Derby, he has played for both Manchester clubs, United and City, appearing in the Manchester Derby, and of course he played for Newcastle and appeared in the Tyne-Wear Derby.

Elliott had also been at Newcastle twice. They sold him to Bolton in 1997 for what was then Bolton's record signing of £2.2m and he came back in 2001 on a free transfer! His time at Bolton saw him teaming up with ex-Newcastle players Alan Thompson, Franz Carr and - you probably guessed it, Peter Beardsley!

Born on July-24:

Year	Player	Position	Years
1921	Albert Clark	Wing Half	1948-1949

July-25

2001: Narrow Win in the Intertoto Cup

A brace from Nobby Solano and a goal from Aaron Hughes gave Newcastle a narrow 3-2 win over 1860 Munchen in the Olympic Stadium, Munich. Having the victory - and three 'away' goals - will certainly ease the pressure for the coming home tie.

First Meeting on July-25:

Year	V	F	A	R	Opposition	Competition
2001	A	3	2	W	1860 Munchen	Intertoto Cup

Born on July-25:

Year	Player	Position	Years
1907	William Chalmers	Inside Right	1928-1931
1966	Darren Jackson	Forward	1986-1988

July-26

1996: In the World Cup Semi-Final at Wembley England take on Portugal and win 2-1. Jack Charlton is in the England team - and so is his brother Bobby. Which is just as well as he scores both goals, 30 and 79 minutes. Portuguese legend Eusebio scored their goal from the penalty spot on 82 minutes.

On the transfer scene...

1978: Midfielder Geoff Nulty departs for Everton

Nulty had made 147 appearances for Newcastle, scoring 14 times in the process. Signed in the same week as Tommy Craig and both making their debuts on Boxing Day 1974 at Carlisle, Nulty was a 'model professional'. A thoroughly efficient midfield ball-winner he was moved back to centre-half on the arrival of Gordon Lee with notable effect. Going to Everton he was reunited with his old Newcastle boss, Lee.

Born on July-26:

Year	Player	Position	Years
1928	Eduardo Oliver Robledo	Left Half	1949 - 1953
1935	Ken Leek	Centre Forward	1961 - 1961

July-27

On the transfer and tour scene...

1978: Full Back Martin Gorry departs for Hartlepool United

1999: Newcastle were playing the seventh game of their pre-season friendly and were coming up against the first opponents that could be said to pose a real challenge - Celtic! Played at Celtic Park in Glasgow in front of a huge crowd - 59,252 being the official figure. That would be huge for most competitive games let alone a friendly.

Celtic were easy 2-0 winners with both goals coming in the second half - one of them scored by Mark Viduka, who would of course be on his way to Newcastle some years later.

Born on July-27:

Year	Player	Position	Years
1975	Alessandro Pistone	Defence	199- 2000

July-28

1999: How's this for a comparison - after yesterday's bumper crowd at Celtic Park Newcastle faced Stoke City in their penultimate pre-season friendly at the Britannia Stadium, the crowd, 6,742. At least Newcastle won this one, 2-1. The goals coming from Franck Dumas and Paul Robinson.

2005: Bad Start to Intertoto Cup Semi-Final

Newcastle suffered a narrow 2-1 defeat at the Estadio Municipal de Riazor in Coruna, Spain against Deportivo. Would the 'away goal' from Bowyer be of any comfort in the home tie?

First Meeting on July-28:

Year	V	F	A	R	Opposition	Competition
2005	A	1	2	L	Deportivo la Coruna	Intertoto Cup

Born on July-28:

Year	Player	Position	Years
1906	Isaac Tate	Goalkeeper	1923-1927
1927	Matthew McNeil	Centre Half	1949-1951
1952	Derek Craig	Central Defence	1969-1975
1985	Mathieu Debuchy	Right Back	2013-2014

July-29

2015: Great Grandads!

The Grandsons of two ex-Newcastle players, Ken Leek and Alan Suddick, made an appearance in the friendly against York City tonight. Karl Darlow, grandson of Ken Leek, ex-Newcastle and Wales Centre Forward, and Lewis Suddick, grandson of ex-Newcastle midfielder, Alan Suddick, were both involved in the friendly tonight against York City at Bootham Cresent.

Whilst they weren't on the pitch together, with Darlow playing the first half in goal and being replaced by Elliott at half-time, and Suddick coming on as a 70th minute substitute for Mitrovik, it was nice to see Newcastle "keeping it in the family".

July-30

1966: World Cup Winner!

In the World Cup Final at Wembley England faced West Germany and won 4-2 after extra-time. Jack Charlton is in the England team - and of course picks up a World Cup Winners medal.

England's goals did of course come from a hat-trick by Geoff Hurst and a one from Martin Peters.

2013, in the penultimate game of their pre-season matches Newcastle were back in Scotland and at St Mirren Park where goals from Papiss Cisse - wearing the Wonga sponsored shirt - and Mathieu Debuchy sealed a 2-0 victory over Scottish Premiership side St Mirren.

Born on July-30:

Year	Player	Position	Years
1932	Alex Gaskell	Centre Forward	1953-1954

July-31

1956: Livingstone Dismissed

Whilst Doug Livingstone had indeed been the manager, much to his chagrin the 'Directors Committee' still had a lot of influence, and indeed the final say on team selection.

In submitting his team to the board for the FA Cup Final against Manchester City at Wembley in 1955, Livingstone had made one great omission - he had sensationally left out Jackie Milburn. The board immediately told him Milburn was playing - he duly went on to score the fastest goal ever scored in a FA Cup Final!

He subsequently spent only one more season at Newcastle, moving down to take charge of the Juniors for a while before eventually leaving altogether today in 1956 and taking up the manager's job at Fulham.

Livingstone was replaced by the same Directors Committee led by Stan Seymour that he himself had replaced upon his appointment.

Born on July-31:

Year	Player	Position	Years
1944	Thomas Robson	Left Wing	1966-1968
1959	Peter Manners	Midfield	1977-1979
1966	Robert McKinnon	Defence	1984-1986

AUGUST

August-01

1954: Livingstone Appointed

Doug Livingstone appointed as manager (replacing Stan Seymour/Directors Committee).

2001: 6-3 Aggregate Win Takes Newcastle to Intertoto Final

Gary Speed on 5 minutes, Lomano LuaLua on 80 minutes and a 90th minute Nobby Solano penalty saw Newcastle win 3-1 on the night against 1860 Munchen at St James's Park, making it 6-3 on aggregate - the Intertoto Cup Final awaits!

Born on August-01:

Year	Player	Position	Years
1892	Robert McIntosh	Right Half	1920 - 1924

August-02

1975: Losing Start to the Anglo-Scottish Campaign

Newcastle made a losing start to their Anglo-Scottish campaign at Brunton Park going down by 2-0, both goals scored by Bobby Owen, in the English Group 1 tie against Carlisle United.

August-03

1974: Tyne-Wear Derby No. 108

Newcastle travelled to Roker Park for a Group 4 fixture in the Texaco Cup against Sunderland, the 108th Tyne-Wear Derby. As holders of the Texaco Cup perhaps Newcastle's expectations were a little high, but they were brought back to reality quickly in their attempt to retain it.

With Vic Halom and Bobby Kerr both scoring for Sunderland, and there being only a single John Tudor goal in replay it was a disastrous start to the new campaign.

2005: Out of the Intertoto Cup

Newcastle go out of the Intertoto Cup at the Semi-Final stage having suffered another 2-1 defeat to Deportivo making it a 4-2 aggregate defeat overall.

Debut on August-03:

Year	Player	Opposition
2005	Scott Matthew Parker (Midfield) Emre Belozoglu (Midfield)	Deportivo la Coruna

Born on August-03:

Year	Player	Position	Years
1966	Gary Kelly	Goalkeeper	1984-1989
1973	Nikos Dabizas	Defender	1998-2001

August-04

On the transfer scene...

1978: Forward Mickey Burns departs for Cardiff City
1987: Forward Tony Cunningham departs for Blackpool
2007: Goalkeeper Tim Krul departs, temporarily, for a loan spell with Falkirk
2011: Midfielder Wayne Routledge departs for Swansea City

Cunningham has the distinction of being the first black player to sign for Newcastle, but he was not the first to play - that honour goes to Howard Gayle who was briefly on loan from Liverpool at St James's Park in the latter stages of the 1982-83 season.

Gayle was Liverpool's first black player also. Despite making only a handful of appearances for the Reds, he achieved quite a cult status there, nothing to do with his colour - more about his fantastic work ethic.

August-05

2006: Roeder Appointed Full-Time

Glenn Roeder appointed full-time manager after an appeal to the Premier League Managers Association as he does not have the "Pro License" stipulated by UEFA. He could only be appointed if the majority of the Premier League managers voted for it - which they did!

Born on August-05:

Year	Player	Position	Years
1974	Antoine Sibierski	Midfield	2006- 2007
1978	Michael Bridges	Forward	2003-2004

August-06

2011: Friendly Abandoned

The pre-season friendly at St James's Park against AFC Fiorentina, whom Newcastle had beaten in the 1974 Anglo-Italian Cup final, was abandoned after 64 minutes due to very heavy rain.

More like a monsoon really!

It was coming down that heavy you could hardly see a couple of feet in front you and even though the St James's Park pitch has excellent drainage it couldn't handle the deluge. The score was 0-0 at the time.

1975: Tyne-Wear Derby No. 109

Newcastle played hosts to Sunderland for an Anglo-Scottish Group 1 tie, the 109th Tyne-Wear Derby. Goals from Vic Halom and Pop Robson gave Sunderland a 2-0 victory.

Born on August-06:

Year	Player	Position	Years
1880	Ronald Orr	Inside Forward	1901-1908
1916	Ernest Hall	Centre Half	1933-1937
1933	Ken Waugh	Full Back	1952-1956
1992	Mehdi Abeid	Midfield	2011-2015

August-07

1971 Newcastle got their Anglo-Scottish Tournament campaign off to a good start in their English Group 4 fixture at Bramall Lane against Sheffield United. A single goal in the second half was enough to give them the victory.

Unfortunately the same could not be said for the start of their Premiership campaign in **1999** as they lost 1-0 to Aston Villa at Villa Park.

2001: Intertoto Cup Final - First Leg

Newcastle travelled to France to play Troyes at the Stade de l'Aube in the First Leg of the Intertoto Cup Final.

It was a 0-0 draw, so all to play for in the Second Leg at St James's Park.

First Meeting on August-07:

Year	V	F	A	R	Opposition	Competition
2001	H	0	0	D	Troyes	Intertoto Cup

Debut on August-07:

Year	Player	Opposition
1999	Kieron Courtney Dyer (Midfield) Franck Dumas (Defence) Elena Sierra Marcelino (Defence) Paul Robinson (Forward) Alain Goma (Defence/Centre Back)	Aston Villa

Born on August-07:

Year	Player	Position	Years
1939	William Salmond Thomson Penman	Midfield	1963-1966

August-08

1997 saw Newcastle travel to Saltergate, the home of Chesterfield, for a pre-season friendly. The result is a 1-1 draw.

2009 saw the only one competitive game played on this day. It was a Championship fixture against West Bromwich Albion at The Hawthorns. Albion took a 1-0 lead into the break but Damien Duff equalised for Newcastle in the second half thus the game ended all-square at 1-1.

Debut on August-08:

Year	Player	Opposition
2009	Nile Ranger (Forward)	West Bromwich Albion

Born on August-08:

Year	Player	Position	Years
1905	Joeseph Devine	Inside Right	1930 - 1931
1913	Harry Johnson	Left Back	1933 - 1937
1978	Louis Laurent Saha	Forward	1998 - 1999
1994	Chancel Mbemba Mangulu	Central Defence	2015 - current

August-09

1969 saw Newcastle lose the opening fixture of League Division 1 to West Ham United at Upton Park. The only goal of the game coming from Geoff Hurst in the second half. However they won the first game of the **1997-98** Premiership season against Sheffield Wednesday 2-1 at St James's Park courtesy of two goals from Tino Asprilla. It was back to losing ways though in **1999** when they travelled to White Hart Lane for the opening game of the **1999-2000** Premiership season, Tottenham Hotspur being comfortable 3-1 winners, a certain Les Ferdinand being on the score sheet for Spurs. Nobby Solano getting Newcastle's only goal.

1973: William Aitken, R.I.P.
William, or "Billy", was a consistent striker in Scotland and was considered to be a virtual 'steal' from Rangers. He was bought ostensibly as a striking partner for Stan Seymour and Tom McDonald. Although Aitken only scored 10 goals in his four seasons at Newcastle he was a real asset to the team. He had an abundance of skill on the ball and would weave his way between the opposition, often leaving them bewildered and dumped on their backsides. On leaving Aitken had made 110 appearances in total..

Debut on August-09:

Year	Player	Opposition
1975	Alan Gowling (Forward)	Middlesbrough
1997	Alessandro Pistone (Defence) Stuart Pearce (Defence) Temuri Ketsbaia (Midfield/Forward) Shay Given (Goalkeeper) Jon Dahl Tomasson (Striker/Midfield)	Sheffield Wednesday

Born on August-09:

Year	Player	Position	Years
1896	William Duncan Cowan	Inside Forward	1923-1926
1915	Tom Swinburne	Goalkeeper	1934-1947

August-10

1974 saw a good win for Newcastle against against Middlesbrough in the Texaco Cup at St James's Park. Goals from Malcolm Macdonald, Tommy Cassidy, John Tudor and Mickey Burns giving then a 4-0 victory.

They also had a win in their UEFA Cup 2nd Qualifying Round, 1st Leg tie against Futbola Klubs Ventspils in **2006**.

Played at the Stadionas Skonto, which is not Ventspil's usual 'home' (that being Ventspils Olimpiskais Stadions) it was a Titus Bramble goal that gave Newcastle a 1-0 victory.

1985: Charlton Jacks It In!

After less than a year in charge Jackie Charlton resigned as manager. Rumours of unrest between himself and the Newcastle hierarchy are abundant. Given the success he went on to have perhaps the hierarchy - and some of the fans - should have listened to Charlton a bit more!

First Meeting on August-10:

Year	V	F	A	R	Opposition	Competition
2006	A	1	0	W	Futbola Klubs Ventspils	UEFA Cup

Debut on August-10:

Year	Player	Opposition
2006	Damien Duff (Midfield/Forward)	Futbola Klubs Ventspils

Born on August-10:

Year	Player	Position	Years
1908	John James Murray	Wing Half	1932-1936
1967	Phillipe Albert	Central Defence	1994-1999

August-11

1996: Charity Shield Defeat

Newcastle faced Manchester United at Wembley in the season 'curtain raiser', the Charity Shield. They were however soundly beaten 4-0!

2007: Opening Day Victory

Newcastle opened the Premiership season with a 3-1 victory over Bolton Wanderers at the Reebok Stadium, Newcastle's goals coming from Charles N'Zogbia and two from Obafemi Martins.

Bolton's team is worth a mention here as it contained Abdoulaye Faye, who was to become a Newcastle player in a matter of days - 20 to be precise, Kevin Nolan who was to arrive at Newcastle the coming January and ex-Newcastle favourite Gary Speed.

Debut on August-11:

Year	Player	Opposition
1996	Alan Shearer (Centre Forward)	Manchester United
2007	Alan Smith (Forward) David Sebastian Rozehnal (Defence) Mark Viduka (Forward) Geremi (Defence/Midfield)	Bolton Wanderers

Born on August-11:

Year	Player	Position	Years
1971	Michael Richard Jeffrey	Forward	1993-1995

August-12

1972: Opening Day Victory

Newcastle opened their League Division 1 season with a 2-1 victory over Wolverhampton Wanderers at St James's Park, Newcastle's goals coming from John Tudor and Tony Green. The game is notable for a couple of other reasons, not least that Wolves' manager on the day was Bill McGarry who would land the Newcastle managers position in 1977, but also that it pitched the Hibbitt brothers against each other. Terry playing for Newcastle of course and Kenny playing for Wolves.

August-13

1979: Edward Stanley Dixon, R.I.P.

Using his middle name Dixon was always called Stan. He signed for Newcastle just before the onset on the Great War (WWI) so his career was halted for the duration of the hostilities. In all Stan played 53 times for Newcastle and scored ten goals..

First Meeting on August-13:

Year	V	F	A	R	Opposition	Competition
1997	H	2	1	W	NK Croatia	Champions League

Debut on August-13:

Year	Player	Opposition
2011	Yohan Cabaye (Midfield) Demba Ba (Forward) Gabriel Antoine Obertan (Right Wing)	Arsenal

Born on August-13:

Year	Player	Position	Years
1970	Alan Shearer	Centre Forward	1996-2006

August-14

1984: Charlton is Choice

Born into a very famous local footballing family, his mother's cousin was none other than the legendary Jackie Milburn, "Big Jack" Charlton was a Newcastle fan through and through. He never got to play for his boyhood heroes however but instead ended up at Leeds United after quitting his job in the Ashington coal mines.

A 1966 World Cup winner and with good managerial experience behind him, having earned promotion to the top-flight with Middlesbrough in his first season there - and winning the Manager of the Year Award, he had also been in charge at Sheffield Wednesday when they got promoted to the Second Division.

There were certainly high hopes at St James's Park upon his appointment.

First Meeting on August-14:

Year	R	F	A	V	Opposition	Competition
2002	W	1	0	A	Zeljeznicar Sarajevo	European Champions League

Debut on August-14:

Year	Player	Opposition
1968	Thomas Gibb (Midfield)	Sheffield Wednesday
1971	Malcolm Macdonald (Centre Forward) Terry Hibbitt (Midfield)	Crystal Palace
1993	Nicos Papavasiliou (Midfield) Malcolm Allen (Forward)	Tottenham Hotspur
2002	Hugo Viana (Midfield) Titus Malachi Bramble (Defence)	Zeljeznicar Sarajevo
2004	Nicky Butt (Midfield) James Phillip Milner (Midfield) Stephen Babeson Carr (Defence) Patrick Stephan Kluivert (Forward)	Middlesbrough

August-15

1992: Scoring Debut

Paul Bracewell scored on his debut today in the League Division 1 fixture against Southend United.

It was an important goal too, as together with an 'own goal' from Southend's Spencer Prior and a goal from Lee Clark it ensured Newcastle had a slender 3-2 victory at St James's Park. Newcastle had taken a 2-0 lead into the break. David Martin an Ian Benjamin scored for Southend.

Debut on August-15:

Year	Player	Opposition
1992	Paul Bracewell (Midfield) Barry Venison (Full-Back/Midfield) John Beresford (Defence (Left Back)	Southend United
1998	Laurent Charvet (Defence/Full Back) Dietmar Hamann (Midfield)	Charlton Athletic
1999	John Karelse (Goalkeeper)	Southampton

Born on August-15:

Year	Player	Position	Years
1924	Ray King	Goalkeeper	1946-1947
1948	Stuart Alderson	Right Wing	1965-1967
1976	Dereck Vivian Hamilton	Full Back/Midfield	1997-2000

August-16

1942: Bob Foyers, R.I.P.

Coming to Newcastle from Edinburg St Bernards, Foyers proved to be a tough, uncompromising, full-back and was soon elevated to club captain. This is quite remarkable given that he only made a total of 39 appearances for Newcastle.

Debut on August-16:

Year	Player	Opposition
1980	Ray Clarke (Forward) Fransiscus Koenen (Midfield)	Sheffield Wednesday
2010	James Robert Perch (Defence)	Manchester United

Born on August-16:

Year	Player	Position	Years
1917	John Fairbrother	Goalkeeper	1947 - 1952
1924	Robert Carmichael Mitchell	Outside-Left	1949 - 1961
1964	Barry Venison	Full-Back/Midfield	1992 - 1995
1989	Moussa Sissoko	Midfield	2013 - current

August-17

Newcastle have only played seven games on this day in history. They have lost three, drawn three and therefore only ever won once. They lost 1-0 to Burnley in **1968**, lost 2-0 to Everton in **1996** and lost 2-0 to Manchester City in **2014**. The draws were 1-1 with Southampton in **1985**, 2-2 with Leeds United in **2003** and 1-1 with Manchester United in **2004**.

The solitary win was in **1974** in a League Division 1 fixture against Coventry City at St James's Park. The result was 3-2 to Newcastle with their goals being scored by Alan Kennedy, Malcolm Macdonald and Pat Howard Coventry goals were scored by Brian Alderson and Tom Hutchison, both in the second half.

Debut on August-17:

Year	Player	Opposition
1974	Glenn Keeley (Central Defence) Michael Edward Burns (Forward)	Coventry City
1985	Alan Davies (Wing)	Southampton
2003	Lee David Bowyer (Midfield)	Leeds United
2008	Daniel Sean Guthrie (Midfield) Fabricio Coloccini (Defence) Jonas Manuel Gutierrez (Midfield)	Manchester United
2014	Ayoze Perez (Forward) Jack Raymond Colback (Midfield) Daryl Janmaat (Right Back) Remy Cabella (Midfield) Emmanuel Riviere (Forward) Rolando Aarons (Midfield)	Manchester City

August-18

1951: Six of the Best

Newcastle hosted Stoke city in a League Division 1 fixture and ran out easy winners 6-0. A hat-trick for Jackie Milburn and goals for Charlie Crowe, Bobby Mitchell and Jorge Robledo ensuring the victory.

1962: Scoring Debut

David Hilley scored on his debut today in the League Division 2 fixture against Cardiff City. Though Newcastle were winning 3-1 at half-time Cardiff fought back well and the game ended up with honours even at 4-4 at Ninian Park.

1991: Scoring Debut

Franz Carr scored on his debut today in the League Division 2 fixture against Charlton Athletic. Though it was a scoring debut it was unfortunately not a winning one as Newcastle went down 2-1 at The Valley. On the score sheet that day for Charlton was none other than Rob Lee!

Debut on August-18:

Year	Player	Opposition
1962	David Hilley (Inside Forward)	Cardiff City
1979	Ian Claude Davies (Left Back)	Oldham Athletic
1991	Franz Carr (Wing)	Charlton Athletic
2007	Claudio Roberto da Silva (Defence)	Aston Villa
2012	Vurnon Anita (Midfield)	Tottenham Hotspur

Born on August-18:

Year	Player	Position	Years
1880	Finlay Ballantyne Speedie	Inside Forward	1906 - 1908
1935	Jimmy Harrower	Inside Forward	1961 - 1962

August-19

1967: Scoring Debut

James "Jim" Scott scored on his debut today in the League Division 1 fixture against Southampton.

With Albert Bennett and Thomas Robson also scoring Newcastle were easy 3-0 winners at St James's Park.

1989: Scoring Debuts

All hail the "Mighty Quinn" - Micky Quinn scored FOUR goals on his debut today in the League Division 2 fixture against Leeds United With a goal from John Gallacher thrown in for good measure - on his debut too - Newcastle were 5-2 winners at St James's Park.

1995: Scoring Debut

Leslie "Sir Les" Ferdinand scored on his debut today in the Premiership fixture against Coventry City. With Rob Lee and Peter Beardsley also scoring Newcastle were easy 3-0 winners at St James's Park.

2001: Premiership's First "Pay per View"

Newcastle and Chelsea go into the history books as they contest the first ever "pay per view" game in the top-flight of English football at Stamford Bridge. Though the idea of "pay-per-view" matches was established in February 1999, with Oxford and Sunderland in a First Division match, this was the first time the concept was adopted by English football's elite - a decision which would irrevocably change football in this country and indeed across the world.

The game ended all-square at 1-1 with a 8th minute lead to Chelsea, scored by Zenden, was cancelled out by a goal from Clarence Acuna on 77 minutes.

First Meeting on August-19:

Year	V	F	A	R	Opposition	Competition
1961	H	0	0	D	Leyton Orient	Division 2
1992	H	2	1	W	Mansfield Town	League Cup

Debut on August-19:

Year	Player	Opposition
1967	James Scott (Right Wing/Midfield)	Southampton
1978	Jim Pearson (Forward) John Connolly (Left Wing)	Millwall
1987	Glyn Hodges (Midfield)	Tottenham Hotspur
1989	Micky Quinn (Centre Forward) Kevin Dillon (Midfield) Wayne Fereday (Winger) John Gallacher (Winger)	Leeds United
1995	David Ginola (Left Wing) Leslie Ferdinand (Forward) Neil Shaka Hislop (Goalkeeper) Warren Barton (Right Back)	Coventry City

Debut on August-19:

Year	Player	Opposition
2001	Pierre Laurent Robert (Outside Left)	Chelsea
2009	Daniel Peter Simpson (Right Back)	Sheffield Wednesday

Born on August-19:

Year	Player	Position	Years
1908	Joseph Richardson	Right Back	1929 - 1945
1944	Peter Noble	Midfield/Forward	1964 - 1968
1976	Stephen Babeson Carr	Defence	2004 - 208
1984	Ryan Anthony David Taylor	Defence/Midfield	2009 - 2015

August-20

2011: Tyne-Wear Derby No. 146

Newcastle travelled to the Stadium of Light to face Sunderland in a Premiership fixture, the 146th Tyne-Wear Derby.

A solitary goal in the second half from Ryan Taylor was enough to give Newcastle the victory.

Debut on August-20:

Year	Player	Opposition
1960	William Tuohy (Outside Left)	Preston North End
1966	Ronald George Guthrie (Left Back)	Aston Villa
1969	Jimmy Smith (Midfield)	Sheffield Wednesday
2000	Daniel Cordone (Midfield) Carl Cort (Forward)	Manchester United

August-21

1965: First Named Substitute for Newcastle

Today saw the introduction of "substitutes" into the world of football. Only one substitute could be named, and they could only be brought on to the field of play to replace an injured player. So today, under these new rules, Albert Bennett has the distinction of being Newcastle's first-ever player to be named as a substitute when he took to the bench in the game against Nottingham Forest. Ending in a 2-2 draw Albert was never used, *that distinction falling to Ollie Burton.*

On the subject of substitutes, Charlton Athletic's Keith Peacock, father of Newcastle's Darren, became the first substitute in the Football League when he replaced Mike Rose 11 minutes into their match against Bolton.

2001: Intertoto Cup Final Drawn - But Lost On Away Goals

Newcastle played out a 4-4 draw with Troyes in their second leg of the Intertoto Cup final. With the first leg being a 0-0 draw Troyes win the Intertoto Cup on the 'away goals' rule.

Debut on August-21:

Year	Player	Opposition
1948	Colin Gibson (Outside Right)	Everton
1985	Ian Stewart (Left Wing)	Luton Town
1994	Marc Hottiger (Right Back) Phillipe Albert (Central Defence)	Leicester City

Born on August-21:

Year	Player	Position	Years
1895	John Archibald	Goalkeeper	1922 - 1923
1908	John Dryden	Outside Left	1932 - 1934
1940	James Scott	Right Wing/Midfield	1967 - 1970
1959	Keith Mulgrove	Left Back	1977 - 1980
1992	Haris Vuckic	Midfield	2009 - current

August-22

1953: Tyne-Wear Derby No. 81

Newcastle hosted Sunderland in a League Division 1 fixture, the 81st Tyne-Wear Derby. The game ended 2-1 to Newcastle with Bobby Mitchell and Vic Keeble scoring their goals whilst Sunderland's scorer was none other than Len Shackleton!

2010: Six of the Best!

Newcastle ran out rampant winners 6-0 against Aston Villa at St James's Park. A hat-trick from Andy Carroll, a brace from Kevin Nolan and a goal from Joey Barton ensured there was a happy time on Tyneside today.

Debut on August-22:

Year	Player	Opposition
1953	Jimmy Scoular (Right Half)	Sunderland
1998	Nolberto Solano (Midfield/Right Wing)	Chelsea
2015	Florian Thauvin (Midfield/Wing)	Manchester United

Born on August-22:

Year	Player	Position	Years
1986	Stephen James Ireland	Midfield	2011

August-23

1947: Six of the Best!

Plymouth Argyle were the visitors to St James's Park for a League Division 2 fixture. They gave a very good account of themselves in the first half, which Newcastle just edged by the only goal of the half. The second half was a completely different story and saw six goals being scored - five of them by Newcastle making the final score 6-1.

Newcastle's scorers were Len Shackleton, with two goals, Roy Bentley, Tom Pearson, Tommy Walker and Charlie Wayman.

2012: Draw In Europa League Qualification Campaign

Newcastle began their campaign to get into the Europa League with the first leg of their tie against Atromitos Athens at the Peristeri Stadium. Going behind on 24 minutes to a goal from Epstein, Ryan Taylor snatched an equaliser in first-half injury time. With no further score there was everything to play for back at St James's Park.

First Meeting on August-23:

Year	V	F	A	R	Opposition	Competition
2012	A	1	1	D	Atromitos Athens	Europa League

Debut on August-23:

Year	Player	Opposition
1947	John Fairbrother (Goalkeeper)	Plymouth Argyle
1961	Ken Leek (Centre Forward)	Walsall
1977	Steve Hardwick (Goalkeeper)	Liverpool
1978	Colin Suggett (Midfield)	West Ham United

Debut on August-23:

Year	Player	Opposition
1997	Ian Rush (Forward)	Aston Villa
2012	Adam Campbell (Forward) Gael Bigirimana (Midfield) Romain Amalfitano (Midfield)	Atromitos Athens
2014	Siem de Jong (Midfield)	Aston Villa

Born on August-23:

Year	Player	Position	Years
1938	John Thomas McGrath	Centre Half	1961 - 1968
1957	Peter Cartwright	Midfield	1979 - 1983

August-24

1960: Scoring Debut

Duncan Neale scored twice on his debut today in the League Division 1 fixture against Fulham. With Bob Gilfillan and William Tuhoy also scoring twice and a goal from Len White, Newcastle were easy victors 7-2 at St James's Park.

1963: Scoring Debut

Colin "Cannonball" Taylor scored on his debut today in the League Division 2 fixture against Derby County. With Willie Penman and Ron McGarry also scoring , Newcastle were victors 3-1 at St James's Park.

1994: Comfortable Win Over Coventry

Two goals from Rob Lee, and goals from Steve Watson and Andy Cole, saw Newcastle breeze Coventry City aside in this 4-0 victory in the Premiership at St James's Park.

2006: UEFA Cup Progression

A goalless draw in the second leg of the UEFA Cup 2nd Qualifying Round against Ventspils meant that Newcastle, winning the first leg 1-0, progressed to the next round.

Debut on August-24:

Year	Player	Opposition
1960	Duncan Neale (Wing Half)	Fulham

Debut on August-24:

Year	Player	Opposition
1963	Gordon Marshall (Goalkeeper) Colin Taylor (Outside Left) Alwyn Derek Burton (Wing Half)	Derby County

Born on August-24:

Year	Player	Position	Years
1930	Arnold James Woollard	Right Back	1952-1956
1940	Colin Taylor	Outside Left	1963-1964

August-25

1956: Tyne-Wear Derby No. 88

Newcastle travelled to Roker Park to face Sunderland in a League Division 1 fixture, the 88th Tyne-Wear Derby. The game ended 2-1 to Newcastle with their scorers being Reg Davies and Jackie Milburn. Sunderland's scorer was once again none other than Len Shackleton!

1958: One and Only Appearance

Today saw the one and only appearance for Newcastle of Centre Forward, Carl Wilson. Newcastle travelled to Bloomfield Road to face Blackpool in a League Division 1 fixture.

The Newcastle attack force were useless on the day and Newcastle were beaten 3-0 quite easily. Carl's father, Joseph Wilson also played a single game for Newcastle at Centre Half in 1929.

1999: Tyne-Wear Derby No. 130

Newcastle hosted Sunderland in a Premiership fixture, the 130th Tyne-Wear Derby.

Despite Newcastle going into the break a goal to the good, scored by Keiron Dyer, the game ended 2-1 to Sunderland. Their scorers being Niall Quinn and Kevin Phillips.

First Meeting on August-25:

Year	V	F	A	R	Opposition	Competition
2010	A	3	2	W	Accrington Stanley	League Cup

Debut on August-25:

Year	Player	Opposition
1934	Thomas Leach (Centre Half) Robert Shankley (Inside Forward)	Nottingham Forest
1958	Carl Wilson (Centre Forward) William Wright (Outside Left)	Blackpool
1979	Peter Cartwright (Midfield)	Charlton Athletic
1984	Malcolm Brown (Right Back)	Leicester City
2010	Shane Ferguson (Midfield)	Accrington Stanley
2011	Sylvain Marveaux (Midfield)	Scunthorpe United

Born on August-25:

Year	Player	Position	Years
1878	Edward Birnie	Right Half	1898 - 1905

August-26

2000: One and Only Appearance

Today saw the one and only appearance for Newcastle of Forward, Jamie Coppinger. Newcastle played hosts to Tottenham Hotspur in a Premiership fixture and Jamie came on as a 79th minute substitute for Daniel Cordone, one of Newcastle's two scorers that day, the other being Gary Speed. Newcastle won 2-0.

2001: Tyne-Wear Derby No. 134

Newcastle hosted Sunderland for a Premiership fixture, the 134th Tyne-Wear Derby. A goal from Craig Bellamy for Newcastle and Kevin Phillips for Sunderland, both in the first half, saw the game end honours even, 1-1.

Debut on August-26:

Year	Player	Opposition
1922	Alexander Mutch (Goalkeeper)	Everton
1978	Peter Withe (Forward)	Luton Town
1989	Mark Stimson (Defence)	Leicester City
2000	Jamie Coppinger (Forward)	Tottenham Hotspur
2008	Sebastien Bassong (Defence)	Coventry City
2009	Haris Vuckic (Midfield) Tamas Kadar (Defence)	Huddersfield Town

Born on August-26:

Year	Player	Position	Years
1884	William Hampson	Right Back	1914 - 1927
1910	Wilfred Feeney	Inside Left	1930 - 1932
1938	Bryan Harvey	Goalkeeper	1958 - 1961

August-27

1938: Scoring Debuts

Henry "Harry" Clifton and Ralph Birkett both scored on their debut today in the League Division 2 fixture against Plymouth Argyle. It was just as well they did as it was their goals that gave Newcastle the slender 2-1 victory at St James's Park.

1980: One and Only Appearance

Today saw the one and only appearance for Newcastle of Midfielder, Phillip Leaver. Newcastle played hosts to Bury in the League Cup Round 2, First Leg tie. Goals from Bill Rafferty, scoring twice, and Alan Shoulder gave Newcastle a 3-1 advantage to take into the second leg, though Phillip of course was to take no further part.

1998: Dalglish Dismissed - Gullit Appointed

Kenny Dalglish was dismissed as Newcastle manager and within minutes of that being announced a further message from St James's Park stated that Ruud Gullit was the new manager.

Debut on August-27:

Year	Player	Opposition
1921	Harry Paton (Inside Left)	Huddersfield Town
1938	Henry Clifton (Inside Forward) John Douglas Wright (Wing Half) Ralph Birkett (Outside Right)	Plymouth Argyle
1980	Phillip Leaver (Midfield)	Bury
1983	John Ryan (Left Back/Midfield)	Leeds United
1988	John Grattan Hendrie (Right Wing) David John Beasant (Goalkeeper) Andy Thorn (Central Defence) John Grant Robertson (Forward)	Everton
2006	Obafemi Akinwunmi Martins (Forward)	Aston Villa

Born on August-27:

Year	Player	Position	Years
1973	Dietmar Johann Wolfgang Haman	Midfield	1998 - 1999
1978	Celestine Hycieth Babayaro	Left Back	2005 - 2007
1985	Lewis Guy	Forward	2004 - 2005
1989	Romain Amalfitano	Midfield	2012 - 2014
1990	Luuk de Jong	Forward	2014 - 2014

August-28

1920: Scoring Debut

Stan Seymour scored on his debut today in the League Division 1 fixture against West Bromwich Albion.

It was just as well he did as it was enough to earn Newcastle a 1-1 draw at St James's Park.

1982: Scoring Debut

Kevin Keegan scored on his debut today in the League Division 2 fixture against Queens Park Rangers. With it being the only goal of the game it ensured that the points stayed at St James's Park.

1999: Gullit Gone!

In the fall-out from the game against Sunderland played in torrential rain and with Gullit leaving out both Shearer and Ferguson from the starting line-up it wasn't only the weather that was causing a storm. This however was a storm Gullit could not survive,

Following the defeat he resigned - a year and a day after being appointed.

2013: More History Created by the Ameobi Brothers

With Shola scoring on 84 minutes and Sammy scoring on 94 minutes the brothers Ameobi grabbed themselves another slice of Newcastle United history - they became the first brothers to score for Newcastle in the same game, to date they are still the only ones.

First Meeting on August-28:

Year	V	F	A	R	Opposition	Competition
2013	A	2	0	W	Morecambe	League Cup

Debut on August-28:

Year	Player	Opposition
1920	Neil Harris (Centre Forward) Edward Ward (Inside Right) Stan Seymour (Outside Left) William John Aitken (Inside Forward)	West Bromwich Albion
1965	Albert Bennett (Centre Forward)	Sheffield Wednesday
1982	Kevin Keegan (Forward) Jeff Clarke (Central Defence)	Queens Park Rangers
2005	Albert Luque (Forward)	Manchester United
2013	Curtis Good (Centre Back)	Morecambe

Born on August-28:

Year	Player	Position	Years
1880	James Lindsay	Right Back	1899 - 1900
1893	George Pyke	Centre Forward	1913 - 1922
1979	Marlon Anderson Harewood	Forward	2009

August-29

We will skip past the disaster in **1928** when Newcastle were thrashed 7-2 at St James's Park by Burnley in a League Division 1 fixture and go to a happier occasion...

1962: Six of the Best

Middlesbrough were the visitors to St James's Park for a League Division 2 fixture. In a close first half Newcastle went into the break 2-1 up. In the second half they scored four goals to win by a very comfortable 6-1 score-line. Their scorers were Barrie Thomas with a hat-trick, Ken Hale with two goals and Dave Hilley.

1979: Tyne-Wear Derby No. 114

Newcastle travelled to Roker Park for a League Cup, Second Round, First Leg tie with Sunderland, the 114th Tyne-Wear Derby.

Sunderland went into the break a goal to the good with a goal from Wilf Rostron on 19 minutes. The second half saw them stretch their lead on 73 minutes thanks to a penalty scored by Pop Robson! Newcastle rescued a draw though with goals from Ian Davies (75) and Peter Cartwright (83).

Debut on August-29:

Year	Player	Opposition
1925	Albert Chandler (Right Back) Oswald Park (Centre Half)	Bolton Wanderers
1928	Edmund Wood (Centre Half)	Burnley
1931	John Allen (Centre Forward)	Liverpool
1936	Robert Francis Dudgeon Ancell (Left Back) Jesse Carver (Centre Half) Ehud Rogers (Outside Right)	Barnsley
1951	Ronald Campbell Simpson (Goalkeeper)	Bolton Wanderers
1970	Stewart Barrowclough (Wing)	Blackpool
1981	Imre Varadi (Forward)	Watford
2007	Jose Sanchez Enrique (Left-Back)	Barnsley

Born on August-29:

Year	Player	Position	Years
1963	Tommy Wright	Goalkeeper	1988 - 1993
1976	Jon Dahl Tomasson	Striker/Midfield	1997 - 1998
1990	Patrick van Aanholt	Defence	2010

August-30

1919: Scoring Debut

James Henderson scored on his debut today in the League Division 1 fixture against Arsenal. With it being the only goal of the game it ensured that Newcastle took the points at Highbury. This is also quite a historic goal as it is the first Newcastle scored since the resumption of the Football League following the cessation of hostilities of the Great War (WWI).

1958: Scoring Debut

John McGuigan scored on his debut today in the League Division 1 fixture against Everton. With William Wright also scoring Newcastle were 2-0 winners at Goodison Park.

1998: Scoring Debut

Stephane Guivarch scored on his debut today in the Premiership fixture against Liverpool. It was however nothing more than a consolation as a hat-trick from a certain Michael Owen helped Liverpool to a comfortable 4-1 victory at St James's Park.

2004: Robson Ousted

After only four games of the new season being played Newcastle chairman Freddy Shepherd announced that Bobby Robson had been dismissed from his post as manager and that John Carver had been appointed as caretaker.

Debut on August-30:

Year	Player	Opposition
1919	John Wilson (Wing Half/Forward) Ray Robinson (Outside Right) Thomas Curry (Right Half) James Henderson (Outside Right)	Arsenal
1930	Duncan Lindsay (Centre Forward) Jimmy Nelson (Right Back) Jimmy Naylor (Left Half) Jack Wilkinson (Outside Right) Ronald Starling (Inside Forward)	Sheffield Wednesday
1958	John McGuigan (Inside Forward)	Everton
1975	John Bird (Central Defence)	Manchester City
1986	Ian Bogie (Midfield)	Luton Town
1998	Carl Serrant (Defence) Stephen Glass (Midfield) Stephane Guivarch (Forward)	Liverpool

Born on August-30:

Year	Player	Position	Years
1951	Peter Withe	Forward	1978-1980
1957	Aiden McCaffery	Centre Half	1975-1978

August-31

1946: Scoring Debut

Roy Bentley scored twice on his debut today in the League Division 2 fixture against Millwall. With Jackie Milburn and Albert Stubbins also scoring Newcastle were comfortable 4-1 winners at The Den.

1960: Scoring Debut

Charles Woods scored on his debut today in the League Division 1 fixture against Fulham. Whilst it may have been a scoring debut it unfortunately wasn't a winning one as though Ivor Allchurch and Gordon Hughes also scored for Newcastle, Fulham were able to breach the Newcastle defence four times, so in a seven goal thriller Newcastle lost 4-3 at Craven Cottage.

1968: Tyne-Wear Derby No. 104

Newcastle travelled to Roker Park for a League Division 1 fixture against Sunderland, the 104th Tyne-Wear Derby.

Newcastle went into the break a goal to the good thanks to a strike from Pop Robson but Sunderland equalised in the second half through Colin Suggett!

1980: McGarry Moves On

Regarded as one of the games strict disciplinarians, McGarry seemed the ideal candidate to take over at Newcastle after the disastrous "player power" reign of Dinnis. There was however nothing he could do to prevent relegation following his appointment. Two rather mediocre seasons followed and just weeks into the 1980/81 season, following a poor run of form that, stretching back to the previous season, saw only two wins in the previous 20 games, he was sacked, *or resigned*, as manager depending upon which reports you believe.

Debut on August-31:

Year	Player	Opposition
1929	Duncan Hutchison (Centre Forward)	Manchester United
1932	John James Murray (Wing Half)	Middlesbrough
1939	David Hamilton (Midfield)	Nottingham Forest
1946	Roy Bentley (Centre Forward) Doug Graham (Full Back) Frank Brennan (Centre-Half) Eric Garbutt (Goalkeeper)	Millwall
1957	Jimmy Hill (Inside Forward)	Tottenham Hotspur
1960	Charles Woods (Forward)	Fulham
2009	Ryan Donaldson (Forward)	Leicester City
2013	Loic Remy (Forward)	Fulham

Born on August-31:

Year	Player	Position	Years
1875	Edward Allen	Left Back	1900 - 1901
1910	Harold Heward	Left Half	1932 - 1934
1954	Alan Kennedy	Left Back	1971 - 1978
1970	Nicos Papavasiliou	Midfield	1993 - 1994

SEPTEMBER

September-01

1906: Tyne-Wear Derby No. 18

Newcastle hosted Sunderland in a League Division 1 fixture, the 18th Tyne-Wear Derby. Two goals from Jock Rutherford and goals from Bill Appleyard and Jim Howie gave Newcastle a 4-2 victory.

Both of Sunderland's goals came from Arthur Bridgett in the second half.

1910: Tyne-Wear Derby No. 28

Newcastle travelled to Roker Park to face Sunderland in a League Division 1 fixture, the 28th Tyne-Wear Derby. Albert Shepherd scored a penalty for Newcastle but it was to no avail as Sunderland ran out 2-1 winners with goals from George Holley and Tim Coleman.

1939: Mather Moves On

The outbreak of war sees Tom Mather ending his association with United. A Directors Committee lead by Stan Seymour was put into place as "manager".

1951: Seven From Nine

Newcastle scored seven times in a nine goal encounter at St James's Park in a League Division 1 fixture against Tottenham Hotspur. Spurs themselves scoring twice.

The goals for Newcastle coming via a hat-trick by Jorge Robledo, two from Bobby Mitchell and one each from Tommy Walker and Ernie Taylor.

1964: Scoring Debut

Bryan "Pop" Robson scored on his debut today in the League Division 2 fixture against Charlton Athletic. With it being the only goal of the game it ensured victory down at The Valley.

1980: Cox Takes Over

Having spent four years as manager of Chesterfield, Arthur Cox was appointed as manager. He was of course assistant manager to Newcastle legend, but then Sunderland manager, Bob Stokoe when they won the FA Cup in 1974.

First Meeting on September-01:

Year	V	F	A	R	Opposition	Competition
1894	A	0	5	L	Darwen	Division 2
1934	H	2	5	L	Brentford	Division 2
1976	A	2	1	W	Gillingham	League Cup

Debut on September-01:

Year	Player	Opposition
1894	Thomas Rendell (Right Half) T Cambell (Outside Right) John Smith (Inside Right)	Darwen
1900	Charles Burgess (Full-Back)	Nottingham Forest
1909	Wilfred Low (Centre Half)	Bolton Wanderers
1913	John King (Inside Forward)	Blackburn Rovers
1937	James Denmark (Centre Half)	Barnsley
1964	Bryan Stanley Robson (Forward)	Charlton Athletic
1976	Alan Guy (Midfield)	Gillingham
1979	Stuart Boam (Central Defence)	Chelsea
1982	John Anderson (Defence)	Blackburn Rovers
1987	Francisco da Silva [Mirandinha] (Forward)	Norwich City

Born on September-01:

Year	Player	Position	Years
1894	Thomas Curry	Right Half	1912-1929
1954	Glenn Keeley	Central Defence	1974-1976

September-02

1893: One and Only Appearance

Both Andrew Ramsey (Goalkeeper) and J. Bowman (Outside Right) made their one and only appearances for Newcastle in the very first Football League match to be played in London - the 2-2 draw with Woolwich Arsenal.

It has to be mentioned though that Ramsey was an ex-Newcastle East End player who had moved to Stockton and then "retuned" to Newcastle when they became "United".

1905: Tyne-Wear Derby No. 16

Newcastle travelled to Roker Park for a League Division 1 fixture against Sunderland, the 16th Tyne-Wear Derby. Ron Orr and Jimmy Howie scored for Newcastle but Sunderland were the victors 3-2 with two goals from Arthur Bridgett and a one from Jimmy Gemmell.

1908: One and Only Appearance

Today saw the one and only appearance for Newcastle of Inside Right, Robert Blanthorne. Newcastle played hosts to Bradford City in a League Division 1 fixture. With Colin Veitch scoring the only goal of the game Newcastle were victorious.

1912: Scoring Debut

John McDonald scored on his debut today in the League Division 1 fixture against Bolton Wanderers. With Jock Rutherford also scoring it ensured a narrow 2-1 victory at Burnden Park.

1939: Newcastle Put 8 Past Swansea Town

Swansea Town came to St James' Park for a League Division 2 fixture and were soundly thrashed 8-1. A hat-trick for Ray Bowden, two for Tom Pearson and one each for David Hamilton, Willie Scott and Billy Cairns made it a sorry journey home for Swansea.

First Meeting on September-02:

Year	V	F	A	R	Opposition	Competition
1893	A	2	2	D	Woolwich Arsenal*	Division 2
1908	H	1	0	W	Bradford City	Division 1
1978	A	0	0	D	Cambridge United	Division 2

*Woolwich Arsenal became Arsenal against whom our first game was 03/09/1904

Debut on September-02:

Year	Player	Opposition
1893	J Bowman (Outside Right) Andrew Ramsay (Goalkeeper)	Woolwich Arsenal
1899	David Richmond Gardner (Left Back)	West Bromwich Albion
1903	James Howie (Inside Right)	Aston Villa
1905	Harold Hardinge (Inside Forward)	Sunderland
1908	James Stewart (Inside Forward) Robert Blanthorne (Inside Right)	Bradford City

Debut on September-02:

Year	Player	Opposition
1911	William Kelly (Inside Forward) James Hay (Left Half)	Bolton Wanderers
1912	John McDonald (Outside Left)	Bolton Wanderers
1914	Bob Pailor (Centre Forward)	West Bromwich Albion
1978	John Brownlie (Right Back)	Cambridge United

Born on September-02:

Year	Player	Position	Years
1900	Robert McKay	Inside Right	1926 - 1928
1925	Ernie Taylor	Inside Forward	1942 - 1951
1953	Paul Cannell	Forward	1972 - 1978
1982	Joseph Barton	Midfield	2007 - 2011

September-03

1930: Record Crowd at St James's Park

The game against Chelsea saw the return to St James's Park of Hughie Gallacher - and with it Newcastle's record crowd of 68,386. Such was the esteem that Gallacher was held in on Tyneside there were an estimated 40,000 outside St James's Park who couldn't get in. Some reports put that figure at 100,000!

Newcastle won the game, a League Division 1 fixture, with the only goal of the game scored by Jackie Cape in the second half.

1932: Newcastle Edge Seven Goal Thriller

This was a 4-3 game against Liverpool that Newcastle did win! They were the visitors to St James's Park for a League Division 1 fixture and though Newcastle went into the break 3-0 up this game was nowhere near over! Back came Liverpool in the second half to score three of their own but luckily Newcastle also got a goal. John Allen, Tommy Lang, Harry McMenemy and a Liverpool 'own goal' giving them the victory.

1999: Robson Takes Over

A boyhood Newcastle fan, often walking miles to his beloved St James's Park, Sir Bobby Robson CBE was appointed as manager. He was already a very accomplished manager at both club and national level, his appointment was greeted with universal approval on Tyneside.

First Meeting on September-03:

Year	V	F	A	R	Opposition	Competition
1898	H	2	4	L	Wolverhampton Wanderers	Division 1
1904	H	3	0	W	Arsenal*	Division 1

*Arsenal were previously Woolwich Arsenal, whom we first played 02/09/1893

Debut on September-03:

Year	Player	Opposition
1904	William McCracken (Full Back)	Arsenal
1906	Robert Blackburn (Outside Right)	Sheffield Wednesday
1947	Norman Dodgin (Wing Half)	Chesterfield

September-04

1897: Scoring Debut
John Campbell scored on his debut today in the League Division 2 fixture with Woolwich Arsenal at St James's Park. With Willie Wardrope getting a brace and a goal from Malcolm Lennox Newcastle were comfortable 4-1 victors.

1929: Scoring Debut
James Richardson scored on his debut today in the League Division 1 fixture against Blackburn Rovers. With goals from Hughie Gallacher, Tommy Lang, Tom McDonald and Tom Urwin to add to Richardson's debut goal Newcastle were comfortable 5-1 winners at St James's Park.

1937: Six of the Best
Newcastle put six past Sheffield United in a League Division 2 fixture at St James's Park. With no reply from Sheffield it was a comfortable 6-0 victory. The goals coming from Tommy Pearson and Archie Livingston, who both scored two, and one each for Bill Imrie and Jimmy Gordon. A rare goal from Gordon, a wing-half, as in his 144 appearances for Newcastle he only ever scored three.

1965: First Ever Substitute
Alwyn Derek "Ollie" Burton has the distinction of being the first-ever substitute to be used by Newcastle when he came on for the injured Trevor Hockey in the 2-0 victory over Northampton Town at St James's Park. Alan Suddick and Bobby Cummings scoring in the second half gave Newcastle the victory in the League Division 1 fixture.

1996: Tyne-Wear Derby No. 128 – Last Roker Park Derby

Newcastle travelled to Roker Park for the last time to face Sunderland in a Premiership fixture, the 128th Tyne-Wear Derby. Goals from Peter Beardsley and Les Ferdinand, with Martin Scott replying for Sunderland gave Newcastle a 2-1 victory.

Debut on September-04:

Year	Player	Opposition
1897	John Harvey (Inside Right) James Jackson (Wing-Back) Thomas Ghee (Right Half) John Campbell (Centre Forward)	Woolwich Arsenal
1898	Matthew Kingsley (Goalkeeper) William Higgins (Centre Half)	Wolverhampton Wanderers
1909	John Finlay (Left Half)	Blackburn Rovers
1920	Robert McIntosh (Right Half)	West Bromwich Albion
1929	James Richardson (Inside Forward)	Blackburn Rovers
1954	Stewart Mitchell (Goalkeeper)	Preston North End

Born on September-04:

Year	Player	Position	Years
1891	Thomas Hall	Centre Forward	1913 - 1920
1940	James Gibson	Centre Forward	1959 - 1961
1941	George Dalton	Full Back	1958 - 1967
1966	John Beresford	Left Back	1992 - 1998

September-05

1899: First South African Association Football Game Abroad

Four weeks prior to the outbreak of the South African War, the Orange Free State Kaffir Football Club toured abroad, the first ever tour by a South African Association Football club.

Their first game was actually supposed to played against Aston Villa but due to the late arrival of the visitors to the UK the honour of hosting this first ever game by a touring black South African side went to St James's Park. The crowd was said to be around 6,000 spectators and Newcastle won the game 6-3.

1925: One and Only Appearance
Today saw the one and only appearance for Newcastle of goalkeeper, Allan Taylor. Despite being beaten three times Newcastle were still victorious in this game, see immediately below...

1925: Six of the Best in Nine Goal Encounter
Newcastle played hosts to Notts County in a League Division 1 fixture. Having a two goal advantage going into the break, being 3-1 up, Newcastle never really lost control of the game despite conceding a further two in the second-half, as they themselves scored a further three. The final score being 6-3 to Newcastle. Their scorers on the day being Tom Mitchell, Tom McDonald, Neil Harris, two from Willie Cowan and a County 'own goal'.

1979: Tyne-Wear Derby No. 115
Newcastle played hosts to Sunderland for a League Cup , Round 2, 2nd Leg tie, the 115th Tyne-Wear Derby. Goals from Stuart Boam and Alan Shoulder for Newcastle, and two for Sunderland's Alan Brown saw the tie end in a 2-2 draw. All the goals being scored in the second half, with Brown's second being a last-minute equaliser.

Debut on September-05:

Year	Player	Opposition
1896	Charles Watts (Goalkeeper) Richard Smellie (Centre Forward) John White (Left Back)	Small Heath
1908	Stanley Allan (Half Back)	Leicester City
1925	Allan Taylor (Goalkeeper)	Notts County
1931	David Bell (Full Back) Harry McMenemy (Inside Left)	Grimsby Town
1981	Peter Haddock (Defence)	Queens Park Rangers

Born on September-05:

Year	Player	Position	Years
1939	Tommy Knox	Outside Left	1965 - 1967
1964	William Francis O'Brien	Midfield	1988 - 1994

September-06

1913: Scoring Debut
Thomas Hall scored on his debut today in the League Division 1 fixture against Sunderland. This was a bit of a double-whammy for Sunderland as

Newcastle had just signed Hall from them! See below...

1913: Tyne-Wear Derby No. 37

Newcastle travelled to Roker Park for a League Division 1 fixture against Sunderland, the 37th Tyne-Wear Derby. The game was level at 1-1 at half-time but Newcastle took the game with a goal in the second half and ran out 2-1 winners. Their goals were courtesy of debutant Thomas Hall and John King. Sunderland's goal was scored by George Holley.

1937: One and Only Appearance

Today saw the one and only appearance for Newcastle of Centre Forward, John "Jack" Sheil. Newcastle travelled to the Oakwell Stadium for a League Division 2 fixture with Barnsley and were comprehensively beaten 3-0.

1986: Scoring Debut

Kevin Scott scored on his debut today in the League Division 1 fixture against Sheffield Wednesday. Unfortunately it wasn't enough as Newcastle were narrowly beaten 3-2 at St James's Park.

2000: Shearer nets his 200th League goal

Alan Shearer scored his 200th League goal in his 375th League appearance as he converted a 30th minute penalty against Coventry City at Highfield Road. Kevin Gallacher made it 2-0 on 58 minutes and that's the way the game ended.

Debut on September-06:

Year	Player	Opposition
1902	William Agnew (Full-Back)	Stoke City
1913	Thomas Hall (Centre Forward)	Sunderland
1922	James Keen (Outside Left)	Birmingham City
1937	John Shiel (Centre Forward)	Barnsley
1952	Tommy Casey (Wing Half) Bobby Robinson (Goalkeeper)	Burnley
1986	Kevin Watson Scott (Central Defence)	Sheffield Wednesday
2000	Brian Kerr (Midfield)	Coventry City

Born on September-06:

Year	Player	Position	Years
1956	Steve Hardwick	Goalkeeper	1976-1983
1970	Stephane Guivarch	Forward	1998-1999

September-07

1889: First Games in the "new" Northern League

The very first games in the Northern League took place today and one involved Newcastle East End with them beating Darlington 2-1 at their ground in Heaton with a reported gate of 1,500.

1895: Eight Debutants in Team

Newcastle handed debuts to eight players in their Division 2 game against Loughbrough Town at St James's Park, yet still won 3-0. All three of Newcastle's goals were scored by a debutant, they being - Andy Aitken, James Logan and Willie Wardrope.

1912: Tyne-Wear Derby No. 32

Newcastle hosted Sunderland in a League Division 1 fixture, the 32nd Tyne-Wear Derby.

Newcastle went into the break a goal to the good courtesy of Albert Shepherd but Sunderland equalised in the second half through Jackie Mordue and the game ended 1-1.

1985: One and Only Appearance

Today saw the one and only appearance for Newcastle of Defender Robert "Rab" McKinnon. Newcastle travelled to White Hart Lane for a League Division 1 fixture with Tottenham Hotspur and were soundly beaten 5-1 by a rampant Spurs side.

First Meeting on September-07:

Year	V	F	A	R	Opposition	Competition
1895	H	3	0	W	Loughborough Town	Division 2

Debut on September-07:

Year	Player	Opposition
1895	James Stott (Inside Left) Andrew Aitken (Centre Half) Robert Foyers (Left Back) John Henderson (Goalkeeper) James Logan (Centre Forward) William McKay (Centre Forward) Willie Wardrope (Inside Forward) William Miller (Right Half)	Loughborough Town

Debut on September-07:

Year	Player	Opposition
1901	Rob Bennie (Right Back) Richard Roberts (Left Wing) Ronald Orr (Inside-Forward)	Blackburn Rovers
1907	Alexander Hall (Centre Forward)	Sheffield Wednesday
1985	Robert McKinnon (Defence)	Tottenham Hotspur

Born on September-07:

Year	Player	Position	Years
1900	William Wilson	Goalkeeper	1925 - 1929
1943	David Turner	Midfield	1960 - 1963
1953	Chris Guthrie	Forward	1970 - 1972
1976	Garry Brady	Midfield	1998 - 2001
1980	Emre Belozoglu	Midfield	2005 - 2008

September-08

1906: Debut Hat-Trick

Harry Brown scored a hat-trick on his debut today in the League Division 1 fixture against Birmingham City. Together with a penalty from Colin Veitch it gave Newcastle a 4-2 victory at St Andrews.

1982: Scoring Debut

Mick Channon scored on his debut today in the League Division 2 fixture against Middlesbrough. It was enough to earn Newcastle a 1-1 draw at St James's Park.

2008: Keegan Quits Again!

Once again Kevin Keegan turns his back on Newcastle and walks away - fully justified it has to be said!

After an acrimonious struggle with owner Mike Ashley and the rest of the so-called 'decision makers' Keegan leaves and the club is in turmoil - again.

First Meeting on September-08:

Year	V	F	A	R	Opposition	Competition
1971	H	2	1	W	Halifax Town	League Cup

Debut on September-08:

Year	Player	Opposition
1906	Harry Brown (Inside Forward)	Birmingham City
1923	William Duncan Cowan (Inside Forward)	Sheffield United
1951	John Duncan (Forward)	Preston North End
1956	Gordon Hughes (Outside Right) Richard Keith (Right Back)	Manchester United
1962	James Iley (Wing Half)	Plymouth Argyle
1982	Michael Roger Channon (Forward)	Middlesbrough

Born on September-08:

Year	Player	Position	Years
1957	Alan Guy	Midfield	1975 - 1979
1969	Gary Speed	Midfield	1998 - 2004

September-09

Newcastle lost 7-1 to Blackburn Rovers at St James's Park in **1925**. In **1929** they lost 5-1 to West Ham United at Upton Park. A slighter better result against West Ham though was to follow.

1936: Five From Eight

West Ham United came to St James's Park for a League Division 2 fixture and in somewhat of a revenge for 1929 Newcastle were victorious 5-3.

Their goals coming courtesy of four goals for Billy Cairn's and a one for Harry McMenemey.

Debut on September-09:

Year	Player	Opposition
1899	John Fraser (Outside Left)	Everton
1905	Joseph Donnachie (Winger)	Birmingham City
1914	Curtis Booth (Centre Forward)	Sheffield Wednesday
1925	William Wilson (Goalkeeper)	Blackburn Rovers
1929	Albert Fidler (Goalkeeper) George Nevin (Full Back)	West Ham United
1933	John Kelly (Centre-Forward)	Derby County
2000	Foluwashola Ameobi (Forward)	Chelsea
2006	Giuseppe Rossi (Forward)	Fulham

Born on September-09:

Year	Player	Position	Years
1931	Stan Keery	Wing Half	1952 - 1957
1943	Frank Albert Clark	Left Back	1962 - 1975
1962	Kevin Brock	Midfield	1988 - 1994

September-10

There have been some very high scoring games on this day over the years. In **1949** Newcastle were beaten 6-3 by Charlton Athletic in a League Division 1 fixture at The Valley. It was worse in **1958** when despite scoring five times at Stamford Bridge against Chelsea they lost - still beaten 6-5! There were though better days...

1927: Seven Heaven

Newcastle put seven goals past Manchester United at St James's Park in a League Division 1 fixture. The goals coming via Stan Seymour, who scored two, Tom McDonald, Hughie Gallacher, Tom Urwin, Joe Harris and an 'own goal'. Manchester did get a consolation so the final score was 7-1 to Newcastle.

1952: Tyne-Wear Derby No. 79

Newcastle hosted Sunderland in a League Division 1 fixture, the 79th Tyne-Wear Derby.

Sunderland took a 1-0 lead into the break and they scored again in the second half but Newcastle scored twice, well once through Reg Davies, their other goal being an 'own goal' from Jack Stelling. The two goals Sunderland did score 'in the right goal' came from Tommy Wright and Willie Watson.

1975: Six of the Best

Newcastle put six past Southport in a League Cup Second Round tie at St James's Park. Alan Gowling scored four and Paul Cannell two in a 6-0 victory.

1985: McFaul Moves Into The Hot Seat

Willie McFaul appointed as manager. McFaul had a long and distinguished playing career with Newcastle, making 377 appearances for the first team.

As the No.1 goalkeeper he was a vital part of the Fairs Cup and Anglo-Italian Cup winning squads, and also played in the 1974 FA Cup Final.

After spells as Coach and Assistant Manager he finally became Newcastle's manager in his own right when succeeding Jack Charlton. As manager he was responsible for giving a then 18 year-old Paul Gascoigne his first start at the club, and with Malcolm Macdonald was instrumental in bringing Mirandinha, the first Brazilian to play in the English top flight, to Newcastle.

First Meeting on September-10:

Year	V	F	A	R	Opposition	Competition
1898	A	0	3	L	Everton	Division 1
1910	A	2	0	W	Oldham Athletic	Division 1
1996	H	4	0	W	Halmstads Bollklubb	UEFA Cup

Debut on September-10:

Year	Player	Opposition
1924	Tom Urwin (Outside Left)	Blackburn Rovers
1966	Stuart Alderson (Right Wing)	Burnley
2005	Michael Owen (Forward)	Fulham

Born on September-10:

Year	Player	Position	Years
1961	Ian Stewart	Left Wing	1985 - 1987

September-11

1946: Scoring Debut

George Stobbart scored twice on his debut today in the League Division 2 fixture against Coventry City. Together with a goal from Charlie Wayman it secured Newcastle a 3-1 win at St James's Park.

First Meeting on September-11:

Year	V	F	A	R	Opposition	Competition
1968	H	4	0	W	Feyenoord	Inter Cities Fairs Cup

Debut on September-11:

Year	Player	Opposition
1897	Ronald Allan (Outside Right)	Walsall
1946	Thomas Jackson Walker (Outside Right) George Stobbart (Inside Forward)	Coventry City

Debut on September-11:

Year	Player	Opposition
2004	Charles N'Zogbia (Midfield)	Blackburn Rovers
2010	Hatem Ben Arfa (Winger/Midfield)	Blackpool

Born on September-11:

Year	Player	Position	Years
1975	Chris Holland,	Midfield	1994 - 1996

September-12

2001: Extra Time Hat-Trick

Craig Bellamy wrote himself into Newcastle's history books today when he became the only Newcastle player to ever score a hat-trick in 'extra-time'. This in the Worthington Cup Second Round tie against Brentford.

A goal from Llyod Owusu on 17 minutes had given the lead to Brentford. This they held until the 59th minute when Shola Ameobi equalised. With no further goals being scored inside the 90 minutes the game into extra-time.

Bellamy then scored his history making hat-trick with his third being in extra-time stoppage-time!

Debut on September-12:

Year	Player	Opposition
1908	Andrew Anderson (Outside Left)	Arsenal
1934	Tom Swinburne (Goalkeeper)	Blackpool
1953	Joe Cooper (Half Back)	Preston North End

Born on September-12:

Year	Player	Position	Years
1927	Andy Graver	Centre Forward	1947 - 1950
1975	Carl Serrant	Defence	1998 - 2001
1980	Steven Caldwell	Central Defence	1998 - 2003

September-13

1917: Thomas Cairns, R.I.P.

Cairns died whilst on active service during the Great War (WWI). He has no known grave and is commemorated on the Arras Memorial to the Missing at the Faubourg-d'Amiens Cemetery in France.

1930: Eleven Goal Thriller at Old Trafford

Newcastle came out 7-4 winners at Old Trafford today. With the match delicately poised at 3-2 in favour of Newcastle at half-time they scored four more in the second half to take the game and the points. The goals were scored by Jackie Cape, with a hat-trick, Ron Starling scoring twice and one each for Duncan Lindsay and Jimmy Richardson.

1993: Scoring Debut

Alex Mathie scored on his debut today in the Premiership fixture against Sheffield Wednesday. With two goals from Andy Cole and another from Malcolm Allen it secured Newcastle a 4-2 win at St James's Park.

1994: Five Star EUFA Cup Performance

A hat-trick from Rob Lee and goals from Scott Sellars and Stevie Watson saw Newcastle easily beat Royal Antwerp 5-0 at the Bosuil Stadion in their EUFA Cup First Round, First Leg tie.

2004: Souness Appointed as New Boss

Graeme Souness appointed as manager.

2008: Scoring Debut

Francisco Jimenez "Xisco" Tejada scored on his debut today in the Premier League fixture against Hull City. Unfortunately with two goals from Hull's Marlon King it was not enough to prevent Newcastle losing 2-1 at St James's Park.

First Meeting on September-13:

Year	V	F	A	R	Opposition	Competition
1972	A	0	0	D	Ayr United	Texaco Cup
1994	A	5	0	W	Royal Antwerp	UEFA Cup

Debut on September-13:

Year	Player	Opposition
1913	Thomas Goodwill (Outside Right)	Everton

Debut on September-13:

Year	Player	Opposition
1967	William Eric Ross (Midfield)	Lincoln City
1993	Alexander Mathie (Forward)	Sheffield Wednesday
1997	John Charles Bryan Barnes (Midfield)	Wimbledon
2008	Francisco Jimenez Tejada (Forward) Ignacio Maria Gonzalez Gatti (Midfield)	Hull City

Born on September-13:

Year	Player	Position	Years
1909	Edwin Bowden	Inside-Right	1937-1939
1964	Paul Bodin	Left Back	1991-1992

September-14

5-1 has been a popular score-line on this day, occurring three times, but not always in Newcastle's favour! In **1895** they were beaten 5-1 by Liverpool at Anfield in a League Division 2 fixture. The other two were much better news for Newcastle fans.

1901: Five Star Performance

Newcastle beat Stoke City 5-1 in a League Division 1 fixture at St James's Park. The goals courtesy of two each for Richard Roberts and Ron Orr and a goal for Tom Niblo.

1927: Newcastle Edge Seven Goal Encounter

Derby County were the visitors to St James's Park in a League Division 1 fixture. This game was evenly matched throughout, the score being 1-1 at half-time and ending 4-3 in Newcastle's favour. Bob McKay scored a hat-trick and Hughie Gallacher scored the other.

1938: Four for Cairns

Newcastle beat West Bromwich Albion 5-1 in a League Division 2 fixture, again at St James's Park. Billy Cairns scored four goals and Albert Stubbins netted the other.

2006: Scoring Debut

Antoine Sibierski scored on his debut today in the UEFA Cup fixture against FC Levadia Tallinn. Being the only goal of the game it gave Newcastle a strong away win in this First Round, First Leg game at the Le Coq Arena.

First Meeting on September-13:

Year	V	F	A	R	Opposition	Competition
1907	H	1	0	W	Chelsea	Division 1
1977	A	0	0	D	Bohemians	UEFA Cup
2006	A	1	0	W	FC Levadia Tallinn	UEFA Cup

Debut on September-13:

Year	Player	Opposition
1901	Willie Stewart (Outside Right)	Stoke City
1936	John Bluey Park (Right Wing)	Bradford Park Avenue
1946	George King (Centre Forward)	Tottenham Hotspur
1977	Ralph Callachan (Midfield)	Bohemians
2006	Antoine Sibierski (Midfield)	FC Levadia Tallinn

Born on September-13:

Year	Player	Position	Years
1957	George Reilly	Forward	1985 - 1985

September-15

1951: Seven Heaven - Four for Robledo!

Burnley were the visitors to St James's Park for a League Division 1 fixture and were soundly beaten 7-1. The result was never in any doubt, Newcastle were already leading 4-1 at half-time and scored three more in the second. Jorge Robledo scored four, George Hannah scored two and Bobby Mitchell got the other.

1976: Beaten and Expelled!

Following the 3-0 defeat by Ayr United at Somerset Park in the Anglo-Scottish Cup Newcastle were expelled from the competition for fielding a 'weakened' side.

When you look at Newcastle's team that day, and who else was available, I don't think it could be construed as a 'weakened' side by any stretch of the imagination.

The team was: Mick Mahoney, Irving Nattrass, Alan Kennedy, Tommy Cassidy, Aiden McCaffery, Geoff Nulty, Stewart Barrowclough, Paul Cannell, Mickey Burns, Alan Gowling and Tommy Craig.

2001: Own Goal Separates the United's in 7 Goal Thriller

Manchester United were the visitors to St James's Park for a Premiership fixture and it took an own goal to separate the two. Newcastle took the lead on 5 minutes through Laurent Robert, Manchester equalised on 29 minutes through van Nistelrooy. Rob Lee put Newcastle back in front on 34 minutes and the half ended with Newcastle leading 2-1.

The second half was equally exciting, and equally nip-and-tuck. Newcastle extended their lead on 52 minutes through Dabizas. Manchester then pulled it back to level the score through two quick-fire goals, Giggs on 62 and Vernon on 64. The score remained at 3-3 until eight minutes to go when Wes Brown turned the ball into his own net to give Newcastle a 4-3 victory.

First Meeting on September-15:

Year	V	F	A	R	Opposition	Competition
1969	A	2	1	W	Dundee United	Inter Cities Fairs Cup
1971	A	0	1	L	Heart of Midlothian	Texaco Cup

Debut on September-15:

Year	Player	Opposition
1894	W.A. Ward (Goalkeeper)	Grimsby Town
1900	Jimmy Laidlaw (Inside Left) Edward Allen (Left Back)	Stoke City
1906	Jimmy Soye (Forward)	Everton
1928	David Flannigan (Left Half)	Aston Villa
1990	Neil Simpson (Midfield)	Port Vale
2001	Sylvain Distin (Defence)	Manchester United

Born on September-15:

Year	Player	Position	Years
1875	James Jackson	Wing-Back	1897 - 1899

September-16

Who said 7 was lucky? In the 23 times Newcastle have played on this day they have lost 7 and drawn 7. One of those loses was a 7-3 defeat at the hands of West Bromwich Albion in **1953** in a League Division 1 fixture - and it was at St James's Park as well.

You also have to go back 7 games between the two to find a Newcastle win.

First Meeting on September-16:

Year	V	F	A	R	Opposition	Competition
1999	A	2	0	W	CSKA Sofia	UEFA Cup
2004	H	2	0	W	Hapoel Bnei Sakhnin	UEFA Cup

Born on September-16:

Year	Player	Position	Years
1906	Robert Bradley	Right Back	1928
1912	Albert Harris	Wing	1935 - 1936
1923	Colin Gibson	Outside Right	1948 - 1949
1957	David McCreery	Midfield	1982 - 1989
1977	Paul Brayson	Forward	1996 - 1998
1994	Aleksandar Mitrovic	Forward	2015 - current

September-17

1924: Hat-Trick Harris

Neil Harris scored a hat-trick and Tom McDonald scored one to give Newcastle a 4-1 victory over West Ham United in a League Division 1 fixture at St James's Park.

1949: Scoring Debut

George Hannah scored on his debut today in the League Division 1 fixture against Manchester City.

With goals from Jackie Milburn, Jorge Robledo and Tommy Walker it was enough to see Newcastle winning 4-2 at St James's Park.

1952: Tyne-Wear Derby No. 80

Newcastle travelled to Roker Park to face Sunderland in a League Division 1 fixture, the 80th Tyne-Wear Derby. Newcastle scored in each half, with a goal in from Bobby Mitchell and one from Jorge Robledo, without reply from Sunderland.

Newcastle therefore being victorious, 2-0.

1955: Milburn Hat-Trick

Jackie Milburn scored a hat-trick and Vic Keeble scored one to give Newcastle a 4-1 victory over Charlton Athletic in a League Division 1 fixture at St James's Park.

First Meeting on September-17:

Year	V	F	A	R	Opposition	Competition
1997	H	3	2	W	Barcelona	European Champions League
1998	H	2	1	W	Partizan Belgrade	European Cup Winners Cup

Debut on September-17:

Year	Player	Opposition
1898	Edward Birnie (Right Half)	Notts County
1924	Isaac Tate (Goalkeeper)	West Ham United
1949	George Hannah (Inside Forward) Alf McMichael (Left-Back)	Manchester City
2007	Habib Beye (Defence) Abdoulaye Diagne Faye (Defence)	Derby County

Born on September-17:

Year	Player	Position	Years
1987	Paul Huntingdon	Centre Half	2004-2007

September-18

1909: Tyne-Wear Derby No. 26

Newcastle travelled to Roker Park to face Sunderland in a League Division 1 fixture, the 26th Tyne-Wear Derby. Newcastle scored in each half with no reply from Sunderland so were victorious 2-0. Their scorers were Albert Shepherd and Jimmy Stewart.

2010: Five Games - Five Yellow Cards!

James Perch became the first player in the history of the Premiership to play the first 5 games of a season and get a yellow in each!

Not a very good title to have, and of course he also got an automatic one match suspension.

First Meeting on September-18:

Year	V	F	A	R	Opposition	Competition
2002	A	0	2	L	FK Dynamo Kyyiv	European Champions League

Debut on September-18:

Year	Player	Opposition
1963	Alan Kirkman (Inside Forward)	Southampton
1971	Pat Howard (Central Defence)	Wolverhampton Wanderers
2010	Cheick Ismael Tiote (Midfield)	Everton

Born on September-18:

Year	Player	Position	Years
1904	John Little	Full Back	1927 - 1928
1939	Ken Hale	Inside Forward	1956 - 1962
1974	Sulzeer Jeremiah Campbell	Defence	2010 - 2011
1975	Richard Appleby	Midfield	1991 - 1995

September-19

Bristol City were on the end of 5-0 defeats to Newcastle in both **1992**, goals from Liam O'Brien, Gavin Peacock (with two), Franz Carr and Kevin Brock, and **1995**, this time Darren Peacock, Scott Sellars, Les Ferdinand, Keith Gillespie and Rob Lee.

Coventry were beaten 5-1 in **1998**, Alan Shearer (with two), Nicos Dabizas, Gary Speed and Stephen Glass.

The best however was to be in **1999** when Bobby Robson had his 'home' debut as manager and Newcastle beat poor Sheffield Wednesday by eight goals.

1999: Record Premiership Win!

Five goals from Alan Shearer (30, 33 [Pen], 42, 81, 84 [Pen]) and goals from Aaron Hughes (11) Kieron Dyer (46) and Gary Speed (78) secured Newcastle's record win in the Premiership.

First Meeting on September-19:

Year	V	F	A	R	Opposition	Competition
1973	A	2	1	W	Morton	Texaco Cup

Debut on September-19:

Year	Player	Opposition
1998	Paul Kenneth Dalglish (Forward)	Coventry City

Born on September-19:

Year	Player	Position	Years
1919	Arnold Grundy	Left Half	1936-1944
1939	Brian Wright	Wing Half	1956-1963
1944	William Eric Ross	Midfield	1967-1969
1962	Gary Nicholas Brazil	Forward	1989-1990
1986	Leon Julian Best	Forward	2010-2012

September-20

1975: Five Star Performance

Newcastle beat Wolverhampton Wanderers 5-1 at St James's Park in a League Division 1 fixture. The scorers being Alan Gowling with a hat-trick and one each for John Tudor and Tommy Cassidy.

2011: Brothers in Arms

For the first time in Newcastle's history two brothers entered the field of play at the same time as substitutes when Shola and Sammy Ameobi came on in the 70th minute in the Carling (League) Cup Third Round tie against Nottingham Forest. A game which Newcastle eventually won in extra-time after Forest had come back from behind on three occasions.

2012: European Brothers in Arms!

When young Sammy Ameobi came on as a 53rd minute substitute in the Europa League game against Maritimo he joined his brother Shola - making them the first brothers to play for Newcastle in a European match. The Group D game ended in a goalless draw.

First Meeting on September-20:

Year	R	F	A	V	Opposition	Competition
1986	A	1	0	W	Wimbledon	Division 2
2012	A	0	0	D	Club Sport Maritimo	Europa League

Debut on September-20:

Year	Player	Opposition
1926	James Boyd (Outside Right)	Cardiff City
1958	Reg Evans (Outside Left) Bryan Harvey (Goalkeeper)	Wolverhampton Wanderers

Debut on September-20:

Year	Player	Opposition
1986	Andy Thomas (Forward) Gary Kelly (Goalkeeper)	Wimbledon
2011	Mehdi Abeid (Midfield) Robert Elliot (Goalkeeper)	Nottingham Forest

Born on September-20:

Year	Player	Position	Years
1910	Joe Ford	Centre Forward	1931 - 1934
1927	William Anderson	Goalkeeper	1946 - 1948

September-21

1957: Tyne-Wear Derby No. 90

Newcastle travelled to Roker Park to face Sunderland in a League Division 1 fixture, the 90th Tyne-Wear Derby.

Sunderland scored in each half through Don Revie and Colin Grainger to take the victory 2-0.

2002: Tyne-Wear Derby No. 136

Newcastle hosted Sunderland in a Premiership fixture, the 136th Tyne-Wear Derby.

Craig Bellamy opened the scoring after only two minutes and Alan Shearer doubled Newcastle's lead on 39 minutes. With no further goals being scored Newcastle were victorious 2-0.

Debut on September-21:

Year	Player	Opposition
1968	Alan Duffy (Forward)	Manchester United
1991	Andrew Walker (Forward)	Millwall

Born on September-21:

Year	Player	Position	Years
1884	William Hibbert	Inside Left	1911 - 1920
1930	Bob Stokoe	Centre Half	1947 - 1961

September-22

1934: Scoring Debut

Jack Smith scored on his debut today in the League Division 2 fixture against Plymouth Argyle. With goals from Jimmy Boyd and Thomas Leach it helped Newcastle to a 3-1 victory at Home Park.

1984: Ten Goals Shared at Loftus Road

Newcastle went to Loftus Road for a League Division 1 fixture against Queens Park Rangers and in a game that saw ten goals honours were even. Newcastle's five coming courtesy of a hat-trick from Chris Waddle and one each for Neil McDonald and Kenny Wharton.

2010: Newcastle Edge Seven Goal Encounter

Newcastle went to Stamford Bridge for a League Cup Third Round tie against Chelsea and came away with a very credible 4-3 victory. Newcastle's goals coming from Shola Ameobi with two and one each for Nile Ranger and Ryan Taylor.

Debut on September-22:

Year	Player	Opposition
1894	Richard Hedley (Outside Right)	Notts County
1934	Jack Smith (Centre Forward) Tom Russell (Left Back)	Plymouth Argyle
2009	Ben Tozer (Defence) James Henry Tavernier (Defence)	Peterborough United
2010	Sulzeer Jeremiah Campbell (Defence)	Chelsea

Born on September-22:

Year	Player	Position	Years
1878	Peter McWilliam	Left Half	1902 - 1911
1936	Robert Whitehead	Full Back	1954 - 1962
1957	Stephen Carney	Defence	1979 - 1985

September-23

1893: One and Only Appearance

The League Division 2 defeat by Burton Swifts at Peel Croft was the single appearance made by J. Barr, Newcastle's Right Half that day.

First Meeting on September-23:

Year	V	F	A	R	Opposition	Competition
1893	A	1	3	L	Burton Swifts	Division 2
1970	A	1	1	D	Internationale Milan	Inter Cities Fairs Cup

Debut on September-23:

Year	Player	Opposition
1893	J Barr (Right Half) C Quinn (Outside Right) Joe Ryder (Goalkeeper)	Burton Swifts
1922	Edward Richardson (Outside Left)	Preston North End
1992	Robert Martin Lee (Midfield)	Middlesbrough
2000	Lomano Tresor LuaLua (Forward)	Charlton Athletic

Born on September-23:

Year	Player	Position	Years
1903	Thomas Leach	Centre Half	1934 - 1936
1936	George Eastham	Inside Forward	1956 - 1960
1989	Wesley Ngo Baheng	Forward	2008 - 2010

September-24

1952: One and Only Appearance

Today saw the one and only appearance for Newcastle of Inside Forward, Neville Black, the 1952 Charity Shield match against Manchester United.

1952: Newcastle Beaten in Six Goal Charity Shield Encounter

Manchester United won the 'toss of a coin' to decide the venue for the Charity Shield, they also went on to win the Shield itself with a final score of 4-2.

Newcastle had ended up the first half well in control, leading by 2-0, a Vic Keeble brace, but a second half collapse saw them conceding four times.

1989: Tyne-Wear Derby No. 120

Newcastle travelled to Roker Park to face Sunderland in a League Division 2 fixture, the 120th Tyne-Wear Derby. With no goals being scored honours were even.

First Meeting on September-24:

Year	V	F	A	R	Opposition	Competition
1892	A	1	5	L	Sheffield United	Northern League
2003	H	5	0	W	NAC Breda FC	UEFA Cup

Debut on September-24:

Year	Player	Opposition
1898	Joseph Rogers (Outside Right)	Stoke City
1919	George Pyke (Centre Forward)	Derby County
1927	Tommy Lang (Outside Left) John Little (Full Back)	Cardiff City
1952	Neville Black (Inside Forward)	Manchester United
1983	Peter Andrew Beardsley (Forward)	Barnsley

Born on September-24:

Year	Player	Position	Years
1877	Thomas Bruce	Forward	1898 - 1908
1933	John Nesbitt	Centre Half	1955 - 1959
1966	Franz Carr	Wing	1991 - 1993

September-25

1935: Naughty Newcastle

With their failure to enter into the Northumberland FA Senior Cup Newcastle United were reported to the Football Association.

1974: League Cup Replay Win

Newcastle faced a League Cup Second Round Replay against Nottingham Forest at St James's Park. The original tie at the City Ground had ended 1-1 but Newcastle made short work of Forest today with a 3-0 victory.

Malcolm Macdonald, Mickey Burns and Glenn Keeley getting the goals.

Debut on September-25:

Year	Player	Opposition
1957	John Nesbitt (Centre Half)	Sheffield Wednesday
1963	Leonard Walker (Defence)	Preston North End
1965	Peter Noble (Midfield/Forward)	Chelsea

Debut on September-25:

Year	Player	Opposition
1982	Neil McDonald (Right Back/Midfield)	Barnsley
1993	Michael Dudley Hooper (Goalkeeper)	West Ham United

Born on September-25:

Year	Player	Position	Years
1895	Tom McDonald	Inside Left	1921 - 1931
1952	Ray Clarke	Forward	1980 - 1981
1962	Chris Withe	Left Back	1979 - 1983

September-26

1931 saw two goals from Jimmy Boyd, a Harry Bedford penalty and a goal from Jack Allen secure a 4-1 victory over Sheffield Wednesday.

1964: Five Star Performance

Newcastle defeated Preston North End 5-2 in a League Division 2 fixture at St James's Park. Ron McGarry scored two, Bobby Cummings and Dave Hilley scored one each the other being a Preston 'own goal'.

2008: Kinnear Appointed as "Interim" Boss

Ex-Wimbledon boss Joe Kinnear appointed as interim manager. This after a notable list of candidates, including ex-England manager Terry Venables, had turned Newcastle down.

2009: Hat-Trick for Nolan

Kevin Nolan scored a hat-trick and Ryan Taylor also scored to give Newcastle a 4-0 victory over Ipswich Town in a Premiership fixture at St James's Park.

The first two of Nolan's hat-trick coming in only two minutes! He scored on 30 and 32 minutes. Taylor's goal followed in another two minutes on 34. Nolan's third was on 51 minutes.

Debut on September-26:

Year	Player	Opposition
1987	John Cornwell (Midfield)	Southampton
2009	Zurab Khizanishvili (Defence) Marlon Anderson Harewood (Forward)	Ipswich Town

Born on September-26:

Year	Player	Position	Years
1877	Andrew Gardner	Outside Right	1902 - 1903
1943	Christopher Napier	Centre Forward	1965 - 1966
1958	Kenneth Graham Sansom	Left Back	1988 - 1989
1972	Alan Neilson	Defence	1990 - 1995
1991	Paul Dummett	Defence	2008 - current

September-27

1902 saw West Bromwich Albion beating Newcastle 6-1 in a League Division 1 fixture at The Hawthorns. Jock Rutherford scoring Newcastle's consolation goal as they were already 3-1 down at the break. Better news was to come though.

1994: Five Star Performance - Ten on Aggregate

Newcastle beat Royal Antwerp 5-2 in the Second Leg of their UEFA Cup 1st Round tie.

Having already beaten them 5-0 in the away leg Newcastle were comfortable 10-2 winners on aggregate. The five today came from an Andy Cole hat-trick and one each for Rob Lee and Peter Beardsley.

September-28

1901: Tyne-Wear Derby No. 7

Newcastle hosted Sunderland in a League Division 1 fixture, the 7th Tyne-Wear Derby. A solitary goal in the second half from Sunderland's Jimmy Gemmell handing them the win.

1929: Five Star Performance

Two goals from Hughie Gallacher and one each for Bill Chamber, Jock McCurley and Tom Urwin gave Newcastle a 5-2 victory over Huddersfield Town in a League Division 1 fixture at St James's Park.

1935: Scoring Debuts

Harry Ware and Albert Harris both scored on their debut today in the League Division 2 fixture against Fulham. Together with a brace from Tom Pearson and a Billy Cairns goal Newcastle were easy 6-2 winners at St James's Park.

Debut on September-28:

Year	Player	Opposition
1901	Tom Davidson (Left Back)	Sunderland
1907	David Willis (Wing Half)	Nottingham Forest
1935	Harry Ware (Inside Right) Albert Harris (Winger)	Fulham
1957	Robert Whitehead (Full Back)	Burnley
1968	Keith Dyson (Forward)	Tottenham Hotspur

Born on September-28:

Year	Player	Position	Years
1985	James Robert Perch	Defence	2010 - 2013

September-29

1928 saw Newcastle lose 5-0 to Manchester United at Old Trafford. In a League Division fixture.

Already 3-0 down going into the break you could say that Newcastle were never really in this match. However it was not all bad news on this day.

1906: Scoring Debut

Finlay Speedie scored twice on his debut today in the League Division 1 fixture against Sheffield Wednesday.

His brace, together with goals from Bill Appleyard, Albert Gosnell and James Kirkcaldy ensured Newcastle were easy 5-1 winners at St James's Park.

1962: Six of the Best

Jimmy Fell, Jimmy Kerray, Barrie Thomas (with two) Alan Suddick and Dave Hilley all scored today in a 6-0 thrashing of Walsall in a League Division 2 fixture at Fellows Park.

First Meeting on September-29:

Year	V	F	A	R	Opposition	Competition
1894	H	2	0	W	Leicester Fosse*	Division 2
1934	H	2	0	W	Norwich City	Division 2

*Leicester Fosse became Leicester City, whom we first played on 14/11/1896

Debut on September-29:

Year	Player	Opposition
1906	Finlay Speedie (Inside Forward)	Sheffield Wednesday
1984	Pat Heard (Defence/Midfield)	West Ham United
1990	Lee Robert Clark (Midfield)	Bristol City

Born on September-29:

Year	Player	Position	Years
1910	Joseph William Wilson	Centre Half	1927-1930
1911	Joe Wilson	Inside Right	1933-1936

September-30

This was a triple historic day in **1893** for the newly named Newcastle United as it not only represented their first-ever victory in the FA Football League but it saw their first hat-trick and then their first double hat-trick!

1893: One and Only Appearance

Related to Newcastle's goalkeeper Joe Ryder, though never appearing in the same side, Isaac Ryder, Inside Left, made his one and only appearance for Newcastle. It was a historic one, as it represented United's first win in League football - and what a win!

1893: Six of the Best with Two Hat-Tricks

This was the first "official FA League" game to be played at St James's Park. Depending upon which report you read the crowd was anywhere between 2,000 and 6,000. The majority would have went home extremely happy as Newcastle outclassed, and out gunned the Gunners. A 6-0 victory over Arsenal saw both Willie Thompson and Joe Wallace each get a hat-trick.

Debut on September-30:

Year	Player	Opposition
1893	Isaac Ryder (Inside Left) W Lowery (Goalkeeper)	Woolwich Arsenal
2000	Steven Caldwell (Centre-Back)	Manchester City

Born on September-30:

Year	Player	Position	Years
1899	Thomas Mitchell	Outside Left	1920 - 1926

OCTOBER

October-01

1892: One and Only Appearance

Included here, for no other reason than it occurs in the season in which Newcastle changed from "East End" to "United", is the single appearance made by John Barker. Technically it was for 'East End' in the 3-1 over Middlesbrough at St James's Park in the Northern League.

1960: Five Star Performance

Two goals from George Luke, two goals from Len White and a goal from Bobby Mitchell gave Newcastle a 5-0 victory over Cardiff City in a League Division 1 fixture at St James's Park.

1961: Mitten Moved Out

Charlie Mitten was sacked as manager and replaced by Norman Smith on a "temporary" basis.

1991: Twelve Goals and it takes Penalties to Separate the Sides

Newcastle faced Tranmere Rovers in a Zenith Data Systems Cup tie at Prenton Park - and what a tie! 2-2 at half-time, 3-3 at full time, 6-6 after extra time! The game went to penalties and Tranmere won 4-3. During the course of the game itself Micky Quinn scored a hat-trick, Gavin Peacock grabbed two and Lee Clark also got on the score sheet.

First Meeting on October-01:

Year	V	F	A	R	Opposition	Competition
1892	H	3	1	W	Middlesbrough	Northern League
1997	A	2	2	D	Dynamo Kiev	European Champions League
2002	A	0	2	L	Juventus	European Champions League

Debut on October-01:

Year	Player	Opposition
1892	Harry Reay (Outside-Right) John Barker (Forward)	Middlesbrough
1904	Jimmy Lawrence (Goalkeeper)	Manchester City
1927	Mick Burns (Goalkeeper)	Blackburn Rovers
1938	Jimmy Woodburn (Left Half)	Coventry City
1960	James Wilson (Outside Left)	Cardiff City

Debut on October-01:

Year	Player	Opposition
1966	John Edward Craggs (Right Back)	Everton
1994	Paul Kitson (Forward)	Aston Villa

Born on October-01:

Year	Player	Position	Years
1927	Alf McMichael	Left Back	1949 - 1963
1939	Duncan Neale	Wing Half	1959 - 1963
1943	William Stewart McFaul	Goalkeeper	1966 - 1975

October-02

Newcastle have twice been beaten 4-2 today, the first in **1954** by Cardiff City, then again in **1962** by Leyton Orient. Both games were away from home, the Cardiff game being a League Division 1 fixture, the Orient game being a League Cup Second Round Replay.

1982: Five Star Performance - with Four from Keegan!

Four goals from Kevin Keegan and a goal from Kevin Todd gave Newcastle a 5-1 victory in an away League Division 2 fixture over Rotherham United.

Debut on October-02:

Year	Player	Opposition
1948	Ron Batty (Left Back)	Portsmouth
1961	Colin Clish (Left Back)	Sheffield United
1971	Raymond Ellison (Full Back)	Derby County

Born on October-02:

Year	Player	Position	Years
1959	Billy Askew	Left Midfield	1990-1992
1964	John Grant Robertson	Forward	1988-1988

October-03

1889: Players Suspended

J.W. Angus, John Barker and James Miller all suspended for "violations of the rules". No confirmation of what those violations were...

1925: Gunners Smashed for Seven

Newcastle smashed seven goals past Arsenal with no reply in their League Division 1 fixture today at St James's Park.

A hat-trick from Bob Clark, two from Stan Seymour and a goal apiece from Jimmy Loughlin and Tom Urwin put Tyneside in seventh heaven!

1981: Varadi Hat-Trick

Imrie Varadi scored a hat-trick and Ian Davies scored a penalty to secure a 4-0 win over Cardiff City in a League Division 2 fixture at Ninian Park.

First Meeting on October-03:

Year	V	F	A	R	Opposition	Competition
1964	A	1	3	L	Ipswich Town	Division 2

Debut on October-03:

Year	Player	Opposition
1901	Sandy Caie (Centre Forward) Thomas Bamlett (Left Back)	Notts County
1953	Ron Greener (Centre Half)	Charlton Athletic
1999	Kevin William Gallacher (Forward)	Middlesbrough

Born on October-03:

Year	Player	Position	Years
1888	John George Peart	Centre Forward	1912-1913

October-04

1902: Six of the Best

Notts County visited St James's Park for a League Division 1 fixture. Newcastle were already 5-0 up going into the break and 'took their foot off' in the second half when Notts County scored a goal of their own, Newcastle however scored in the second half too making it a comfortable 6-1 victory.

The Newcastle goals coming via two from Jock Rutherford and one each for Bob McColl, Ron Orr, Willie Stewart and John Carr.

First Meeting on October-04:

Year	V	F	A	R	Opposition	Competition
2012	H	3	0	W	FC Girondins de Bordeaux	Europa League

Debut on October-04:

Year	Player	Opposition
1919	Alexander Parrott Ramsay (Outside Left)	Liverpool
1989	John Burridge (Goalkeeper)	Reading
1995	Jimmy Crawford (Midfield) Paul Brayson (Forward)	Bristol City

Born on October-04:

Year	Player	Position	Years
1989	Frank Wiafe Danquah	Forward	2008 - 2010

October-05

1946: Record Win - 13-0

Newcastle recorded their highest ever score when they demolished Newport County 13-0 at St James's Park in the League Division 2 clash today!

Len Shackleton - *on his debut* - scored six of those goals - the most goals scored by a debutant. Charlie Wayman scored four, Jackie Milburn scored two and the remaining goal was scored by Roy Bentley.

1993: Seven Past Notts County

An Andy Cole hat-trick, two goals from Malcolm Allen and a goal apiece from Peter Beardsley and Rob Lee saw Newcastle brush aside Notts County in this League Cup clash at the County Ground. County did get a second half consolation goal with the game ending 7-1 to Newcastle.

First Meeting on October-05:

Year	V	F	A	R	Opposition	Competition
1901	A	1	3	L	Birmingham City*	Division 2
1983	H	1	1	D	Oxford United	League Cup

*Birmingham City were previously Small Heath whom we first met on 28/10/1893

Debut on October-05:

Year	Player	Opposition
1929	Albert McInroy (Goalkeeper)	Sheffield United
1946	Len Shackleton (Inside Forward)	Newport County

Born on October-05:

Year	Player	Position	Years
1925	Ronald Batty	Left Back	1945 - 1958
1958	Peter Johnson	Left Back	1980 - 1983
1972	Alain Goma	Centre Back	1999 - 2001

October-06

1894: Scoring Debuts

John McNee and Charles Dickson both scored on their debuts today in the League Division 2 fixture with Burslem Port Vale. A game which ended in a 4-4 draw at Vale's Athletic Ground. This after Newcastle had been leading 4-2 at half-time!

1900: Tyne-Wear Derby No. 5

Newcastle travelled to Roker Park to face Sunderland in a League Division 1 fixture, the 5th Tyne-Wear Derby. Andy McCombie scored for Newcastle in the first half - but he was still four years away from being a Newcastle player! So Newcastle went into the break 1-0 up thanks to his 'own goal'. Sunderland equalised though in the second half through Geordie Livingstone so the game ended honours even at 1-1. Oh, but the irony of the scorers says it all.

1951: Scoring Debut

Reg Davies scored on his debut today in the League Division 1 fixture against Wolverhampton Wanderers. Together with a brace from Jackie Milburn, Newcastle were a 3-1 winners at St James's Park.

Debut on October-06:

Year	Player	Opposition
1894	John McNee (Inside Right) Charles Dickson (Outside Left)	Burslem Port Vale
1928	Robert Thomson (Left Back)	Leeds United
1951	Reg Davies (Inside Forward)	Wolverhampton Wanderers
1956	George Eastham (Inside Forward)	Luton Town
1971	Derek Craig (Central Defence)	Arsenal
1982	David McCreery (Midfield)	Leeds United

Born on October-06:

Year	Player	Position	Years
1919	Albert Sibley	Outside Right	1947 - 1950
1935	John Harold Taylor	Outside Right	1952 - 1960
1981	Zurab Khizanishvili	Defence	2009

October-07

1899: Six of the Best

Newcastle put six past Notts County in a League Division 1 fixture at St James's Park. Newcastle scored three goals in either half and with no reply from County were easy 6-0 winners. The goals coming from Jack Fraser, who scored two, Sandy MacFarlane, Jock Peddie, Jimmy Stevenson and Willie Wardrope.

First Meeting on October-07:

Year	V	F	A	R	Opposition	Competition
1893	A	1	2	L	Lincoln City	Division 2

Debut on October-07:

Year	Player	Opposition
1893	Toby Gillespy (Inside Left)	Lincoln City
1911	Robert Gibson (Outside Right)	West Bromwich Albion
1961	Alan Suddick (Midfield/Forward)	Charlton Athletic

Born on October-07:

Year	Player	Position	Years
1881	James Tildesley	Full Back	1903 - 1906
1912	Billy Cairns	Inside Forward	1933 - 1944
1913	John Bluey Park	Right Wing	1936 - 1941
1947	Pat Howard	Central Defence	1971 - 1976

October-08

1908: James Stott, R.I.P.

Arriving at Newcastle from Grimsby Town, Stott was a hard-tackling and intelligent player who became club captain and guided Newcastle to their first promotion in the 1897-88 season.

Described as being a snappy dresser, but with a short temper (*on and off the pitch*), upon his retirement he became licensee at the Blue Star public house on Westgate Road in Newcastle. It is reported that Stott, sadly, contracted a brain tumour, and died in a lunatic asylum in Newcastle.

1973: Six of the Best

A Malcolm Macdonald hat-trick, two goals from Keith Robson and a rare goal from Frank Clark (one of only two goals he ever scored for the club in 484 appearances, *but then again he was a left-back*) secured easy progression in the League Cup against Doncaster Rovers at St James's Park.

2010: Carroll Signs New Five Year Deal

Andy Carroll has committed himself to Newcastle for the next five years after signing an extension to his current contract. History will show that he never saw this out!

Debut on October-08:

Year	Player	Opposition
1910	Robert Hewison (Right Half)	Notts County
1977	John Blackley (Central Defence)	Derby County

Born on October-08:

Year	Player	Position	Years
1896	Alfred Maitland	Left Back	1924 - 1930
1990	Karl Darlow	Goalkeeper	2014 - current

October-09

1904: Newcastle Cleared in McCracken Transfer

At their meeting tonight, at 104 High Holborn, the Football Association Committee decided there was no evidence against Newcastle United and Bill McCracken over his transfer and the case against them was dismissed.

1920: Tyne-Wear Derby No. 43

Newcastle hosted Sunderland in a League Division 1 fixture, the 43rd Tyne-Wear Derby. In this they recorded their biggest win over their local rivals as they beat them 6-1.

With a hat-trick from Neil Harris, two from Andy Smailes, and one from Stan Seymour it was Tyneside who were celebrating the Derby in style. For the record Charlie Buchan scored Sunderland's goal.

1948: Tyne-Wear Derby No. 71

Newcastle travelled to Roker Park to face Sunderland in a League Division 1 fixture, the 71st Tyne-Wear Derby. With first half goals from George Hair for Newcastle, and that man Len Shackleton for Sunderland, honours even at 1-1.

1954: Tyne-Wear Derby No. 83

Newcastle travelled to Roker Park to face Sunderland in a League Division 1 fixture, the 83rd Tyne-Wear Derby. Sunderland took this game 4-2. Ted Purdy and Billy Bingham gave them a 2-0 lead at the break. Jackie Milburn pulled one back two minutes after the re-start. Bingham scored again to extend Sunderland's lead and they went further ahead with a goal from Ken Chisholm. Bobby Mitchell converted a penalty late on but there was to be no great comeback for Newcastle.

1963: Tyne-Wear Derby No. 96

Newcastle travelled to Roker Park to face Sunderland in a League Division 2 fixture, the 96th Tyne-Wear Derby. Len Ashurst and George Herd scored for Sunderland whilst Newcastle could only manage one through Colin Taylor. Sunderland win 2-1.

1988: Jackie Milburn, R.I.P.

There are times when the word 'legend' seems to be used too easily, but in the case of Jackie Milburn - Wor Jackie - the word legend seems inadequate, but he surely was a true giant and legend for Newcastle. The news of his passing brought a huge sense of sorrow to Tyneside. He had made 401 appearances for Newcastle and in doing so had scored 202 goals.

Milburn was the first footballer to be made a Freeman of the City of Newcastle upon Tyne and in 1987 when Newcastle United opened their new West Stand at St James' Park it was named 'The Milburn Stand', in his honour.

Born on October-09:

Year	Player	Position	Years
1905	Jimmy Loughlin	Forward	1924-1927
1975	Mark Viduka	Forward	2007-2009

October-10

1959: One and Only Appearance

Walter Malcolm, Forward, made his one and only appearance today for

Newcastle as they welcomed Nottingham Forest to St James's Park in a League Division 1 fixture. Newcastle won the game 2-1, with a goal from Len White and a Forest 'own goal'.

1964: Five Star Performance

Newcastle put five past Leyton Orient without reply in a League Division 2 fixture at St James's Park. The scorers were Pop Robson and Stan Anderson, with two each and a single from Jim Iley.

1988: McFaul Dismissed

Willie McFaul dismissed as manager - Colin Suggett appointed caretaker.

First Meeting on October-10:

Year	V	F	A	R	Opposition	Competition
1960	A	1	4	L	Colchester United	League Cup

Debut on October-10:

Year	Player	Opposition
1936	Tom Mooney (Outside Left)	Leicester City
1959	Walter Grant Malcolm (Forward)	Nottingham Forest
1960	George Dalton (Full Back)	Colchester United
1981	Kevin Todd (Forward)	Derby County

Born on October-10:

Year	Player	Position	Years
1916	Willie Scott	Centre Forward	1938 - 1946
1935	Bill Redhead	Half Back	1954 - 1959
1935	Albert Joseph Scanlon	Outside Left	1960 - 1962
1963	Bjorn Kristensen	Centre Back	1989 - 1993

October-11

1958: Scoring Debut

Ivor Allchurch scored twice on his debut today in the League Division 1 fixture against Leicester City.

Together with a goal from Len White Newcastle ran out with a 3-1 victory at St James's Park.

1961: One and Only Appearance

Billy Wilson, Right Half, made his one and only appearance today for Newcastle as they hosted Sheffield United at St James's Park in a League Cup Second Round Replay. Newcastle lost the game 2-0.

Debut on October-11:

Year	Player	Opposition
1958	Ivor Allchurch (Inside-Forward)	Leicester City
1961	Billy Wilson (Right Half)	Sheffield United

Born on October-11:

Year	Player	Position	Years
1909	Ronald William Starling	Inside Forward	1930 - 1932
1930	Ronald Campbell Simpson	Goalkeeper	1951 - 1960
1960	Kevin John Pugh	Midfield	1976 - 1982

October-12

1895: Eight Goal Spree

Newcastle, then of the second division, faced non-league side West Hartlepool Rangers in a FA Cup First Qualifying Round tie and put eight goals past them. James Collins and James Logan both scored two each and the others came from Willie Thompson, Jimmy Stott, William Graham and a Rangers 'own goal'.

1907: One and Only Appearance

George Hedley, Midfield/Wing, made his one and only appearance today for Newcastle as they hosted Manchester United at St James's Park in a League Division 1 fixture. It was a 'baptism of fire', as they say, for Hedley as Newcastle were roasted 6-1 by Manchester. Apparently not only was this Hedley's only appearance for Newcastle but it was his only appearance for anyone at Football League level.

1932: Newcastle Beaten in Charity Shield

FA Cup winners Newcastle and League Champions Everton contested the Charity Shield and despite scoring three goals Newcastle were still beaten with Everton scoring five. The game was played at St James's Park. Newcastle's scorers were Harry McMenemy, with two goals and Jimmy Boyd, but goal scoring legend Dixie Dean scored four for Everton with their other coming from Tommy Johnson.

First Meeting on October-11:

Year	V	F	A	R	Opposition	Competition
1895	A	8	0	W	West Hartlepool Rangers	FA Cup
1935	H	1	2	L	Charlton Athletic	Division 2

Debut on October-11:

Year	Player	Opposition
1907	George Hedley (Midfield/Wing)	Manchester United
1991	Gavin Maguire (Central Defence)	Leicester City

Born on October-11:

Year	Player	Position	Years
1884	John Rutherford	Right Wing	1902 - 1913
1891	Curtis Booth	Centre Forward	1913 - 1920
1915	David Smith	Outside Right	1935 - 1936
1935	Bill Curry	Centre Forward	1953 - 1959
1959	Paul Goddard	Forward	1986 - 1988
1981	Foluwashola Ameobi	Forward	2000 - 2014
1981	Brian Kerr	Midfield	1999 - 2004

October-13

1962: Tyne-Wear Derby No. 94

Newcastle hosted Sunderland in a League Division 2 fixture, the 94th Tyne-Wear Derby. Both sides scored a goal in the first half and with no other goals in the second half honours were even at 1-1. Jimmy Kerray scored for Newcastle and Brian Clough scored for Sunderland.

1988: Newcastle came to a standstill today as the funeral of Jackie Milburn took place. There were over 1,000 mourners at St Nicholas's Cathedral in Newcastle and tens upon tens of thousands of people lined the streets to watch the cortege pass.

First Meeting on October-13:

Year	V	F	A	R	Opposition	Competition
1979	H	1	0	W	Shrewsbury Town	Division 2

Debut on October-13:

Year	Player	Opposition
1951	William Isiah Foulkes (Outside Right)	Huddersfield Town
1990	Scott Sloan (Forward)	Oxford United

Born on October-13:

Year	Player	Position	Years
1932	Ken Prior	Outside Left	1952 - 1957
1946	Anthony Green	Midfield	1971 - 1973
1952	Gordon Henry Hodgson	Midfield	1971 - 1974
1964	John Cornwell	Midfield	1987 - 1988
1980	Scott Matthew Parker	Midfield	2005 - 2007

October-14

1893: One and Only Appearance

M. Keir, playing as one of Newcastle's forwards against Notts County in the League Division 2 fixture at the County Ground, Meadow Lane, picked up an injury and was never to recover from it sufficiently enough to be selected again for Newcastle. It was said that he moved back to Scotland, but very little is really known about him. Notts County won the game 3-1.

1911: Tyne-Wear Derby No. 30

Newcastle travelled to Roker Park to face Sunderland in a League Division 1 fixture, the 30th Tyne-Wear Derby. A goal from John Scott and a penalty from Bill McCracken gave Newcastle a 2-1 victory. Sunderland's goal coming from George Holley.

1978: Tyne-Wear Derby No. 112

Newcastle travelled to Roker Park to face Sunderland in a League Division 1 fixture, the 112th Tyne-Wear Derby.

Newcastle went into the break a goal to the good thanks to Peter Withe but Roy Greenwood equalised for Sunderland in the second half. The game therefore ending honours even at 1-1.

First Meeting on October-14:

Year	V	F	A	R	Opposition	Competition
1893	A	1	3	L	Notts County	Division 2

Debut on October-14:

Year	Player	Opposition
1893	John Inglis (Outside Right) M Keir (Forward)	Notts County
1933	Thomas Usher Pearson (Left-Wing)	Arsenal

Born on October-14:

Year	Player	Position	Years
1979	Olivier Jimmy Wilfrid Bernard	Left Back	2001 - 2007

October-15

There has been some high scoring games on this day over the years, Newcastle beat Sheffield Wednesday 4-3 in **1927**, they beat Tranmere Rovers 5-1 in **1938** and in **1960** eight goals were shared with Wolverhampton Wanderers.

1949: Tyne-Wear Derby No. 73

Newcastle hosted Sunderland in a League Division 1 fixture, the 73rd Tyne-Wear Derby. Newcastle took a 2-1 lead into the break with goals from Jorge Robledo and Tommy Walker (Tommy Wright getting Sunderland's goal). However a goal from Sunderland's Dickie Davies equalised the score in the second half and the game ended honours even at 2-2.

1977: Scoring Debut

Dennis Martin scored on his debut today in the League Division 1 fixture with Manchester United. Although Newcastle scored again through Mickey Burns it was not enough as they lost 3-2 at Old Trafford.

1997: Scoring Debut

Dereck Vivian "Des" Hamilton scored on his debut today in the League Cup tie with Hull City. With Ian Rush adding a 83rd minute goal to Hamilton's opener on 47 minutes Newcastle easily progressed from this Round 3 tie 2-0 at St James's Park.

First Meeting on October-15:

Year	V	F	A	R	Opposition	Competition
1938	H	5	1	W	Tranmere Rovers	Division 2
1996	A	2	3	L	Ferencvaros	UEFA Cup

Debut on October-15:

Year	Player	Opposition
1955	Ken Waugh (Full Back)	Arsenal
1977	Dennis Martin (Right Wing/Midfield)	Manchester United
1997	Des Hamilton (Full Back/Midfield)	Hull City

Born on October-15:

Year	Player	Position	Years
1899	Henry Bedford	Inside Forward	1930 - 1932
1909	Ehud Rogers	Outside Right	1936 - 1938
1934	Joe Cooper	Half Back	1952 - 1959
1979	Andrew Alexander Cole	Centre Forward	1993 - 1995

October-16

1920: Tyne-Wear Derby No. 44

Newcastle travelled to Roker Park to face Sunderland in a League Division 1 fixture, the 44th Tyne-Wear Derby.

Two second half goals, one from Stan Seymour the other from Neil Harris gave Newcastle a 2-0 victory.

1954: Eight Goals Shared

Newcastle and Tottenham Hotspur met at St James's Park in a League Division 1 fixture and between them scored eight goals.

Newcastle's goals were scored by Ivor Broadis, with two, Charlie Crowe and Len White.

Debut on October-16:

Year	Player	Opposition
1954	Bill Paterson (Centre Half)	Tottenham Hotspur
2011	Davide Santon (Defence)	Tottenham Hotspur

Born on October-16:

Year	Player	Position	Years
1876	Thomas Blyth	Centre Forward	1896 - 1898
1929	Ivor Allchurch	Inside-Forward	1958 - 1962

October-17

1896: Scoring Debut

John Auld scored on his debut today in the League Division 2 fixture with Manchester City at Hyde Road. With Richard Smellie also scoring for Newcastle they were victorious by 2 goals to 1.

1925: Tyne-Wear Derby No. 53

Newcastle hosted Sunderland in a League Division 1 fixture, the 53rd Tyne-Wear Derby. This turned out to be a rather unique Derby in that of the 153 held to date (end of 2014-15 season) only nine have resulted in a goalless draw. Eight have been at Sunderland (all at Roker Park, i.e. prior to their move to the Stadium of Light) so this represents not only the first goalless draw at St James's Park in a Tyne-Wear Derby, but the only time there had been one.

Debut on October-17:

Year	Player	Opposition
1896	John Connell (Inside Right) John Robertson Auld (Centre-Half)	Manchester City
1959	George Luke (Outside Left)	Fulham

Born on October-17:

Year	Player	Position	Years
1939	John Bell	Wing Half	1956 - 1962
1977	Habib Beye	Defence	2007 - 2009

October-18

1907: One and Only Appearance

Errington "Ike" Keen, Left Half, made his one and only appearance today for Newcastle as they hosted Derby County in a League Division 1 fixture. Newcastle were comprehensively beaten 5-2.

Tommy Lang scoring both Newcastle goals, one from the penalty spot. Keen actually went on to sign for Derby County and became an England international.

1924: Tyne-Wear Derby No. 51

Newcastle travelled to Roker Park to face Sunderland in a League Division 1 fixture, the 51st Tyne-Wear Derby. A goal each in the first half being the only scores saw honours even. Newcastle scored through Bob Clarke and Sunderland through Bobby Marshall.

1992: Tyne-Wear Derby No. 126

Newcastle travelled to Roker Park to face Sunderland in a League Division 1 fixture, the 126th Tyne-Wear Derby. An 'own goal' from Sunderland's Gary Owers gave Newcastle a first half lead. Liam O'Brien scored a second for Newcastle after the restart and the game ended with Newcastle winners 2-1.

First Meeting on October-18:

Year	V	F	A	R	Opposition	Competition
1994	H	3	2	W	Athletic Bilbao	UEFA Cup

Debut on October-18:

Year	Player	Opposition
1902	Peter McWilliam (Left Half)	Middlesbrough
1930	Errington Ridley L Keen (Left Half)	Derby County
1986	Darren Jackson (Forward)	Arsenal

October-19

1929: Tyne-Wear Derby No. 61

Newcastle travelled to Roker Park to face Sunderland in a League Division 1 fixture, the 61st Tyne-Wear Derby. A single goal in the first half from Sunderland's Gordon Gunson gave them the victory.

1991: Peacock Hat-Trick as Newcastle Edge 7 Goal Encounter

Oxford United visited St James's Park for a League Division 2 fixture and were just edged in a thrilling 4-3 victory for Newcastle.

As mentioned, Gavin Peacock scored a hat-trick, and it was Andy Hunt who scored Newcastle's other goal.

First Meeting on October-19:

Year	V	F	A	R	Opposition	Competition
1968	H	3	2	W	Queens Park Rangers	Division 1
1977	A	1	2	L	Bastia	UEFA Cup
2006	H	1	0	W	Fenerbache Spor Kulubu	UEFA Cup

Debut on October-19:

Year	Player	Opposition
1963	Leslie O'Neill (Midfield)	Portsmouth

Born on October-19:

Year	Player	Position	Years
1892	John Finlay	Left Half	1909 - 1927
1924	Jeremiah Lowery	Goalkeeper	1947 - 1952
1961	Phillip Leaver	Midfield	1977 - 1982
1989	Mark Doninger	Midfield	2005 - 2009

October-20

1894: Eight Goals Shared

Filbert Street saw eight goals being shared equally between Newcastle and Leicester Fosse in a League Division 2 fixture. Newcastle's scorers being Charles Dickson, Willie Thompson, Bobby Willis and a penalty by Jock Smith.

1996: A Day To Never Forget

When Phillipe Albert chipped Peter Schmeichel to make it 5-0 at St James's Park against Manchester United people in Sunderland would have heard the cheers! Etched in the memory of the Toon Army is: 1-0 Peacock (12), 2-0 Ginola (30), 3-0 Ferdinand (62), 4-0 Shearer (74) and that glorious chip from Albert (83) making it 5-0.

Born on October-20:

Year	Player	Position	Years
1895	James Clark	Inside Left	1921 - 1924
1961	Ian Rush	Forward	1997 - 1998

October-21

1905: One and Only Appearance

Thomas Sowerby "Tom" Rowlandson, Goalkeeper, made his one and only appearance today for Newcastle as they hosted Bury in a League Division 1 fixture.

With goals from Ron Orr, Bill Appleyard and Colin Veitch Newcastle were quite comfortable 3-1 winners.

1933: Tyne-Wear Derby No. 69

Newcastle hosted Sunderland in a League Division 1 fixture, the 69th Tyne-Wear Derby. Sammy Weaver scored in both halves for Newcastle and Sunderland scored a single goal in the second half to make it a 2-1 victory for Newcastle.

2012: Tyne-Wear Derby No. 148

Newcastle travelled to the Stadium of Light to face Sunderland in a Premiership fixture, the 148th Tyne-Wear Derby. Yohann Cabaye put Newcastle ahead after only three minutes and it took a Demba Ba 'own goal' on 85 minutes to provide Sunderland with an equaliser and the game ended honours even at 1-1.

First Meeting on October-21:

Year	V	F	A	R	Opposition	Competition
1970	H	2	0	W	Pesci Doza	Inter Cities Fairs Cup
1999	A	2	1	W	FC Zurich	EUFA Cup
2004	A	1	0	W	Panionios Athen	UEFA Cup

Debut on October-21:

Year	Player	Opposition
1905	Thomas Rowlandson (Goalkeeper)	Bury
1911	William Hibbert (Inside Left)	Blackburn Rovers

Born on October-21:

Year	Player	Position	Years
1959	Kevin Sheedy	Left Midfield	1992 - 1993

October-22

1910: Six of the Best - Shepherd with Four

Newcastle put six past Liverpool in a League Division 1 fixture at St James's Park. The goals coming from the four by Albert Shepherd and one each for Jimmy Stewart and Sandy Higgins. Liverpool did get a consolation goal in the second half through Ernest Peake.

1966 saw six of the worst though as Newcastle were beaten 6-0 by Blackpool in a League Division 1 fixture at Bloomfield Road.

First Meeting on October-22:

Year	V	F	A	R	Opposition	Competition
1997	A	0	1	L	PSV Eindhoven	European Champions League

Debut on October-22:

Year	Player	Opposition
1980	Chris Roland Waddle (Midfield) Chris Withe (Left Back)	Shrewsbury Town
2007	Joseph Barton (Midfilder)	Tottenham Hotspur

Born on October-22:

Year	Player	Position	Years
1911	Harry Ware	Inside Right	1935 - 1937
1993	Gael Bigirimana	Midfield	2012 - current

October-23

1893: Newcastle fined for fielding unregistered player

Newcastle United were fined 2 Guineas at a meeting of the Football Management Committee held at the Midland Hotel, Birmingham, for fielding a player called "Davies" without having registered him. The reports don't state the date on which 'Davies' actually played or the opposition against whom he played.

We can only assume that this happened whilst "United" were still "East End" or that it was not in a league fixture as Newcastle did not have anyone with the surname of Davies playing for them at the time in their 'first' team.

1893: One and Only Appearance

John Patten made his one and only appearance today for Newcastle as they travelled to Hyde Road to face Ardwick in a League Division 2 fixture. Whilst Newcastle won the game, 3-2, Patten was never to appear for them again.

1926: Six of the Best

Newcastle put six past Blackburn Rovers in a League Division 1 fixture at St James's Park. The goals coming from a Stan Seymour hat-trick with one each for Bob Clark, Tom McDonald and Roddie MacKenzie. Rovers did get a consolation goal but the end result was a comfortable 6-1 victory to Newcastle.

2005: Tyne-Wear Derby No. 138

Newcastle hosted Sunderland for a Premiership fixture, the 138th Tyne-Wear Derby. Two goals from Shola Ameobi and one from Emre Belozoglu gave Newcastle a 3-2 victory. Sunderland's goals being scored by Liam Lawrence and Stephen Elliott.

First Meeting on October-23:

Year	V	F	A	R	Opposition	Competition
1893	A	3	2	W	Ardwick*	Division 2

*Ardwick became Manchester City against whom our first game was 04/01/1896

Debut on October-23:

Year	Player	Opposition
1893	John Patten (Forward)	Ardwick
1954	John Thompson (Goalkeeper) Bill Curry (Centre Forward)	Manchester United
1971	Chris Guthrie (Forward)	Manchester United

Born on October-23:

Year	Player	Position	Years
1915	Jimmy Gordon	Wing Half	1934 - 1945
1930	Alan Monkhouse	Forward	1953 - 1956

October-24

1914: Newcastle Edge 7 Goal Encounter

Sheffield United visited St James's Park for a League Division 1 fixture and were just edged in a 4-3 victory for Newcastle. Curtis Booth, Tom Hall, with two, and Frank Hudspeth with a penalty ensured the victory.

1995 saw Newcastle progress in the League Cup by disposing of Stoke 4-0 at St James's Park in the Third Round tie. The goals coming from Peter Beardsley, with two, and one apiece from Les Ferdinand and Darren Peacock.

2004: Newcastle Edge 7 Goal Encounter

Manchester City visited St James's Park for a League Division 1 fixture and were just edged in a 4-3 victory for Newcastle. The first half finished 0-0 and there was no indication within it that we would see seven goals in the second half but that's exactly what happened. Newcastle went 2-0 up through Laurent Robert and Alan Shearer, City pulled it back to 2-2 through Shaun Wright-Phillips and Robbie Fowler. Newcastle took the lead again through Robbie Elliott, City equalised again through a second goal from Wright-Phillips and with less than a minute left on the clock Craig Bellamy scored the winner for Newcastle.

Debut on October-24:

Year	Player	Opposition
1959	Robert Gilfillan (Forward)	Bolton Wanderers

Born on October-24:

Year	Player	Position	Years
1905	Robert Thomson	Left Back	1928 - 1934
1963	John Grattan Hendrie	Right Wing	1988 - 1989
1989	Jack Raymond Colback	Midfield	2014 - current

October-25

1947: Five Star Performance

Newcastle put five past Southampton in a League Division 2 fixture at St James's Park, with no reply from Southampton this was a very comfortable victory.

Two goals from Tommy Walker and the others from Jackie Milburn, Tom Pearson and George Stobbart sealed the victory.

1980 saw six of the worst as Chelsea demolished Newcastle 6-0 in a League Division 2 fixture at Stamford Bridge.

2008: Tyne-Wear Derby No. 142

Newcastle travelled to the Stadium of Light to face Sunderland in a Premiership fixture, the 142nd Tyne-Wear Derby.

The game was finely balanced at 1-1 going into the break after Shola Ameobi had equalised Sunderland's opener from Djibril Cisse. Keiran Richardson scored a goal in the second half to give Sunderland the win 2-1.

First Meeting on October-25:

Year	V	F	A	R	Opposition	Competition
2012	H	1	0	W	Brugge	Europa League

Debut on October-25:

Year	Player	Opposition
1980	Bruce Halliday (Central Defence)	Chelsea
1986	Peter Jackson (Central Defence)	Aston Villa

Born on October-25:

Year	Player	Position	Years
1940	Walter Grant Malcolm	Forward	1957 - 1960
1950	Mick Mahoney	Goalkeeper	1975 - 1978

October-26

1901: Eight is Great!

Newcastle put eight past Notts County with no reply in a League Division 1 fixture at St James's Park. Ron Orr scored four, Jock Peddie got a hat-trick and Richard Roberts netted a goal too.

1912: Six of the Best

Newcastle put six past Everton with no reply in a League Division 1 fixture at Goodison Park. Wilf Low, John McTavish and Jimmy Stewart each scored twice.

1994: One and Only Appearance

Midfielder Stephen Guppy, , made his one and only appearance today for Newcastle as they hosted Manchester United in a League Cup Second Round tie. With goals from Phillipe Albert and Paul Kitson giving Newcastle a 2-0 victory they progressed to the next round.

Born on October-26:

Year	Player	Position	Years
1971	Stephen Norman Howey	Central Defence	1989 - 2000
1971	Elena Sierra Marcelino	Central Defence	1999 - 2003

October-27

1894: Newcastle Edge Nine Goal Encounter

Newcastle entertained Ardwick in a League Division 2 fixture and the fans were treated to a nine goal thriller with Newcastle just edging it 5-4. Their goals courtesy of a Willie Thompson hat-trick and one apiece for Charles Dickson and William Graham.

1928: Tyne-Wear Derby No. 59

Newcastle travelled to Roker Park to face Sunderland in a League Division 1 fixture, the 59th Tyne-Wear Derby. Sunderland took the game 5-2. Newcastle's scorers being Jimmy Boyd and Roddie MacKenzie.

1962: Six of the Best

Newcastle put six past Swansea Town with no reply in a League Division 2 fixture at St James's Park. Two goals each for Jimmy Fell and Alan Suddick where complemented with a goal from Barrie Thomas and a Swansea 'own goal'.

2013: Tyne-Wear Derby No. 150

Newcastle travelled to the Stadium of Light to face Sunderland in a Premiership fixture, the 150th Tyne-Wear Derby. Steven Fletcher gave Sunderland a 1-0 lead going into the break. Mathieu Debuchy equalised for Newcastle on 57 minutes but with only 6 minutes left Fabio Borini gave Sunderland the victory 2-1.

First Meeting on October-27:

Year	V	F	A	R	Opposition	Competition
1934	A	3	1	W	Port Vale	Division 2

Debut on October-27:

Year	Player	Opposition
1928	John Hill (Centre Half)	Sunderland
1979	William Rafferty (Forward)	Cambridge United
1990	Matty Appleby (Centre Back)	West Bromwich Albion
2004	Ronny Johnsen (Defence)	Norwich City

Born on October-27:

Year	Player	Position	Years
1947	Dennis Martin	Right Wing/Midfield	1977 - 1978
1972	Lee Robert Clark	Midfield	1988 - 2006
1986	Matthew Joseph Pattison	Centre Midfield	2005 - 2008

October-28

1893: One and Only Appearance

William Simm, Outside Right, made his one and only appearance today for

Newcastle as they entertained Small Heath at St James's Park in a League Division 2 fixture. Newcastle lost the game 2-0 and Simm was never to appear for them again.

2009: Hughton Given Managers Job

It was today confirmed that Chris Hughton had been appointed to the manager's job on a permanent basis until the end of the 2010-11 season. This after he had been caretaker manager and installed Newcastle at the top of the Championship.

2009: Newcastle NOT for sale!

In a long running saga owner Mike Ashley has once again taken the club off the market after failing to attract a buyer. This was after it was confirmed that leading contender Chris Moat failed to come up with the £80m asking price.

First Meeting on October-28:

Year	V	F	A	R	Opposition	Competition
1893	H	0	2	L	Small Heath*	Division 2

*Small Heath became Birmingham City, whom we first met on 05/10/1901.

Debut on October-28:

Year	Player	Opposition
1893	William Simm (Outside Right)	Small Heath
1899	Colin Veitch (Half Back)	Wolverhampton Wanderers
2000	Clarence Acuna (Midfield)	West Ham United

Born on October-28:

Year	Player	Position	Years
1920	Dick Burke	Full Back	1946 - 1947
1980	Alan Smith	Forward	2007 - 2012
1984	Obafemi Akinwunmi Martins	Forward	2006 - 2009

October-29

1966: Tyne-Wear Derby No. 100

Newcastle hosted Sunderland in a League Division 1 fixture, the 100th Tyne-Wear Derby.

What would have hopefully turned out to be a 'centenary' celebration at St James's Park certainly didn't turn out that way - Sunderland took the game 3-0 with goals from John O'Hare, Neil Martin and George Mulhall.

1977: Eight Goals Shared

Newcastle and Everton contested a League Division 1 fixture at St James's Park. Alan Gowling scored twice and there were goals from Tommy Craig and Tommy Cassidy, but these were matched by Bob Latchford scoring twice and Pejic and Lyons scoring for Everton.

1983: Five Star Performance

Newcastle put five past Manchester City, with no reply, in a League Division 2 fixture at St James's Park. The goals coming from a Peter Beardsley hat-trick with Kevin Keegan and Chris Waddle getting one each.

1991: One and Only Appearance

Justinus Soni "Justin" Fashanu, Forward, made his one and only appearance today for Newcastle when they travelled to London Road for their League Cup Third Round tie against Peterborough United. Fashanu, who was only on loan at Newcastle, came on as a substitute for Andy Hunt but was unable to make any impact, Newcastle lost 1-0 to a goal from Charlery.

Debut on October-29:

Year	Player	Opposition
1898	Alexander MacFarlane (Inside Left)	Preston North End
1927	Jonathan Wilkinson (Forward)	Aston Villa
1966	Ronald Wyn Davies (Forward)	Sunderland
1991	Justin Fashanu (Forward)	Peterborough United

Born on October-29:

Year	Player	Position	Years
1903	William Gillespie	Right Back	1927 - 1929
1932	John McGuigan	Inside Forward	1958 - 1962
1951	Stewart Barrowclough	Midfield/Wing	1970 - 1978
1970	Anthony Lormor	Forward	1987 - 1990

October-30

1897: Six of the Best

Newcastle put six past Willington Athletic with no reply in a FA Cup

Qualifying Round 3 tie. Andy Aitken scored four, the other two coming from Johnny Campbell and James Jackson.

1926: Tyne-Wear Derby No. 55

Newcastle travelled to Roker Park to face Sunderland in a League Division 2 fixture, the 55th Tyne-Wear Derby. With a goal in each half (Halliday & Death) Sunderland took the victory 2-0.

1993 saw a hat-trick from Peter Beardsley, complemented with a goal from Andy Cole, earn Newcastle a 4-0 victory over Wimbledon at St James's Park in a Premiership fixture.

First Meeting on October-30:

Year	V	F	A	R	Opposition	Competition
1897	A	6	0	W	Willington Athletic	FA Cup
1968	A	1	1	D	Sporting Lisbon	Inter Cities Fairs Cup

Debut on October-30:

Year	Player	Opposition
1971	Anthony Green (Midfield)	Everton
1973	David Crosson (Right Back)	Birmingham City
1982	Chris Hedworth (Defence)	Leeds United

Born on October-30:

Year	Player	Position	Years
1895	Neil Harris	Centre Forward	1920 - 1926
1924	Charlie Crowe	Left Half	1944 - 1957

October-31

1931 saw Newcastle destroyed 8-1 by Everton at Goodison Park in a League Division 1 fixture. However this day would also see Newcastle do some destroying of their own...

2010: Tyne-Wear Derby No. 144

In the 144th Tyne-Wear Derby - nicknamed the "Demolition Derby" a hat-trick from Kevin Nolan and a brace from Shola Ameobi thoroughly destroyed Sunderland, though they did get a last-gasp consolation goal from Darren Bent on 90 minutes.

Not only did the game see 6 goals but it also saw no fewer than 9 yellow cards and 1 red card for Titus Bramble - who was now a Sunderland player.

The Yellows were: Danny Simpson, Cheick Tiote and Andy Carroll for Newcastle and for Sunderland, Phillip Bardsley, Michael Turner, Nedum Onuoha, Lee Cattermole, Steed Malbranque and John Mensah who had only been on the pitch six minutes after coming on as a substitute on 76 minutes.

Debut on October-31:

Year	Player	Opposition
1903	James Tildesley (Full Back)	Wolverhampton Wanderers
1953	Ivor Broadis (Inside Forward)	Sheffield United

Born on October-31:

Year	Player	Position	Years
1898	Tom Phillipson	Outside Right	1919 - 1921
1910	Tom Mooney	Outside Left	1936 - 1944
1935	Jimmy Hill	Inside Forward	1957 - 1958
1948	John Edward Craggs	Right Back	1964 - 1983
1956	Eddie Edgar	Goalkeeper	1973 - 1976
1991	James Henry Tavernier	Defence	2009 - 2014

Milburn Stand
viewed from Barrack Road

NOVEMBER

November-01

1902: One and Only Appearance
Ord Richardson, Inside Right, made his one and only appearance today for Newcastle when they travelled to Molineux for a League Division 1 fixture against Wolverhampton Wanderers. With a goal in the first half and two in the second half Wolves were easy winners as Newcastle drew a blank.

1930 saw two goals each from Joe Devine and Duncan Lindsay enough to beat Leeds United 4-1 at St James's Park in a League Division 2 fixture.

1989: Five Star Performance
An 'own goal' by Don Goodman, others from Gary Brazil, Kevin Brock, Liam O'Brien and Mark McGhee saw Newcastle run out 5-1 winners at The Hawthorns in a League Division 2 fixture against West Bromwich Albion. An interesting substitute was made by West Bromwich Albion, they brought on a certain Sam Allardyce.

1997: Last Gasp Equaliser - *in both halves*
In a Premiership fixture at St James's Park against Leicester City Newcastle took the lead on 4 minutes through John Barnes. Leicester equalised then took the lead, this through two goals from Ian Marshall. Then into first half injury time Jon Dahl Tomasson equalised so that at the break it was 2-2. In the second half Leicester again took the lead and it was not until the last minute that John Beresford equalised again for Newcastle and the game ended 3-3. A very exciting game indeed.

Debut on November-01:

Year	Player	Opposition
1902	Ord Richardson (Inside Right) Samuel Graham (Outside Right)	Wolverhampton Wanderers
1913	Angus Douglas (Outside Right)	Burnley
1919	William Bradley (Goalkeeper)	Preston North End
1952	George Brander (Winger)	Derby County
1969	John Cowan (Midfield) Jimmy Thomson (Midfield)	Burnley
1980	Peter Johnson (Left Back)	Watford
2000	Christian Bassedas (Midfield)	Bradford City

Born on November-01:

Year	Player	Position	Years
1921	Norman Dodgin	Wing Half	1940 - 1950
1929	George Brander	Wing Half	1952 - 1954
1942	Preben Arentoft	Midfield	1969 - 1971
1977	Carl Cort	Forward	2000 - 2004
1982	Bradley Orr	Midfield	2002 - 2004

November-02

2006: 100th Goal in the EUFA Cup

Albert Luque's 37th minute header, the only goal of the game, against U.S. Città di Palermo becomes Newcastle's 100th goal in the UEFA Cup.

2009: Keith Kettleborough, R.I.P.

The sad news came today that Keith Kettleborough had died this morning following an illness. Kettleborough, and all his experience, was brought to Newcastle to ensure a successful fight against relegation in 1966.

As the fashion in the sixties was for 'long' hair Kettleborough cut an unmistakable figure on the pitch with his balding head - even though he was only 31 himself. His impact on the team was equally unmistakable though as Newcastle regained some lost confidence.

Leaving for a player-manager position Kettleborough went to Doncaster Rovers and finally Chesterfield where he completed his football career. As well as being a professional footballer, Kettleborough was also a professional cricketer.

First Meeting on November-02:

Year	V	F	A	R	Opposition	Competition
2006	H	1	0	W	RC Celta de Vigo	UEFA Cup

Debut on November-02:

Year	Player	Opposition
1991	Alan Thompson (Midfield)	Swindon Town
2006	Andrew Carroll (Striker) Tim Krul (Goalkeeper)	U.S. Cittá di Palermo

Born on November-02:

Year	Player	Position	Years
1888	Scott Duncan	Outside Right	1908 - 1913
1965	Neil Raymond McDonald	Right Back	1982 - 1988
1994	Remie Streete	Defence	2012 - 2015

November-03

A 4-1 defeat at the hands of Bury in **1894** and Portsmouth in **2007** were somewhat atoned for in both **1928** and **1934** when Newcastle recorded 4-1 victories over Huddersfield Town, scorers being Hughie Gallacher, with two, Jimmy Boyd and Tommy Lang, and Barnsley, scorers being Jack Smith, with two, Jimmy Boyd and Jimmy Murray, respectively.

1971: Five Star Performance

Newcastle put five past Coventry City in a Texaco Cup Second Round, Second Leg tie at St James's Park. Two goals from John Tudor and one each for Malcolm Macdonald and Irving Nattrass were complemented by an 'own goal' from Coventry's Jeff Blockley. This rounded off a 5-1 win for Newcastle and as the first leg had been drawn 1-1, Newcastle progressed to the next round with a 6-2 aggregate score.

First Meeting on November-03:

Year	V	F	A	R	Opposition	Competition
1894	A	1	4	L	Bury	Division 2

Debut on November-03:

Year	Player	Opposition
1951	Hugh Cameron (Left Wing)	Liverpool
1973	Ray Hudson (Midfield)	Stoke City

November-04

The very first meeting between Liverpool and Newcastle in **1893** did not fare well, as Liverpool ran out 5-1 winners at Anfield. However revenge was to come.

1922: Tyne-Wear Derby No. 47

Newcastle hosted Sunderland in a League Division 1 fixture, the 47th Tyne-Wear Derby. Billy Aitken and Tom McDonald scored one each in either half and Sunderland got a second half goal through Charlie Buchan so the game ended 2-1 to Newcastle.

1950: Robledo Hat-Trick Sinks Liverpool

A hat-trick from Jorge Robledo and a goal from Ernie Taylor saw Newcastle come away from Anfield having beaten Liverpool 4-2 in their League Division 1 fixture.

First Meeting on November-04:

Year	V	F	A	R	Opposition	Competition
1893	A	1	5	L	Liverpool	Division 2
2004	H	2	0	W	Dynamo Tbilisi	UEFA Cup

Debut on November-04:

Year	Player	Opposition
1970	Ian Mitchell (Outside Left)	Pecsi Doza

Born on November-04:

Year	Player	Position	Years
1885	Alexander Higgins	Centre Forward	1905 - 1919
1958	Fransiscus Koenen	Midfield	1980 - 1981
1960	Gary Nicholson	Left Wing	1977 - 1981

November-05

1927: Tyne-Wear Derby No. 57

Newcastle hosted Sunderland in a League Division 1 fixture, the 57th Tyne-Wear Derby. The game was finely balanced at 1-1 going into the break but Newcastle applied the pressure in the second half to score twice and earn a 3-1 victory. Newcastle's scorers were Tom McDonald, Bob McKay and Stan Seymour. Bobby Marshall got the Sunderland goal.

Debut on November-05:

Year	Player	Opposition
1898	Jimmy Stevenson (Inside Left)	Liverpool
1904	Albert Arthur Gosnell (Left Wing)	Middlesbrough
1960	William Thompson (Centre Half)	Chelsea
1977	Nigel Walker (Midfield)	Bristol City

November-06

1926: Debut Hat-Trick

Robert "Bob" McKay scored three times on his debut today in the League Division 1 fixture with West Bromwich Albion. Together with a brace from Hughie Gallacher Newcastle ran out comfortable 5-2 winners at St James's Park.

1974: Comfortably Through to Final

Newcastle went to St Andrews for the second leg of their Texaco Cup Semi-Final against Birmingham City and strolled to a 4-1 victory. Alan Kennedy, Paul Cannell, John Tudor and a Gary Pendry 'own goal' secured the victory on the night. With the first leg having ended in a 1-1 draw Newcastle were in the final for the second consecutive season - they were of courses current holders of the Texaco Cup.

First Meeting on November-06:

Year	V	F	A	R	Opposition	Competition
1963	A	1	2	L	Bournemouth	League Cup
2003	A	3	2	W	FC Basel	UEFA Cup

Debut on November-06:

Year	Player	Opposition
1926	Robert McKay (Inside Right)	West Bromwich Albion
1937	Edwin R. Bowden (Inside-Right)	Southampton
1963	Joe Butler (Right-Back) David James Craig (Full Back)	Bournemouth
1965	Christopher Napier (Centre Forward)	Blackpool
2002	Michael Chopra (Forward)	Everton

Born on November-06:

Year	Player	Position	Years
1958	Kevin Carr	Goalkeeper	1976 - 1985

November-07

1953 saw Newcastle put four past Cardiff City at St James's Park with no reply in a League Division 1 fixture, goals from Ivor Broadis, with two, George Hannah and Jackie Millburn. There was better to come.

1959: Eight is Great!

A hat-trick from Len White, two goals from Ivor Allchurch, one each for George Luke, Gordon Hughes and George Eastham ensured a handsome 8-2 victory for Newcastle over Everton at St James's Park in a League Division 1 fixture. The only down side being that they allowed Everton's Thomas to get two second half goals. But when you've scored eight you can be forgiven.

1981: One and Only Appearance

Kevin John Pugh, Midfield, made his one and only appearance today for Newcastle when they travelled to Stamford Bridge for a League Division 2 fixture against Chelsea.

Trailing 2-0 at half-time Newcastle did manage to pull one back in the second half with a Chris Waddle goal but Chelsea ran out eventual winners 2-1.

First Meeting on November-07:

Year	V	F	A	R	Opposition	Competition
1936	A	2	2	D	Coventry City	Division 2

Debut on November-07:

Year	Player	Opposition
1953	Alan Monkhouse (Forward)	Cardiff City
1959	George Heslop (Centre Half)	Everton
1970	Tommy Cassidy (Defence/Midfield)	Southampton
1981	Kevin John Pugh (Midfield) Alan Brown (Forward) Wesley Saunders (Central Defence)	Chelsea
1987	Michael O'Neill (Midfield)	Luton Town

Born on November-07:

Year	Player	Position	Years
1917	George Joseph Bradley	Defence	1938 - 1946
1959	John Anderson	Right Back	1982 - 1992
1962	Darron Karl McDonough	Midfield	1992 - 1994
1963	John Charles Bryan Barnes	Midfield	1997
1967	Marc Hottiger	Right Back	1994 - 1996

November-08

1969: Tyne-wear Derby No. 106

Newcastle hosted Sunderland in a League Division 1 fixture, the 106th Tyne-Wear Derby. Two goals from Keith Dyson and a goal from Wyn Davies secured a 3-0 victory for Newcastle.

Debut on November-08:

Year	Player	Opposition
1902	Andrew Gardner (Outside Right)	Liverpool
1952	Tommy Mulgrew (Inside Forward)	Blackpool
1986	Paul Goddard (Forward)	Leicester City
1998	Giorgos Georgiadis (Midfield)	Manchester United

Born on November-08:

Year	Player	Position	Years
1885	James Kirkcaldy	Half Back	1904 - 1907
1946	Roger Jones	Goalkeeper	1975 - 1977
1979	Aaron William Hughes	Defence	1997 - 2005
1983	Michael James Williamson	Defence	2010 - current

November-09

1895: Second Half Collapse Sees Eight Goals Shared

Newcastle took a 3-0 lead into the break in their League Division 2 fixture against Darwen at Barley Bank. In a huge turnaround Darwen scored four times in the second half, though Newcastle did score once more themselves, the game ending 4-4. Newcastle's scorers were Willie Wardrope, Andy Aitken, Willie Thompson and James Collins.

1901: Scoring Debut

Robert "Bob" McColl scored a penalty on his debut in the League Division 1 fixture with Manchester City. Together with goals from Richard Roberts and Ron Orr Newcastle ran out comfortable 3-0 winners at St James's Park.

1935: Hat-Trick Saves The Day

A hat-trick from John Smith and a goal from Wilf Bott secured a narrow 4-3 victory for Newcastle over Bury in a League Division 1 fixture at Gigg Lane. Newcastle had been leading 2-1 going into the break and perhaps did not foresee the Bury fight back.

1977: Dinnis Dismissed

Richard Dinnis, arriving at St James's Park along with Gordon Lee found himself surprisingly in charge at Newcastle because of so-called "player power"! Upon Lee's resignation, the players demanded that Dinnis be given the manager's job, threatening to strike otherwise. Dinnis was duly appointed but within 40 games, and only 12 wins, he was duly sacked. This gave Dinnis the perhaps most unwanted distinction of being Newcastle's shortest serving manager. (*Until 2008 and Sam Allardyce that is.*)

Debut on November-09:

Year	Player	Opposition
1895	Malcolm Lennox (Outside Right)	Darwen
1901	Robert Smyth McColl (Centre Forward)	Manchester City
1963	Stan Anderson (Right-Half) Trevor Hockey (Midfield)	Cardiff City

Born on November-09:

Year	Player	Position	Years
1952	Mike Larnach	Inside Forward	1977 - 1978

November-10

1894: Scoring Debut

Robert McDermidd scored on his debut today in the League Division 2 fixture with Burton Wanderers.

With Willie Thompson and Jock Smith also scoring for Newcastle they were victorious by 3-1 at St James's Park.

1923 and **1928** saw Newcastle facing Manchester City, on both occasions Newcastle scored four times.

The first being a 4-1 victory at St James's Park, the second a 4-2 victory at Maine Road saw Hughie Gallacher scoring a hat-trick. Both games were in League Division 1.

2007: Tyne-wear Derby No. 140

Newcastle travelled to the Stadium of Light to face Sunderland in a Premiership fixture, the 140th Tyne-Wear Derby. Danny Higginbotham put Sunderland in the lead on 54 minutes but James Milner equalised 12 minutes later and the game ended honours even at 1-1.

First Meeting on November-10:

Year	V	F	A	R	Opposition	Competition
1894	H	3	1	W	Burton Wanderers	Division 2

Debut on November-10:

Year	Player	Opposition
1894	Robert McDermidd (Right Back)	Burton Wanderers
1973	George Hope (Forward)	Leicester City
1990	Stephen Craig Watson (Defence)	Wolverhampton Wanderers

Born on November-10:

Year	Player	Position	Years
1876	John Fraser	Outside Left	1899-1901
1895	Alfred Hagan	Inside Left	1919-1923
1928	Tommy Thompson	Inside Forward	1946–1950
1946	Geoffrey Allen	Outside Left	1964–1970
1969	Faustino Hernan Asprilla Hinestroza	Forward	1996–1998
1976	Shefki Kuqi	Forward	2011

November-11

1905: Eight is Great!

Newcastle scored eight times, with no reply, against Wolverhampton Wanderers at St James's Park in a League Division 1 fixture. A hat-trick from Bill Appleyard, two each from Ron Orr and Jim Howie together with a penalty from Colin Veitch wrapped up a comfortable win.

1922: Tyne-wear Derby No. 48

Newcastle travelled to Roker Park to face Sunderland in a League Division 1 fixture, the 48th Tyne-Wear Derby. Two second half goals, one from Jock Paterson the other by Arthur Hawes gave Sunderland a 2-0 victory.

First Meeting on November-11:

Year	V	F	A	R	Opposition	Competition
1961	A	0	0	D	Rotherham United*	Division 2
1992	A	1	1	D	AS Lucchese Libertas	Anglo-Italian Cup

*Previously Rotherham Town whom we first played on 20/01/1894.

Born on November-11:

Year	Player	Position	Years
1941	Alwyn Derek Burton	Wing Half	1963 - 1973
1945	Bryan Stanley Robson	Forward	1962 - 1971
1990	Georginio Wijnaldum	Midfield	2015 - current
1993	Jamaal Lascelles	Defence	2014 - current

November-12

1892: Five Star Performance

One of the last games for Newcastle East End - a Northern League fixture against Darlington saw Newcastle score five without reply. Jock Sorely scored twice, Willie Graham, Willie Thompson and James Collins got the others. Darlington were however down to ten men for the whole of the second half as McDonald was injured in the first half and did not come out for the second. This was of course well before the days of substitutes!

1955: Six of the Best

Newcastle scored six past Huddersfield Town in a League Division 1 fixture at Leeds Road. This included four goals for Vic Keeble. Len White and Charlie Crowe scoring the other two.

2010: Three Match Ban for Barton

Following an incident in the game against Blackburn Rovers on Wednesday, 10/11/2010, midfielder Joey Barton was found guilty of violent conduct and handed a three match ban by the Independent Regulatory Commission hearing.

First Meeting on November-12:

Year	R	F	A	V	Opposition	Competition
1892	W	5	0	H	Darlington	Northern League
1898	L	0	2	A	Nottingham Forest	Division 1

Debut on November-12:

Year	Player	Opposition
1966	William McFaul (Goalkeeper)	Liverpool
1977	Tony Smith (Central Defence)	Wolverhampton Wanderers
1988	David Robinson (Forward)	Arsenal

Born on November-12:

Year	Player	Position	Years
1945	David Young	Wing Half	1964 - 1973
1957	Anthony Eugene Cunningham	Forward	1985 - 1987
1966	Joseph Ball Allon	Forward	1984 - 1987
1966	Andy Thorn	Central Defence	1988 - 1989

November-13

1909 saw a 4-0 defeat at the hands of Preston North End in a League Division 1 fixture at Deepdale, whilst **1965** saw a 4-2 defeat against Blackburn Rovers at Ewood Park.

Blackburn had already beaten Newcastle 2-1 in **1937** and if you add the 3-1 defeat by Burnley in **1920** and the 3-2 defeat by Bury in **1926** you could say that if your name begins with a 'B' this has been a good day to play Newcastle!

2002: Last Gasp Winner

Craig Bellamy scored in the last minute of the first half to give Newcastle a 1-0 lead going into the break against Feyenoord at the Stadion Feijenoord (de Kuip) in the European Champions League. Just after the restart Hugo Vianna doubled Newcastle's lead but Feyenoord struck back with two goals of their own to equalise. It was then in the last minute of the game when Bellamy scored his second and Newcastle's third to take the tie 3-2.

Debut on November-13:

Year	Player	Opposition
1897	John Hope Peddie (Centre Forward)	Newton Heath

November-14

1936: Seven Heaven

Newcastle scored seven, with no reply, against Doncaster Rovers at St James's Park in a League Division 2 fixture. The goals coming courtesy of four from Jack Smith, two from Billy Leighton and one from Ehud "Tim" Rogers.

1981 saw a goal from Alan Brown in the League Division 2 fixture against Charlton Athletic at St James's Park, a game Newcastle won quite easily 4-1. Noteworthy because in the five games Brown played for Newcastle he scored three times. Also noteworthy as Brown was only on loan to Newcastle - from Sunderland! Why they let him come to Newcastle, and why they in turn didn't extend his loan still bemuses everyone who can remember Brown.

First Meeting on November-14:

Year	V	F	A	R	Opposition	Competition
1896	H	3	1	W	Leicester City*	Division 2
1914	A	0	1	L	Bradford Park Avenue	Division 1

*Leicester City were originally Leicester Fosse whom we first played on 29/09/1894

Debut on November-14:

Year	Player	Opposition
1925	John Dowsey (Inside Right)	Tottenham Hotspur

Born on November-14:

Year	Player	Position	Years
1906	William Halliday	Inside Left	1927 - 1928
1920	Willie McCall	Outside Left	1948 - 1948
1923	Thomas Jackson Walker	Outside Right	1941 - 1954
1991	Philip Airey	Forward	2010 - current

November-15

1930: Eleven Goal Encounter

There were eleven goals scored in the League Division 1 fixture at St James's Park, but it was not in Newcastle's favour. Portsmouth were the victors by 7-4. Newcastle's four came from two for Duncan Lindsay and one each for Joe Devine and Jack Wilkinson.

First Meeting on November-15:

Year	V	F	A	R	Opposition	Competition
1924	A	1	1	D	Leeds United	Division 1

Debut on November-15:

Year	Player	Opposition
1902	John Watson (Right Back)	Sheffield United

Born on November-15:

Year	Player	Position	Years
1875	Matthew Kingsley	Goalkeeper	1898 - 1904
1918	Billy Pears	Right Half	1935 - 1941
1953	Keith Robson	Forward	1971 - 1974
1961	Neil Simpson	Midfield	1990 - 1991
1967	Gavin Peacock	Midfield	1990 - 1993

November-16

1895: Seven Heaven

Newcastle scored seven goals in a 7-2 victory in League Division 2 against Darwen at St James's Park. The goals coming courtesy of a hat-trick for Willie Wardrope and a goal apiece for Andy Aitken, James Collins, Malcolm Lennox and Bob McDermidd, his first of only two goals he scored in his 64 appearances.

Though he was a right-back so you wouldn't have expected many in those days as defenders were 'real' defenders and didn't venture that often over the half-way line.

1957: Scoring Debut

John "Jackie" Bell scored on his debut today in the League Division 1 fixture with Luton Town. Together with a brace from Len White this ensured Newcastle ran out comfortable winners 3-0 at Kenilworth Road.

1974: Five Star Performance

Newcastle put five past Chelsea at St James's Park, without reply, in a League Division 1 fixture.

The goals courtesy of two from Malcolm Macdonald, and one apiece for Paul Cannell, Alan Kennedy and Stewart Barrowclough.

First Meeting on November-16:

Year	V	F	A	R	Opposition	Competition
1935	H	2	1	W	Doncaster Rovers	Division 2

Debut on November-16:

Year	Player	Opposition
1957	John Russell Bell (Wing Half)	Luton Town

Born on November-16:

Year	Player	Position	Years
1911	Jackie Cape	Outside Right	1930 - 1934
1995	Rolando Aarons	Midfield	2014 - current

November-17

1991: Tyne-wear Derby No. 124

Newcastle travelled to Roker Park to face Sunderland in a League Division 2 fixture, the 124th Tyne-Wear Derby. Peter Davenport gave a 1-0 lead to Sunderland going into the break but Newcastle equalised through Liam O'Brien in the second half and the game ended honours even at 1-1.

Debut on November-17:

Year	Player	Opposition
1923	William Gibson (Left Half)	Preston North End
1934	Norman Tapken (Goalkeeper)	Bradford City

Born on November-17:

Year	Player	Position	Years
1935	Robert Douglas Cummings	Centre Forward	1954 - 1965

November-18

1977: McGarry Moves In

Bill McGarry appointed as manager. Regarded as one of the game's strict disciplinarians, McGarry seemed the ideal candidate to take over at Newcastle after the disastrous "player power" reign of Dinnis.

2000: Tyne-wear Derby No. 132

Newcastle hosted Sunderland in a Premiership fixture, the 132nd Tyne-Wear Derby. Gary Speed gave Newcastle a 1-0 lead going into the break but Don Hutchison and Niall Quinn scored for Sunderland in the second half to take the game 2-1.

First Meeting on November-18:

Year	V	F	A	R	Opposition	Competition
1893	A	3	5	L	Northwich Victoria	Division 2
1969	A	0	0	D	FC Porto	Inter Cities Fairs Cup

Born on November-18:

Year	Player	Position	Years
1950	Tommy Cassidy	Midfield	1970 - 1980

November-19

1910: Tyne-wear Derby No. 29
Newcastle hosted Sunderland in a League Division 1 fixture, the 29th Tyne-Wear Derby. Albert Shepherd scored for Newcastle, Tim Coleman scored for Sunderland, both goals coming in the first half, and the game ended honours even at 1-1.

1921: Tyne-wear Derby No. 45
Newcastle hosted Sunderland in a League Division 1 fixture, the 45th Tyne-Wear Derby. Newcastle took a 2-0 lead into the break thanks to goals from Tom McDonald and Bob McIntosh. However Sunderland scored twice themselves in the second half and the game ended honours even at 2-2.

1938: One and Only Appearance
George Joseph Bradley, Defender, made his one and only appearance today for Newcastle when they travelled to Ewood Park for a League Division 2 fixture against Blackburn Rovers. Trailing 3-0 at half-time Newcastle could not score, and Blackburn didn't add to their score, so that was how the game ended, a comfortable 3-0 win for Blackburn.

1957: John Allen, R.I.P.
John, more commonly known as Jack, scored 41 times in his 90 appearances for Newcastle, a very impressive record. Of course who could forget what were probably his two most important goals? He scored both goals in Newcastle's 2 - 1 win over Arsenal in the 1932 FA Cup Final.

2007: Ken Leek, R.I.P.
Ken only made 14 appearances for Newcastle, but in doing so he scored six goals. In 2014 his grandson, Karl Darlow, was signed by Newcastle.

First Meeting on November-19:

Year	V	F	A	R	Opposition	Competition
1892	A	2	3	L	Middlesbrough Ironopolis	Northern League
1996	A	1	1	D	Metz	UEFA Cup

Debut on November-19:

Year	Player	Opposition
1892	Peter Watson (Right Back)	Middlesbrough Ironopolis
1938	George Joseph Bradley (Defence) Benny Craig (Right-Back)	Blackburn Rovers
1988	William Francis O'Brien (Midfield) Rob McDonald (Midfield)	Millwall

November-20

In the 16 games Newcastle have played on this day they have won ten, drawn one and lost the other five.

Within those five defeats two of them saw Newcastle conceding five goals.

1965 saw then lose 5-1 to Leicester City in a League Division 1, at St James's Park, and **2010** saw them lose 5-1 to Bolton Wanderers in a Premiership fixture at of the Reebok Stadium.

There however some better news...

1926: Five Star Performance

Newcastle put five past Birmingham City in a League Division 1 fixture at St James's Park. The goals coming from Hughie Gallacher, Frank Hudspeth, Tom McDonald, Bob McKay and Stan Seymour.

Birmingham did score one themselves in the second half so the game ended 5-1 in Newcastle's favour.

1968: Fairs Cup Progression

Newcastle won the second leg of their Fairs Cup Second Round tie with Sporting Lisbon at St James's Park with a single goal scored by Pop Robson on 10 minutes.

With the first leg having been drawn 1-1 it was enough to see Newcastle through to the next round.

First Meeting on November-20:

Year	V	F	A	R	Opposition	Competition
1991	H	3	2	W	Southend United	Division 2

Debut on November-20:

Year	Player	Opposition
1971	Alex Reid (Midfield)	Nottingham Forest

Born on November-20:

Year	Player	Position	Years
1978	Paul Robinson	Forward	1999 - 2000

November-21

1931: Five Star Performance

Newcastle put five past West Bromwich Albion in a League Division 1 fixture at St James's Park. The goals coming from John Allen, Jimmy Boyd, Jimmy Richardson, with two, and Sammy Weaver. West Bromwich did score one themselves in the second half so the game ended 5-1 in Newcastle's favour.

1934: Jimmy Lawrence, R.I.P.

Lawrence has appeared for Newcastle more times than any other player in their history - 498 - and is surely their greatest ever goalkeeper. His consistency was legendary, much to the disappointment of several good goalkeepers at Newcastle who could not get a game because of him.

In a team that was to be renowned throughout the country as the "Edwardian Masters" Lawrence won three League Championships, and the FA Cup. When making his last appearance for Newcastle in April 1922 Lawrence was 42 years old!

Born on November-21:

Year	Player	Position	Years
1950	Thomas Brooks Craig	Midfield	1974 - 1978
1968	Mark Robinson	Defence	1993 - 1994
1995	Jamie Sterry	Defence	2015 - current

November-22

1919: Tyne-wear Derby No. 41

Newcastle hosted Sunderland in a League Division 1 fixture, the 41st Tyne-Wear Derby. With a goal in either half from Charlie Buchan, Sunderland took the game 2-0.

1924: Harris Hat-Trick

Neil Harris scored a hat-trick in the 4-0 victory over Birmingham City in a League Division 1 fixture at St James's Park. Newcastle's other goal was scored by Willie Cowan.

1930: Tyne-wear Derby No. 63

Newcastle travelled to Roker Park to face Sunderland in a League Division 1 fixture, the 63rd Tyne-Wear Derby.

With two goals each for Jimmy Connor and Billy Eden and a one from Bobby Gurney, Sunderland took the game 5-0.

Debut on November-22:

Year	Player	Opposition
1958	John Mitten (Winger)	West Bromwich Albion
1978	Gary Nicholson (Left Wing)	Cambridge United

Born on November-22:

Year	Player	Position	Years
1983	Peter Iain Ramage	Defence	2004 - 2008

November-23

1895: Five Star Performance

Newcastle put five past Rendall without reply in their FA Cup Qualifying Round 3 tie at St James's Park. It was two for Andy Aitken with one apiece for Willie Wardrope, James Logan and Willie Thompson.

1907: Eight is Great!

Newcastle scored eight goals, without reply, against Birmingham City in a League Division 1 fixture at St James's Park. A Jock Rutherford hat-trick, two each from Jim Howie and Colin Veitch and one from Bill Appleyard gave Newcastle a very comfortable 8-0 victory.

1935: Scoring Debut

Archie Livingstone scored on his debut today in the League Division 2 fixture with Sheffield United.

Unfortunately it was nothing more than a consolation goal for Newcastle as they suffered a heavy 5-1 defeat at Bramall Lane.

First Meeting on November-23:

Year	V	F	A	R	Opposition	Competition
1895	H	5	0	W	Rendall	FA Cup
2006	H	2	1	W	RC Celta de Vigo	UEFA Cup

Debut on November-23:

Year	Player	Opposition
1912	James Fleming (Centre Forward)	Tottenham Hotspur
1935	Archie Livingstone (Inside Forward)	Sheffield United
1998	Garry Brady (Midfield)	Everton

Born on November-23:

Year	Player	Position	Years
1909	Tom Russell	Left Back	1934 - 1935
1966	Kevin William Gallacher	Forward	1999 - 2001

November-24

1951 saw Newcastle at Maine Road for a League Division 1 fixture against Manchester City. A goalless first half was instantly forgotten about as the second half produced five goals, with Newcastle just shading it 3-2. Their goals coming from Jackie Milburn, Bobby Mitchell and Jorge Robledo.

The League Division 2 fixture in **1979** against Swansea City at Vetch Field had a bizarre turn of events. Shortly after Swansea scored their second goal the referee - listed in "The Pink" as "Mrs E Read (Bristol)" - collided with Swansea's Robbie James and, with Read grounded, clutching his back, Newcastle's Stuart Boam picked up the whistle and was the one who stopped play. Newcastle won the game 3-2, with goals from Terry Hibbitt, Billy Rafferty and Alan Shoulder.

First Meeting on November-24:

Year	V	F	A	R	Opposition	Competition
1906	A	1	2	L	Bristol City	Division 1
1979	A	3	2	W	Swansea City*	Division 2
1992	H	0	1	L	Ascoli	Anglo-Italian Cup

*Swansea City were previously Swansea Town, first played on 30/01/1915.

Debut on November-24:

Year	Player	Opposition
1984	Gary Megson (Midfield)	Southampton
1990	Tommy Gaynor (Forward)	Watford

Born on November-24:

Year	Player	Position	Years
1952	David Crosson	Right Back	1972 - 1975
1957	David McLean	Midfield	1975 - 1978
1958	Robert Sime Aitken	Central Defence	1990 - 1991
1967	Gavin Maguire	Central Defence	1991

November-25

1933: Scoring Debut

Ron Williams scored on his debut today in the League Division 1 fixture with Aston Villa. It helped Newcastle to a narrow 3-2 victory at Villa Park. Tommy Lang and Sammy Weaver scoring Newcastle's other two goals.

1950: Second Half Recovery

Charlton Athletic took a 1-0 lead into the break at St James's Park in a League Division 1 fixture. They scored again in the second half but Newcastle through two goals from Jackie Milburn and one from Tommy Walker managed to secure a 3-2 victory.

1967 and **2004** saw Newcastle earning 4-0 victories over Sheffield Wednesday and FC Sochaux Montbeliard. The first, a League Division 1 fixture at St James's Park the goals came from Albert Bennet, with two, Wyn Davies and David Elliott. The second at Stade Auguste Bonal in the UEFA Cup the goals came from Lee Bowyer, Shola Ameobi and Laurent Robert.

First Meeting on November-25:

Year	V	F	A	R	Opposition	Competition
2004	A	4	0	W	FC Sochaux Montbeliard	UEFA Cup

Debut on November-25:

Year	Player	Opposition
1893	Thomas Rogers (Left Back)	Liverpool
1899	Alexander Gardner (Right Half)	Preston North End

Debut on November-25:

Year	Player	Opposition
1933	Ronald Williams (Centre Forward)	Aston Villa

Born on November-25:

Year	Player	Position	Years
1897	James Keen	Outside Left	1922 - 1923
1965	David Kelly	Forward	1991 - 1993

November-26

1892: Seven Heaven in East End's Penultimate Game

Newcastle East End, in their penultimate appearance before becoming 'United' faced Darlington at Feethams in the Northern League. Newcastle duly put seven past them with no reply. The goals coming courtesy of a hat-trick from Joe Wallace, one apiece from Harry Reay, Willie Thompson, Jock Sorely and a Darlington 'own goal'.

1921: Tyne-wear Derby No. 46

Newcastle travelled to Roker Park to face Sunderland in a League Division 1 fixture, the 46th Tyne-Wear Derby.

With no goals being scored honours were even at 0-0.

1927: One and Only Appearance

William Halliday, Inside Left, made his one and only appearance today for Newcastle when they travelled to Filbert Street for a League Division 1 fixture against Leicester City.

Trailing 1-0 at half-time Newcastle conceded a further two in the second half and with not being able to score themselves Leicester were the easy winners 3-0.

Incidentally, William's brother, David Halliday, was quite a goal scoring hero, none more so than when he spent four years at Sunderland!

1932: Tyne-wear Derby No. 67

Newcastle travelled to Roker Park to face Sunderland in a League Division 1 fixture, the 67th Tyne-Wear Derby. A goal in either half gave Newcastle a 2-0 victory. The scorers being John Allen and Tommy Lang.

First Meeting on November-26:

Year	V	F	A	R	Opposition	Competition
1898	A	1	3	L	Derby County	Division 1
1938	H	2	2	D	Millwall	Division 2

Debut on November-26:

Year	Player	Opposition
1927	William Halliday (Inside Left)	Leicester City
1960	Albert Joseph Scanlon (Outside Left) Herbert Garrow (Goalkeeper)	Blackburn Rovers
1997	Aaron William Hughes (Defence)	Barcelona

November-27

1974: First Leg of Final Lost

Newcastle faced Southampton in the first leg of the Texaco Cup Final and were beaten 1-0 - well it was at The Dell, no one would have expected Newcastle to come away from there with a win, definitely the most 'hoodoo' ground for them! Newcastle were of course the holders. Incidentally, Mick Channon got Southampton's goal.

2011: Gary Speed MBE, R.I.P

The sad news broke this morning of the death of Gary Speed, former Newcastle star and Wales manager at the time.

Debut on November-27:

Year	Player	Opposition
1982	Howard Gayle (Wing)	Cambridge United

Born on November-27:

Year	Player	Position	Years
1965	Scott Sellars	Midfield	1993 - 1995
1969	David Robinson	Forward	1986 - 1992

November-28

1908: Scoring Debut

Albert Shepherd scored on his debut today in the League Division 1 fixture with Nottingham Forest. With George Wilson, Alex Higgins and Bob

Liddell also scoring, Newcastle were easy 4-0 winners at the City Ground.

1931: Tyne-wear Derby No. 65

Newcastle travelled to Roker Park to face Sunderland in a League Division 1 fixture, the 65th Tyne-Wear Derby. Newcastle took a 3-0 lead into the break and both teams scored one each in the second half, Newcastle therefore taking a 4-1 victory. Their scorers being Jimmy Boyd, Tommy Lang, Harry McMenemey and Jimmy Richardson. Joe Devine who had only just left St James's Park scored Sunderland's goal.

1998: Scoring Debut

Duncan Ferguson scored twice on his debut today in the Premiership fixture with Wimbledon. Nobby Solano also scored for Newcastle thus ensuring a 3-1 win at St James's Park.

Debut on November-28:

Year	Player	Opposition
1903	Tom Wills (Left Back)	Bury
1908	Albert Shepherd (Centre Forward)	Nottingham Forest
1998	Stephen Alan Harper (Goalkeeper) Duncan Ferguson (Forward)	Wimbledon
1999	Cristova Helder (Centre Back) Jose Rodrigues Alves Fumaca (Midfield)	Tottenham Hotspur
2009	Fabrice Pancrate (Wing)	Swansea City

Born on November-28:

Year	Player	Position	Years
1891	John Alderson	Goalkeeper	1913 - 1919
1903	Alec Betton	Centre Half	1931 - 1934
1933	Alex Tait	Centre Forward	1952 - 1960
1948	Michael Roger Channon	Forward	1982 - 1982
1959	Martin Richard Thomas	Goalkeeper	1983 - 1988
1960	Kenny Wharton	Left Back/Midfield	1978 - 1989

November-29

1902 saw Newcastle take a heavy 7-0 defeat at the hands of Aston Villa at Villa Park.

If that wasn't bad enough what happened in 1919 is worse...

1919: Tyne-wear Derby No. 42

Newcastle hosted Sunderland in a League Division 1 fixture, the 42nd Tyne-Wear Derby. Newcastle took a 2-0 lead into the break with goals from Billy Hibbert and Ray Robinson. However it was all Sunderland in the second half and they scored three times through Jackie Mordue and two from Barney Travers to take the game 3-2.

Debut on November-29:

Year	Player	Opposition
1902	Henry Stenhouse (Outside Right)	Aston Villa

November-30

1901: Five Star Performance

Newcastle put five past Grimsby Town in a League Division 1 fixture at St James's Park. A hat-trick from Jock Peddie and one apiece for Richard Roberts and Ron Orr secured the victory. Grimsby did manage a single goal in the second half but it was still a comfortable 5-1 win for Newcastle.

1935: Five Star Performance

Newcastle put five past Nottingham Forest in a League Division 2 fixture at St James's Park. David Fairhurst scored two for Newcastle in this game - the only two goals he scored in 285 appearances. Jack Smith also got two and Albert Harris scored the other. Forest did get a goal themselves so the game ended 5-1 to Newcastle.

1968 saw Newcastle put four past Southampton and **1986** saw them put four past West Ham United. Both were League Division 1 fixtures at St James's Park. Pop Robson, with two, Alan Foggon and Keith Dyson were the scorers against Southampton whilst it was Neil McDonald, Andy Thomas, with two, and Darren Jackson who scored against West Ham United.

First Meeting on November-30:

Year	V	F	A	R	Opposition	Competition
2006	A	0	0	D	Eintracht Frankfurt	UEFA Cup

Debut on November-30:

Year	Player	Opposition
1929	Sammy Weaver (Midfield)	Arsenal
1935	Hugh Bulloch (Centre Half)	Nottingham Forest

DECEMBER

December-01

1950: Martin Moves Out

George Martin resigned as manager (going to Aston Villa) and was replaced by a Directors Committee led by Stan Seymour.

1962: One and Only Appearance

George Watkin, Centre Forward, made his one and only appearance today for Newcastle when they travelled to Gigg Lane for a League Division 2 fixture against Bury. With neither side managing to score honours were even.

1990: Newcastle Lose Nine Goal Thriller

A hat-trick from Micky Quinn and a goal from Liam O'Brien still wasn't enough as Newcastle lost 5-4 to Leicester City at Filbert Street in a League Division 2 fixture. The Foxes goals being a hat-trick from Kelly and a goal apiece for Fenwick and Oldfield.

Debut on December-01:

Year	Player	Opposition
1894	John Hynd (Goalkeeper)	Grimsby Town
1962	George Watkin (Centre Forward)	Bury
1979	Stephen Carney (Defence)	Fulham
1984	Joseph Ball Allon (Forward)	Stoke City
1990	Gavin Peacock (Midfield)	Leicester City

Born on December-01:

Year	Player	Position	Years
1905	Allan Taylor	Goalkeeper	1925 - 1926
1915	Arthur Douglas Frost	Forward	1939 - 1939

December-02

1905: One and Only Appearance

Hugh Bolton, Centre Forward, made his one and only appearance today for Newcastle when they travelled to Bramall Lane for a League Division 2 fixture against Sheffield United. With Newcastle failing to score and Sheffield getting a goal in each half they were victorious by 2-0 that day.

As an aside Bolton went to Everton and was part of their FA Cup winning team of 1906 - when they beat Newcastle in the final!

1961: Tyne-wear Derby No. 92

Newcastle hosted Sunderland in a League Division 1 fixture, the 92nd Tyne-Wear Derby. Newcastle took a 1-0 lead into the break but even though they scored again in the second half Sunderland scored twice so it was honours even at 2-2. John McGuigan and Len White were Newcastle's scorers whilst Brian Clough got both of Sunderland's goals.

Debut on December-02:

Year	Player	Opposition
1899	John Carr (Left Back)	Nottingham Forest
1905	Hugh Bolton (Forward)	Sheffield United
1978	Mick Martin (Midfield)	Crystal Palace

Born on December-02:

Year	Player	Position	Years
1935	Jimmy Kerray	Inside Forward	1962 - 1963
1968	David Batty	Midfield	1996 - 1998
1992	Massadio Haidara	Left Back	2013 - current
1995	Lubomir Satka	Defence	2014 - current

December-03

1892: East End Sign-Off with 5-1 Victory

Newcastle East End played their final game today - as they were to become "United" in a matter of days.

They signed-off in some style too, with a comprehensive 5-1 victory over Stockton in the Northern League.

So the last ever goals for Newcastle East End were scored by Willy Graham, Bobby Crielly, Willie Thompson, Jock Sorley and Joe Wallace.

1904: Scoring Debut

Joe McClarence scored on his debut today in the League Division 1 fixture with Blackburn Rovers. With this being the only goal of the game it ensured the points stayed at St James's Park.

1910: Six of the Best

A hat-trick from Albert Shepherd, a brace from Alex Higgins and a goal from Jim Stewart saw Newcastle brush aside Bradford City by 6-1 in their Division 1 match at St James's Park.

1986: Inauguration of the Full Members Cup

Following the ban of English clubs from European competition for an indefinite period after the Heysel Stadium disaster in 1985 the Full Members Cup was designed as a domestic answer to the void left behind. Newcastle's involvement in this inaugural year ended swiftly at the first hurdle with a 5-2 defeat at the hands of Everton.

2012: Newcastle Welcome Back Brother They Never Used

Wigan Athletic visited St James's Park in a Premiership fixture and in their side was Gary Caldwell, brother of Steven, both at Newcastle at the same time, but Gary never made a senior appearance. Newcastle won comfortably 3-0, with two goals from Demba Ba and one from Gael Bigirimana, however they were playing against ten men from as early as the 12th minute which is when Wigan had Maynor Figueroa sent off for a foul on Papiss Cisse, which gave Newcastle a penalty too, which was the first of Ba's two.

First Meeting on December-03:

Year	V	F	A	R	Opposition	Competition
1892	H	5	1	W	Stockton	Northern League
1898	H	3	0	W	West Bromwich Albion	Division 1

Debut on December-03:

Year	Player	Opposition
1904	Joe McClarence (Inside Forward)	Blackburn Rovers
1910	Francis Hudspeth (Left Back)	Bradford City
1921	James Low (Outside Right)	Middlesbrough
1927	William Carlton (Right Half)	Liverpool
1977	Stuart Robinson (Left Wing)	Leicester City
1986	Anthony Nesbit (Midfield)	Everton
1988	Archibald Gourlay (Midfield)	Luton Town

Born on December-03:

Year	Player	Position	Years
1951	John Burridge	Goalkeeper	1989 - 1991

December-04

1909: Newcastle on Wrong End of 11 Goal Thriller
Four goals by Albert Shepherd and a goal from Jim Howie saw Newcastle going in at half-time at Anfield 5-2 up. In a thrilling second half - *for Liverpool fans anyway* - the score ended up 6-5 in Liverpool's favour. Two of Liverpool's goals coming from Ron Orr whom Newcastle had sold to them in April the previous year.

1976: Eight Goal Game at Highbury Ends in Defeat
Two goals from Mickey Burns and a goal from Alan Gowling weren't enough for Newcastle as they ended up losing this eight goal game against Arsenal at Highbury 5-3.

1988: Smith Takes Over
Jim Smith appointed as manager. Smith arrived at Newcastle with an impressive résumé, having won back-to-back promotions for Oxford United from Division 3 to 2, then 2 to 1 - the first time in Oxford's history they had been in the "top-flight".

Both promotions were as Champions of the respective divisions too. He had also taken Queens Park Rangers to the League Cup final, ironically to lose to Oxford!

Debut on December-04:

Year	Player	Opposition
1920	Andrew Gray (Half Back)	Aston Villa
1974	Peter Anthony Kelly (Full-Back)	Chester City
1993	Michael Richard Jeffrey (Forward)	Tottenham Hotspur

Born on December-04:

Year	Player	Position	Years
1899	Charles William Spencer	Central Midfield	1921 - 1928
1900	Chris Swan	Inside Right	1919 - 1923
1943	Leslie O'Neill	Midfield	1961 - 1965

December-05

1908: Tyne-Wear Derby No. 22 - Black Day on Tyneside
Newcastle suffered heavily at the hands of arch Rivals Sunderland - losing 9-1 at St James's Park!

With the game poised evenly at 1-1 at half-time who was to know, or even remotely guess, at the turmoil that would happen in the second half. Sunderland were rampant scoring eight times - the last five of these coming in a spread of only 9 minutes!

1931: Only Game With No Corners?

It is strongly believed that today's game against Portsmouth was the first, *and possibly only ever*, game played where neither side won a corner. It also ended up with no goals either!

Born on December-05:

Year	Player	Position	Years
1922	Bobby Cowell	Right-Back	1943 - 1956
1937	Ronald James McGarry	Inside Forward	1962 - 1967
1961	Alan Davies	Wing	1985 - 1987

December-06

2010: Hughton Sacked

In a move that stunned most Newcastle fans, *and players so it seems*, Newcastle owner Mike Ashley sacked manager Chris Hughton. Having been 'caretaker' manager on three occasions Hughton had been given the job on a permanent basis after they had been relegated from the Premiership.

He brought them straight back up again - as Champions. It was quite a bombshell to hear the news of his sacking.

Debut on December-06:

Year	Player	Opposition
1919	Andrew Smailes (Inside Right)	Sheffield United
2014	Jak Alnwick (Goalkeeper)	Chelsea

Born on December-06:

Year	Player	Position	Years
1919	Benny Craig	Right Back	1938 - 1950
1951	David Mills	Forward	1982 - 1984
1956	Peter Anthony Kelly	Full-Back	1973 - 1981
1967	Ian Bogie	Midfield	1986 - 1989

December-07

1929: One and Only Appearance

Joseph William Wilson, Centre Half, made his one and only appearance today for Newcastle when they hosted Aston Villa in a League Division 2 fixture. Goals from Hughie Gallacher and Sammy Weaver were not enough to win the game but they did ensure Newcastle shared the spoils as the game ended 2-2.

As fate would have it Joe's son, Carl, was to later sign for Newcastle - and he too was to make only a solitary appearance.

Debut on December-07:

Year	Player	Opposition
1907	James Ridley (Outside Right)	Everton
1929	Joseph William Wilson (Centre Half)	Aston Villa
1935	Alfred Garnham (Defence)	Norwich City
1946	Dick Burke (Full Back)	Plymouth Argyle
1974	Tony Bell (Goalkeeper)	Tottenham Hotspur
1985	Billy Whitehurst (Forward)	Luton Town
1991	David Kelly (Forward) Paul Bodin (Left Back)	Port Vale

December-08

Of the 14 times Newcastle have played on this day they have lost no fewer the eight times! Of the remaining six they have drawn three and therefore only won three.

The first win, in **1923**, was a 2-0 victory in a League Division 1 fixture against Burnley. The second, in **1962**, was a 4-1 victory against Rotherham United in a League Division 2 fixture and the final one was in **2007** which was a Premiership fixture against Birmingham City. All three were played at St James's Park.

In the Burnley game the goals were scored by Stan Seymour and Tom McDonald, in the Rotherham game they came from Ken Hale, with two, William Tuohy and Jimmy Kerray.

In the Birmingham game the scorers were Obafemi Martins and the one and only goal from Habib Beye.

First Meeting on December-08:

Year	R	F	A	V	Opposition	Competition
1992	D	2	2	H	AS Bari	Anglo-Italian Cup

Debut on December-08:

Year	Player	Opposition
1900	Matt Scott (Left Back)	Sheffield United
1906	Chris Duffy (Outside Left)	Sheffield United
1973	Denis Laughton (Midfield)	Birmingham City
1992	Richard Appleby (Midfield)	AS Bari

Born on December-08:

Year	Player	Position	Years
1884	Wilfred Low	Centre Half	1909 - 1924
1912	Clarence Alfred Theaker	Goalkeeper	1938 - 1947
1914	William Leighton	Inside Right	1932 - 1938
1951	Terence McDermott	Midfield	1973 - 1984
1951	Rob McDonald	Midfield	1988 - 1989
1966	Leslie Ferdinand	Forward	1995 - 1997

December-09

1892: United are Born

At the beginning of the season Newcastle East End incorporated what remained of Newcastle West End and moved into their ground of St James's Park and today changed their name to Newcastle United. The rest, as they say, is history...

1925: Scoring Debut

Thomas "Tucker" Mordue scored on his debut in the League Division 1 fixture with Sheffield United. Willie Cowan and Frank Hudspeth also scored making it a 3-1 victory to Newcastle at St James's Park.

2010: Pardew Appointed

Just three days after the sacking of the very popular Chris Hughton as Newcastle's manager they today announced that Alan Pardew would be taking over on a five-and-a-half year deal. It certainly did not go down well with the majority of fans! Nothing to do with Pardew of course, more still the resentment felt over the dismissal of Hughton.

Debut on December-09:

Year	Player	Opposition
1893	Thomas Bartlett (Inside Left)	Notts County
1925	Thomas Mordue (Centre Forward)	Sheffield United
1978	Alan Shoulder (Forward)	Stoke City
2006	Paul Huntingdon (Centre-Half)	Blackburn Rovers

Born on December-09:

Year	Player	Position	Years
1884	Alexander Mutch	Goalkeeper	1922 - 1924
1916	Eddie Connelly	Inside Forward	1935 - 1938
1961	Peter Haddock	Defence	1978 - 1986

December-10

1892: United's First Game

Having officially changed their name yesterday from Newcastle East End to Newcastle United this was the first game to be played and it was against Middlesbrough Ironopolis. Fitting therefore that it was at St James's Park, but on what was said to be a "cold and wintery afternoon" it certainly did not produce the result that was wanted!

In the first half Newcastle were playing downhill[1] and they had the better of the game, and quite a few decent shots on goal, only to find that the 'Nops goalkeeper was in great form. Their defender, Elliott was said to be playing "out of his skin" as well. For almost all of the half Newcastle were on top but could not find a way through. Then towards the end of the half disaster struck when the 'Nops had a good bit of play that saw their forwards break out and McReddie scored. Being the only goal of the half Newcastle were gutted to be going in 1-0 down.

The start of the second half saw the 'Nops pulling out all the stops in an effort to increase their lead and they got a second through McArthur. This spurred Newcastle to go on a charge. Their half-backs started to get more and more into the game, bringing a reward when Reay scored to get one back. With the 'bit between their teeth' now Newcastle piled on the pressure searching for the equaliser, but once again the stout defending and goalkeeping by Ironopolis kept them out so the game ended 2-1 and all their efforts were wasted.

[1] St. James's Park had a very bad slope in those days! It was measured at 18 feet from goal to goal - meaning the goal-line at the Gallowgate end was 18 feet below the one at the Leazes end.

1960: Ten Goals - But No Winner

Newcastle and West Ham United played out a 10 goal thriller today at St James's Park but with the score being 5-5 there was no winner.

Going in a half-time 2-1 down, Newcastle were to fall further behind in the second half and when the score reached 5-1 to West Ham it seemed all done and dusted.

Newcastle however managed to rally themselves and eventually came back with four goals of their own to earn an unexpected 5-5 draw.

Debut on December-10:

Year	Player	Opposition
1927	Thomas Evans (Left Back)	Arsenal
1977	Kevin Carr (Goalkeeper)	Queens Park Rangers
1988	Kevin Brock (Midfield)	Wimbledon

Born on December-10:

Year	Player	Position	Years
1872	William Lindsay	Full Back	1898 - 1900
1885	Albert Shepherd	Centre Forward	1908 - 1914
1926	John Duncan	Forward	1950 - 1953
1990	Kazenga LuaLua	Midfield	2005 - 2011
1991	Bradden Inman	Midfield	2008 - 2013

December-11

1948: One and Only Appearance

Albert Clark, Wing Half, made his one and only appearance today for Newcastle when they hosted Sheffield United in a League Division 1 fixture.

In a tight affair goals from Jackie Milburn, George Stobbart and an 'own goal' from Cox gave Newcastle a narrow 3-2 victory.

1965: Wrong End of 7 Goal Thriller

Newcastle travelled to the Boleyn Ground, Upton Park, to face West Ham

United and in a game that saw seven goals Newcastle were on the wrong end, losing 4-3. They had been losing 3-0 at half-time so it was an impressive second-half performance from them with goals by Albert Bennett, Jim Iley and Bryan 'Pop' Robson but it was to no avail.

1971: Scoring Debut

Viv Busby scored on his debut today in the League Division 1 fixture with West Bromwich Albion. With Malcolm Macdonald getting a brace this was an easy 3-0 victory for Newcastle at The Hawthorns.

1974: Newcastle Win Texaco Cup for the Second Time

Newcastle and Southampton contested the two-legged Texaco Cup final. In this, the second leg, Newcastle won the game 3-0 - with an aggregate score of 3-1 after the game went into extra-time. Goals from John Tudor, Alex Bruce and Paul Cannell ensured the cup stayed on Tyneside, as Newcastle were of course the holders having won it last year against Burnley.

Debut on December-11:

Year	Player	Opposition
1909	Robert Waugh (Right Back)	Aston Villa
1948	Albert Clark (Wing Half)	Sheffield United
1971	Vivian Dennis Busby (Forward)	West Bromwich Albion

Born on December-11:

Year	Player	Position	Years
1928	George Hannah	Inside Forward	1949 - 1957

December-12

1904: Scoring Debut

Hugh Kilpatrick Gallacher - "Wee Hughie" - a goal scoring legend at Newcastle, scored twice on his debut today in the League Division 1 fixture with Everton. Despite this, and a further goal from Stan Seymour, Newcastle could only manage a 3-3 draw at St James's Park. This because of a hat-trick from the Everton's own goal scoring legend, Dixie Dean.

1936: Newcastle Put 5 Past Swansea

Swansea, then known as "Town", not "City" were the visitors to St James's Park today in a League Division 2 fixture. With two goals apiece from Tim Rogers and Jack Smith and one from Tommy Usher Newcastle were the comfortable victors 5-1.

1959: Seven Goal Thriller at Kenilworth Road

Two goals from George Eastham and one apiece for Gordon Hughes and George Luke gave Newcastle an impressive 4-3 victory over Luton Town in this Division 1 fixture . The game had been delicately poised at 2-2 at half-time but Newcastle scored twice again in the second half to take the points.

1964: Newcastle Put 5 Past Northampton

A hat-trick from Ron McGarry, a goal from Trevor Hockey and an own goal gave Newcastle an easy afternoon beating Northampton Town 5-0 at St James's Park in a League Division 2 fixture.

Debut on December-12:

Year	Player	Opposition
1925	Hugh Kilpatrick Gallacher (Forward)	Everton

Born on December-12:

Year	Player	Position	Years
1880	James Hay	Left Half	1911 - 1919
1966	Lee Payne	Left Wing	1988 - 1989
1974	Nolberto Albino Solano	Right Wing	1998 - 2007
1975	Craig Moore	Centre Back	2005 - 2007

December-13

1930: Scoring Debut

Henry "Harry" Bedford scored on his debut today in the League Division 1 fixture with Leicester City.

Together with two goals from Duncan Hutchinson, a goal from Jimmy Boyd and an 'own goal' Newcastle ran out 5-2 winners at St James's Park.

2003: Spurs Sank at St James's Park

Newcastle put four past Tottenham Hotspur today at St James's Park in a Premiership fixture and with no reply from the visitors were easy 4-0 victors.

The goals came courtesy of two goals for Laurent Robert (35 & 55 and two for Alan Shearer (59 & 66). In the Tottenham team that day was defender Stephen Carr who was to come to Newcastle in the close season.

Debut on December-13:

Year	Player	Opposition
1902	William Wilson (Half Back)	Bury
1913	Stanley Hardy (Inside Left)	Sheffield United
1930	Harry Bedford (Inside Forward)	Leicester City

Born on December-13:

Year	Player	Position	Years
1914	Stanley Docking	Inside Left	1934 - 1938
1944	Thomas Gibb	Midfield	1968 - 1975
1955	Glenn Victor Roeder	Central Defence	1983 - 1988
1956	Malcolm Brown	Right Back	1983 - 1985
1970	David Roche	Midfield	1986 - 1993

December-14

1907: Scoring Debut

George Wilson scored twice on his debut today in the League Division 1 fixture with Liverpool. With Jock Rutherford also getting a brace and Bill Appleyard getting in on the act Newcastle were easy 5-1 winners at Anfield.. Parkinson scoring Liverpool's solitary goal.

1929: Elland Road Rout

Newcastle travelled to Elland Road and were well and truly beaten 5-2 by Leeds United in a League Division 2 fixture. Hughie Gallacher scored both Newcastle's goals, one in each half, but with Longden and Jennings each getting two also, and a goal from Wainscoat for good measure, Newcastle were never truly in this game.

Debut on December-14:

Year	Player	Opposition
1907	George Wilson (Outside Left)	Liverpool
1985	Paul Stephenson (Midfield)	Southampton

Born on December-14:

Year	Player	Position	Years
1960	Brian Ferguson	Midfield	1979 - 1980
1960	Chris Roland Waddle	Midfield	1980 - 1985

Born on December-14:

Year	Player	Position	Years
1967	Scott Sloan	Forward	1990 - 1991
1979	Jean Alain Boumsong	Central Defence	2005 - 2006
1979	Michael Owen	Forward	2005 - 2009

December-15

1923: Tyne-Wear Derby No. 49

Newcastle travelled to Roker Park to face Sunderland in a League Division 1 fixture, the 49th Tyne-Wear Derby. Goals from Stan Seymour and Neil Harris weren't enough as Sunderland scored three through Jock Paterson and two for Arthur Hawes. All five goals being scored in the first half.

1951: Newcastle Win Nine Goal Thriller at Stoke

Two goals each from Reg Davis and Jorge Robledo and a goal from John Duncan saw Newcastle edge this Division 1 fixture at the Victoria Ground winning 5-4. It had been 2-2 at half-time but Newcastle triumphed.

Debut on December-15:

Year	Player	Opposition
1962	Ronald James McGarry (Inside Forward)	Cardiff City

Born on December-15:

Year	Player	Position	Years
1935	James Iley	Wing Half	1962 - 1969

December-16

1893: Scoring Debut

Robert "Bobby" Willis scored on his debut today in the League Division 2 fixture with Small Heath. With Tom Crate, Joe Wallace and William Graham also scoring Newcastle were easy 4-1 victors at Muntz Street.

1895: First & Only

Newcastle were drawn against Durham based Tow Law Town of the Northern League in Qualifying Round 4 of the FA Cup. This is the one and only time these two teams have met and Newcastle were easy victors 4-0. Willie Wardrope, Willie Thompson, Malcolm Lennox and James Stott being Newcastle's scorers.

1911: Six for Newcastle in Eight Goal Game

Newcastle scored six times - with six different scorers in this 6-2 victory over Aston Villa at St James's Park in this Division 1 game.

The six scorers were: Sandy Higgins, Billy Hibbert, Jimmy Stewart, Jock Rutherford, James "Dun" Hay and Bill McCracken who scored his from the penalty spot.

2004: One and Only Appearance

Lewis Guy, Forward, made his one and only appearance today for Newcastle when they hosted Sporting Lisbon in their EUFA Cup Round 2, Group D fixture.

Coming on as a 79th minute substitute for Craig Bellamy, who scored Newcastle's only goal of the game, Guy had 11 minutes of first-team football at Newcastle.

The game ended 1-1 with Custodio cancelling out Bellamy's goal.

First Meeting on December-16:

Year	V	F	A	R	Opposition	Competition
1895	W	4	0	H	Tow Law Town	FA Cup
1992	H	2	2	D	AC Cesena	Anglo-Italian Cup

Debut on December-16:

Year	Player	Opposition
1893	Robert Willis (Inside Right)	Small Heath
2004	Lewis Guy (Forward)	Sporting Lisbon

Born on December-16:

Year	Player	Position	Years
1880	William Agnew	Full Back	1902 - 1904
1907	George Nevin	Full Back	1928 - 1930
1944	John Markie	Centre Half	1962 - 1964
1962	Andy Thomas	Midfield/Forward	1986 - 1988
1977	Sylvain Distin	Defence	2001 - 2002

December-17

1892: First Win for "United"
Newcastle "United" won their first game today, their second under the new name.

It was a Northern League fixture against Stockton at St James's Park. Two goals each from Jock Sorely and Tom Crate, plus a goal from Harry Reay gave "United" a 5-2 victory.

1898: One and Only Appearance
Archie Mowatt, Outside Right, made his one and only appearance today for Newcastle as they welcomed Sheffield Wednesday to St James's Park for a League Division 1 fixture.

The game ended with honours even at 2-2, with goals from Sandy MacFarlane and a last minute equaliser from Jock Peddie to earn Newcastle the draw.

1904: Miners Secretary Dies at St James's Park
Ralph Young, Secretary of the Northumberland Miners Association died suddenly during the Newcastle v Sheffield Wednesday game today. It was reported that he was talking to a friend and "*his conversation suddenly ceased and he died where he sat*". Newcastle won the game 6-2. Their goals coming from Jock Rutherford, with two, and one apiece for Ron Orr, Bill Appleyard, Jim Howie and Peter McWilliam.

1921: One and Only Appearance
John Thain, Outside Right, made his one and only appearance today for Newcastle when they hosted Aston Villa in a League Division 1 fixture. Aston Villa were narrow winners, 2-1, in a quite evenly contested game.

First Meeting on December-17:

Year	V	F	A	R	Opposition	Competition
1898	H	2	2	D	Sheffield Wednesday	Division 1

Debut on December-17:

Year	Player	Opposition
1898	Archie Mowatt (Outside Right)	Sheffield Wednesday
1921	John Thain (Outside Right)	Aston Villa

Born on December-17:

Year	Player	Position	Years
1933	George Luke	Outside Left	1950 - 1961
1966	Kevin Watson Scott	Central Defence	1984 - 1994

December-18

1909 saw a heavy 4-0 defeat to Sheffield United at Bramall Lane in a League Division 1 fixture. Whilst **1974** saw Newcastle losing their League Cup Quarter-Final Replay 1-0 against Chester (*Chester City from 1980*) at Sealand Road. It wasn't all bad news on this day though.

1954: Five Star Performance

Two goals each for Bobby Mitchell and Vic Keeble and one for Jackie Milburn gave Newcastle a sterling 5-1 victory over Arsenal at St James's Park in a League Division 1 fixture.

2001: Great Second Half Revival

Again Arsenal were the opponents with this time the fixture being in the Premiership at Highbury. Robert Pires had given Arsenal a 1-0 lead going into the break. The second half though saw goals from Alan O'Brien, an Alan Shearer penalty, and a last minute strike from Laurent Robert to give a 3-1 victory to Newcastle.

Born on December-18:

Year	Player	Position	Years
1922	Ivor Broadis	Inside Forward	1953 - 1955
1955	Michael Barker	Left Back	1972 - 1979
1959	Kevin Dillon	Midfield	1989 - 1991

December-19

1931: Five Star Performance

Newcastle put five past Sheffield United in a League Division 1 fixture at St James's Park, though Sheffield did score three themselves to make it an exciting game. Newcastle's goals came courtesy of a hat-trick by Harry Bedford, and a goal each for Jimmy Boyd and Tommy Lang.

1953: Tyne-Wear Derby No. 82

Newcastle travelled to Roker Park to face Sunderland in a League Division 1 fixture, the 82nd Tyne-Wear Derby.

The game went into the break even at 0-0. Stan Anderson, quite a hero for both Newcastle and Sunderland, scored in the second half, but unfortunately at the time he was with Sunderland! Ivor Broadis, again a player who would be a hero to both teams scored also, but thankfully he was with Newcastle at the time, so honours were even 1-1 at the end of the game.

1973: Newcastle Scrape Into Final

Newcastle won the second leg of their Texaco Cup Semi-Final against Dundee United at St James's Park. The score on the night being 4-1. With the first leg at Tannadice Park being lost 2-0 they just scraped into the final 4-3 on aggregate. Keith Robson, John Tudor, Malcolm Macdonald and Tommy Cassidy being Newcastle's saviours.

Born on December-19:

Year	Player	Position	Years
1919	George Lowrie	Centre Forward	1948 - 1950
1954	Martin Christopher Gorry	Left Back	1976 - 1978
1963	Derek Bel	Midfield	1981 - 1983
1991	Jeff Henderson	Defence	2008 - current

December-20

1919: Scoring Debut

Alfred Hagan scored on his debut today in the League Division 1 fixture with Manchester United. It unfortunately proved to be nothing more than a consolation as Newcastle went down 2-1 at Old Trafford.

1969: Scoring Debut

David Ford scored on his debut today in the League Division 1 fixture with Ipswich Town. With Pop Robson scoring two and Keith Dyson also scoring this was an excellent debut for Ford as Newcastle were very comfortable 4-0 winners at St James's Park, though all four goals did come in the second-half.

2009: Newcastle Break Championship Attendance Record

With an attendance of 49,644 at St James's Park today Newcastle in their match against Middlesbrough smashed the attendance record for the Championship. The record was previously held by Sunderland with a gate of 47,350 against Stoke in May 2005.

Debut on December-20:

Year	Player	Opposition
1919	Alfred Hagan (Inside Left)	Manchester United
1969	David Ford (Inside Forward)	Ipswich Town
1980	John Trewick (Midfield)	Bristol City

Born on December-20:

Year	Player	Position	Years
1909	George Mathison	Right Half	1926 - 1933
1938	David Hilley	Inside Forward	1962 - 1967
1949	Alan Duffy	Forward	1966 - 1970
1952	Irving Nattrass	Midfield	1970 - 1979
1968	Alexander Mathie	Forward	1993 - 1995
1978	Geremi Sorele Njitap Fotso	Central Defence	2007 - 2010
1980	Fitz Benjamin Hall	Central Defence	2010

December-21

1895: Six of the Best

Rotherham Town, who were later to combine with Rotherham County to become Rotherham United, were the visitors to St James's Park today and ended up being soundly defeated 6-1. Two goals each for Willie Wardrope and Malcolm Lennox and singles from Willie McKay and Jimmy Stott were enough to overwhelm Town. Though having only being 1-0 up at half-time it certainly didn't look like the victory would be as comprehensive as it turned out to be.

1907: Tyne-Wear Derby No. 20

Newcastle travelled to Roker Park to face Sunderland in a League Division 1 fixture, the 20th Tyne-Wear Derby.

With Newcastle leading 3-2 at half-time it was still a game that could have went either way but it went Newcastle's way with them adding a fourth to end the game 4-2.

The Newcastle goals came from George Wilson who scored two and one each for Jock Rutherford and Colin Veitch. (Billy Hogg and Arthur Bridgett scoring for Sunderland.)

1935: Edward Birnie, R.I.P.

Today saw the sad passing of Edward, or "Ted", Birnie. He was a tall and fast defender who was a 'jack-of-all-trades' whilst at Newcastle. Indeed his versatility was probably his downfall. Making only 20 appearances for Newcastle he played in no fewer than six positions! Needless to say this hampered any chance he had of commanding any single position.

2014: Tyne-Wear Derby No. 152

Newcastle played hosts to Sunderland in a Premiership fixture, the 152nd Tyne-Wear Derby. A single goal from Adam Johnson in the last minute of the game consigned Newcastle to their fourth Derby defeat in a row.

Born on December-21:

Year	Player	Position	Years
1946	Michael Edward Burns	Forward	1974 - 1978

December-22

1894: Seven Scored in Nine Goal St James's Park Encounter

Newcastle entertained Walsall Town Swifts today and scored 7 of the 9 goals that entertained the St James's Park faithful today. A hat-trick from Jock Smith, a brace from Tom Crate, a goal from Bobby Willis and an 'own goal' saw them winning this League Division 2 fixture very comfortably 7-2.

1923: Tyne-Wear Derby No. 50

Newcastle hosted Sunderland in a League Division 1 fixture, the 50th Tyne-Wear Derby. Two goals from Jock Paterson gave Sunderland a 2-0 victory.

1956: Tyne-Wear Derby No. 89

Newcastle hosted Sunderland in a League Division 1 fixture, the 89th Tyne-Wear Derby. Already leading 3-1 at the break this game was never in any doubt and the score in the second half was 3-1 as well, making it a 6-2 victory to Newcastle. The scorers were Alex Tait with a hat-trick, and one each for Reg Davies, Len White and Tommy Casey. Charlie Fleming scored both of Sunderland's goals.

1999: Six of the Best

Newcastle put six past Tottenham Hotspur in their FA Cup Third Round Replay at St James's Park. Gary Speed, Nikos Dabizas, Duncan Ferguson Kieron Dyer and Alan Shearer (with two) ensured Newcastle progressed at the second attempt. David Ginola also scored, but as he was a Spurs player now the final score was 6-1.

Interestingly, apart from Ginola, Spurs also had Sol Campbell in their side and brought on Ruel Fox as a second half substitute.

2001: Newcastle Edge Elland Road Thriller

Leeds hosted Newcastle in this Premiership fixture and in a game that saw seven goals Newcastle were victorious 4-3. Goals from Craig Bellamy (36), Robbie Elliott (59), Alan Shearer (71 [Pen]) and a last-gasp winner from Nobby Solano on 90 ensured the win.

Looking at Leeds scorers though is interesting - Lee Bowyer and Mark Viduka were among them (Ian Harte getting their other goal). However looking at the Leeds team that day is also interesting, not only did it include Bowyer and Viduka but David Batty also played and they had Jonathan Woodgate and Alan Smith on the bench!

First Meeting on December-22:

Year	V	F	A	R	Opposition	Competition
1906	A	3	1	W	Manchester United*	Division 1

*Manchester United were previously Newton Heath, first meeting on 06/04/1895.

Debut on December-22:

Year	Player	Opposition
1894	Patrick O'Brien (Inside Left)	Walsall Town Swifts
1984	Ian Baird (Centre Forward)	Aston Villa

Born on December-22:

Year	Player	Position	Years
1973	Alan Thompson	Midfield	1989 - 1993

December-23

1899: Tyne-Wear Derby No. 3

Newcastle hosted Sunderland in a League Division 1 fixture, the 3rd Tyne-Wear Derby. Newcastle went into the break 2-1 up but were brought back down to earth as Sunderland scored three in the second half to take the game 4-2.

Newcastle's scorers were Sandy MacFarlane and Alex Gardner. Sunderland's scorers were Bobby Hogg with a hat-trick and Colin McLatchie.

Debut on December-23:

Year	Player	Opposition
1905	John Findlay (Right Half)	Bolton Wanderers
1911	Tommy Lowes (Inside Forward)	Preston North End

Born on December-23:

Year	Player	Position	Years
1952	Alex Bruce	Forward	1974
1983	Michael Chopra	Forward	2000 - 2006

December-24

1898: Tyne-Wear Derby No. 1

Christmas Eve and a trip to Roker Park for the first "Tyne-Wear" Derby between Newcastle United and Sunderland. A 3-2 victory meant that it was the Geordies who would be having a Merry Christmas!

So the honour of being the first players to score in a Tyne-Wear Derby goes to Willie Wardrope and Jock Peddie, who actually scored twice.

Making the first Sunderland player to score in a Tyne-Wear Derby Jim Leslie who scored both of Sunderland's goals.

NB: Both Newcastle East End and Newcastle West End had played Sunderland before this, three times in total, all in the FA Cup. West End playing them on 13/11/1886, winning 1-0 and again on 05/11/1887, this time losing 3-1. East End played them on 10/11/1888 and were beaten 2-0. This however was the first time Newcastle "United" had played Sunderland.

1904: Tyne-Wear Derby No. 14

Newcastle United travelled to Roker Park for a League Division 1 fixture against Sunderland, the 14th Tyne-Wear Derby.

Unfortunately it would not be the Geordies who would be having a Merry Christmas as Sunderland won 3-1. An Andy McCombie 'own goal' and one each for Dicky Jackson and Harold Buckle saw to that! Newcastle's consolation goal was scored by Peter McWilliam in the first half.

Christmas would be better in **1932** as Newcastle put four past Blackpool, with no reply, at Bloomfield Road in a League Division 1 fixture. The goals coming from Jack Allen, with two, Jimmy Boyd and Tommy Lang.

1955: Five Star Performance

Newcastle put five past Preston North End, with no reply, in a League Division 1 fixture at St James's Park. The scorers being: two each for Jackie Milburn and Vic Keeble and one for Bobby Mitchell.

First Meeting on December-24:

Year	V	F	A	R	Opposition	Competition
1898	A	3	2	W	Sunderland	Division 1

Debut on December-24:

Year	Player	Opposition
1966	Graham Winstanley (Centre Back)	Leeds United

Born on December-24:

Year	Player	Position	Years
1909	David Bell	Full Back	1930 - 1934

December-25

Merry Christmas!

The number six is a pretty recurrent one on a Christmas Day where Newcastle are concerned. It certainly was in **1894** and **1895** when Crewe Alexandra were the visitors to St James's Park as Newcastle beat then 6-0 on both occasions. Newcastle also scored six goals in **1934** when they beat Hull City 6-2. However they were on the wrong side of six goals in **1925** when they were beaten 6-3 by Liverpool at Anfield.

Six was the total number of goals in their game against West Bromwich Albion when they were beaten 4-2 at St James's Park in **1946** and if you aggregate the scores in the two games that Newcastle have played Sunderland on a Christmas day it would be 6-6! This with Newcastle losing 5-2 in **1914** but winning 4-1 in **1951**.

1914: Tyne-Wear Derby No. 39

Newcastle hosted Sunderland in a League Division 1 fixture, the 39th Tyne-Wear Derby. It was to turn out to be a thoroughly miserable Christmas Day for Newcastle as they lost 5-2 and didn't even score! Both of their goals being 'own goals' by Sunderland players. When Sunderland did score in the 'right' goal it was Bobby Best with a hat-trick and one each for Charlie Buchan and George Philip - Bah, Humbug!

1934: Scoring Debut

Joe Wilson scored on his debut today in the League Division 2 fixture with Hull City. As mentioned above Newcastle scored six goals in this match, the others coming from Jack Smith, Tom Pearson, who both scored twice, and William Gallantree, *on his 21st birthday*, making it 6-2 at St James's Park.

1950: Scoring Debut

Bob Stokoe scored on his debut today in the League Division 1 fixture with Middlesbrough. Unfortunately it was nothing more than a consolation goal as Newcastle were beaten 2-1 at Ayresome Park.

1951: Tyne-Wear Derby No. 77

Newcastle travelled to Roker Park to face Sunderland in a League Division 1 fixture, the 77th Tyne-Wear Derby. Two goals from Jorge Robledo, and one each for Jackie Milburn and Billy Foulkes gave Newcastle a 4-1 victory. Sunderland's consolation goal came in the second half from Trevor Ford.

First Meeting on December-25:

Year	V	F	A	R	Opposition	Competition
1937	D	0	0	H	Stockport County	Division 1

Debut on December-25:

Year	Player	Opposition
1895	John Carr (Wing Half)	Crewe Alexandra
1924	Alfred Maitland (Left Back)	Everton
1925	Joseph Harris (Right Half)	Liverpool
1929	George Scott (Outside Left)	Middlesbrough
1934	Joe Wilson (Inside-Right)	Hull City
1950	Bob Stokoe (Centre Half) Matthew McNeil (Centre Half) Tom Paterson (Inside Forward)	Middlesbrough
1952	Tommy Cahill (Left Back)	Cardiff City

Born on December-25:

Year	Player	Position	Years
1913	William Gallantree	Outside Right	1931 - 1936
1973	Robert James Elliott	Defence	1990 - 2006

December-26

1903: Tyne-Wear Derby No. 12

Newcastle hosted Sunderland in a League Division 1 fixture, the 12th Tyne-Wear Derby. Two goals for Sunderland's Harold Buckle and one from Arthur Bridgett, with only one goal in reply for Newcastle's Jock Rutherford gave the visitors a 3-1 victory.

1914: Tyne-Wear Derby No. 40

Newcastle travelled to Roker Park to face Sunderland in a League Division 1 fixture, the 40th Tyne-Wear Derby. Having lost 5-2 at home to Sunderland yesterday this was not a wildly anticipated re-match, but Newcastle were to make amends with a 4-2 victory. Two goals from Billy Hibbert and one each for Sandy Higgins and Frank Hudspeth gave Newcastle the much needed revenge.

1933: Newcastle Grab 7 at Goodison

A trip to Merseyside and Goodison Park saw Newcastle deliver some knockout blows to Everton in a game that saw ten goals with Newcastle grabbing seven in a comprehensive 7-3 victory in this Division 1 fixture. A hat-trick from Ron Williams and goals from Jimmy Boyd, Jimmy Richardson, Tommy Lang and a penalty from Sammy Weaver settled this rather one-sided match.

1951: Tyne-Wear Derby No. 78

Newcastle hosted Sunderland in a League Division 1 fixture, the 78th Tyne-Wear Derby. Sunderland took a 1-0 lead into the break and scored again in the second half but this was matched by two goals from Jackie Milburn so the game ended honours even at 2-2.

1953: One and Only Appearance

Alex Gaskell, Centre Forward, made his one and only appearance today for Newcastle when they hosted Middlesbrough in a League Division 1 fixture. With the game evenly balanced, and scoreless, at half-time the second half saw five goals - but three of them were for Middlesbrough so they were 3-2 victors. Newcastle's goals were scored by Ivor Broadis and Bobby Mitchell.

1955: Tyne-Wear Derby No. 85

Newcastle travelled to Roker Park to face Sunderland in a League Division 1 fixture, the 85th Tyne-Wear Derby. Sunderland must have felt pretty much punch-drunk this Boxing Day as Newcastle hit them for six! With Vic Keeble, Jackie Milburn and Bill Curry each grabbing two goals apiece they smashed Sunderland 6-1 on their own turf.

1967: Tyne-Wear Derby No. 102

Newcastle hosted Sunderland in a League Division 1 fixture, the 102nd Tyne-Wear Derby. Goals from Albert Bennet and Wyn Davies gave Newcastle a 2-1 victory. Sunderland's goal coming from Colin Suggett!

1977: One and Only Appearance

Martin Christopher Gorry, Left Back, made his one and only appearance today for Newcastle when they travelled to Maine Road for a League Division 1 fixture against Manchester City. Coming on as a substitute for John Blackley the game was already going badly and Newcastle were soundly beaten 4-0.

2013: Five Star Performance

Going 1-0 down to Stoke City after 29 minutes was not the best start to this Boxing Day fixture in the Premiership, especially in front of your own home crowd. However like a boxer recovering from an early knockdown Newcastle fought back to take the game comfortably 5-1. The goals coming from Loic Remy (44, 56), Yoan Gouffran (48), Yohan Cabaye (66) and Papiss Cisse (80 [Pen]).

First Meeting on December-26:

Year	V	F	A	R	Opposition	Competition
1893	A	2	1	W	Walsall Town Swifts	Division 2

Debut on December-26:

Year	Player	Opposition
1893	John Law (Inside Right)	Walsall Town Swifts
1896	John Ostler (Centre Half) Thomas Stewart (Left Back)	Grimsby Town
1907	John McCormack (Half Back)	Sheffield United
1912	Richard Little (Right Back)	Liverpool
1953	Alex Gaskell (Centre Forward)	Middlesbrough
1970	Martin Burleigh (Goalkeeper)	Leeds United
1974	Thomas Brooks Craig (Midfield) Geoff Nulty (Midfield)	Carlisle United
1977	Martin Christopher Gorry (Left Back)	Manchester City
1980	Mick Harford (Forward)	Grimsby Town
1983	Glenn Victor Roeder (Central Defence)	Blackburn Rovers
1986	Jeffrey Wrightson (Central Defence)	Everton

Debut on December-26:

Year	Player	Opposition
1988	Kenneth Graham Sansom (Left Back) Ray Ranson (Right Back)	Sheffield Wednesday
2006	David Edgar (Centre-Back)	Bolton Wanderers

Born on December-26:

Year	Player	Position	Years
1935	Terry Marshall	Outside Right	1958 - 1961

December-27

1902: Tyne-Wear Derby No. 10

Newcastle travelled to Roker Park to face Sunderland in a League Division 1 fixture, the 10th Tyne-Wear Derby. With no goals being scored the game was honours even at 0-0.

1913: Tyne-Wear Derby No. 38

Newcastle hosted Sunderland in a League Division 1 fixture, the 38th Tyne-Wear Derby. Tommy Goodwill and Billy Hibbert scored for Newcastle and Charlie Buchan for Sunderland. All the goals coming in the second half, thus Newcastle were the victors 2-1.

1955: Tyne-Wear Derby No. 86

Newcastle hosted Sunderland in a League Division 1 fixture, the 86th Tyne-Wear Derby. Having already beaten them 6-1 yesterday at Roker Park Newcastle were looking to capitalise on it, this they did with a 3-1 victory. Sunderland though took a surprising 1-0 lead into the break through Bill Holden but Newcastle redressed this with goals from Vic Keeble, Jackie Milburn and Len White.

1976: Tyne-Wear Derby No. 110

Newcastle hosted Sunderland in a League Division 1 fixture, the 110th Tyne-Wear Derby. Newcastle scored in either half through Paul Cannell and Alan Kennedy with no reply and were therefore winners at 2-0.

First Meeting on December-27:

Year	V	F	A	R	Opposition	Competition
1893	A	1	1	D	Crewe Alexandra	Division 2

Debut on December-27:

Year	Player	Opposition
1924	Jimmy Loughlin (Forward)	Huddersfield Town

Born on December-27:

Year	Player	Position	Years
1936	Billy Day	Outside Right	1962 - 1963
1967	Mark Stimson	Defence	1989 - 1992
1971	Duncan Ferguson	Forward	1998 - 2000

December-28

1912: Tyne-Wear Derby No. 33

Newcastle hosted Sunderland in a League Division 1 fixture, the 33rd Tyne-Wear Derby. A goal in either half from Sunderland's George Holley gave the game to them 2-0.

1996: Seven Heaven

Newcastle put seven past Tottenham Hotspur at St James's Park in a Premiership fixture. Two from Alan Shearer, two from Les Ferdinand, two from Rob Lee and one from Laurent Robert. With two minutes to go Neilsen did get a consolation for Spurs but that was more due to Newcastle relaxing than it was to Spurs being effective.

First Meeting on December-28:

Year	V	F	A	R	Opposition	Competition
1896	A	0	2	L	Gainsborough Trinity	Division 2

Debut on December-28:

Year	Player	Opposition
1901	John Graham (Right Half)	Bury
1957	Ken Hale (Inside Forward) William McKinney (Right Back)	Tottenham Hotspur

Born on December-28:

Year	Player	Position	Years
1886	Stanley Allan	Half Back	1908 - 1911
1980	Lomano Tresor LuaLua	Forward	2001 - 2003

December-29

1894: Match Abandoned But Result Stands!

Newcastle travelled to The Hillary Street Ground to meet Walsall Town Swifts in their League Division 2 fixture. Little did they know what they were walking into!

Both clubs were battling to keep their place in the Football League - and to pay their bills. However the financial problems at Walsall meant that their players were not being paid, and that came to a head before this game. The Walsall players basically refused to play the game unless they got paid and there were "very heated" discussions between them and the committee which ran the club in the dressing room.

These 'discussions' lasted beyond the scheduled kick-off and when finally an agreement was reached the kick-off had been delayed by 20 minutes.

In what were atrocious conditions Newcastle took a 3-0 lead at half-time, courtesy of a hat-trick from Bob Willis. The second half saw Walsall get two goals back, but with the weather worsening, there was rain, sleet and a gale force wind blowing, and the fact that the light was fading, the referee called a halt to the game in the 78th minute.

Normally an abandoned game would need to be replayed but the Football League decided that with Walsall being partly to blame for the abandonment, i.e. causing the late kick-off, they let the result stand.

1956: One and Only Appearance

Bill Redhead, Half Back, made his one and only appearance today when Newcastle hosted Sheffield Wednesday in a League Division 1 fixture. A Bill Curry goal wasn't enough on this day as Sheffield, who had been leading 1-0 at half-time, scored again. The game ending 2-1 to Sheffield.

Debut on December-29:

Year	Player	Opposition
1894	William Milne (Outside Left)	Walsall Town Swifts
1951	George Lackenby (Defence)	Tottenham Hotspur
1956	Bill Redhead (Half Back)	Sheffield Wednesday

Born on December-29:

Year	Player	Position	Years
1978	Kieron Courtney Dyer	Midfield	1999 - 2007
1978	Brian Pinas	Midfield	1997 - 1998
1984	Martin Brittain	Midfield	2003 - 2006

December-30

1905: Tyne-Wear Derby No. 17
Newcastle hosted Sunderland in a League Division 1 fixture, the 17th Tyne-Wear Derby. Ron Orr for Newcastle and Billy Hogg for Sunderland both scored in the first half. There being no other goals the game ended 1-1.

1911: Five Star Performance
Newcastle put five past Bolton Wanderers at St James's Park in a League Division 1 fixture. The goals coming from a Billy Hibbert hat-trick and one apiece for James Hay and Colin Veitch.

1967: Tyne-Wear Derby No. 103
Newcastle travelled to Roker Park to face Sunderland in a League Division 1 fixture, the 103rd Tyne-Wear Derby. Sunderland led 2-1 at the break but the game ended 'all-square' at 3-3. Newcastle's scorers were Ollie Burton with two, and John McNamee. Sunderland's scorers were Colin Suggett with two, and Bruce Stuckey.

1978: One and Only Appearance
Keith Mulgrove, Left Back, made his one and only appearance today as Newcastle travelled to the Goldstone Ground for a League Division 2 fixture against Brighton & Hove Albion. A goal in each half for Brighton ensured Newcastle came home empty handed.

First Meeting on December-30:

Year	V	F	A	R	Opposition	Competition
1893	H	2	1	W	Burslem Port Vale*	Division 2

*Became simply 'Port Vale' against whom we first played on 27/10/1934

Debut on December-30:

Year	Player	Opposition
1978	Keith Mulgrove (Left Back)	Brighton & Hove Albion
1989	Darren Bradshaw (Right Back/Midfield)	Swindon Town

Born on December-30:

Year	Player	Position	Years
1948	Colin Suggett	Midfield	1978 - 1981
1950	William Rafferty	Forward	1979 - 1980

December-31

Unfortunately New Years Eve has not traditionally been a good day for Newcastle. Of the 16 games played they have lost nine, the one in **1960** being a 5-3 defeat to Burnley and in **1966** it was a 4-0 defeat by Tottenham Hotspur. Both 'away' fixtures in League Division 1. Two of the 16 games were drawn 0-0, in **1898** and **1938**, against Wolverhampton Wanderers and Sheffield United respectively.

However that means we can 'sign off' with five wins!

Newcastle beat Arsenal 2-0 at Highbury **1904**, goals by Jock Rutherford and Colin Veitch. Newcastle beat Manchester United 3-0 at St James's Park in **1921**, goals by Neil Harris (with two) and Tom McDonald. Newcastle beat Bolton Wanderers 3-1 at St James's Park in **1932**, goals by Jimmy Boyd (with two) and Jack Allen. Newcastle beat Aston Villa 1-0 at Villa Park in **1949**, George Hannah with the only goal. Finally in **1983** Newcastle beat Oldham Athletic 2-1 at Boundary Park, Kevin Keegan scoring twice.

Debut on December-31:

Year	Player	Opposition
1949	Eduardo Oliver Robledo (Left-Half)	Aston Villa
1966	Thomas Robson (Left Wing) John McNamee (Central Defence) David Elliott (Midfield)	Tottenham Hotspur
1977	Mike Larnach (Inside Forward)	Liverpool

Born on December-31:

Year	Player	Position	Years
1899	William Bertram	Inside Left	1920 - 1921
1950	Raymond Ellison	Full Back	1968 - 1973

QUICK REFERENCE

January

First Meetings:

Aberdare Athletic, Bedford, Carlisle United, Cheltenham Town, Chester City, Clapton Orient, Crystal Palace, Glossop North End, Hartlepool United, Hendon, Hereford United, Huddersfield Town, Manchester City, Newport County, Peterborough United, Portsmouth, Preston North End, Reading, Rotherham Town, Real Zaragoza, Scunthorpe United, Southport, Stevenage Borough, Swansea Town, Torquay United, Wigan Athletic, Wrexham, Yeading, York City

Debut:

AIREY Philip, AITKEN Robert Sime, ALDERSON John, ALLEN John, BABAYARO Celestine Hycieth, BARTON David, BETTON Alec, BOTT Wilfred, BOUMSONG Jean Alain, CAIRNS Billy, CAPE Jackie, CLARK James, CONNELLY Eddie, CORBETT Bobby, COWELL Bobby, CROWE Charlie, DEBUCHY Mathieu, DOCKING Stanley, DOMI Didier, DRYDEN John, DUMMETT Paul, FAYE Amady Moustapha, FEENEY Wilfred, FORD Joe, FRASER Robert, GALLANTREE William, GILLESPIE Keith Robert, GILLESPIE William, GOSLING Daniel, GOUFFRAN Yoan, GRAVER Andy, HAIR George, HAMPSON William, HARVEY Joe, HODGSON Ken, HOUGHTON Frank Calvert, HUCKERBY Darren, HUGHES John, HUNTER James, KEERY Stan, KETTLEBOROUGH Keith Frank, KING Ray, LAVERICK J, LORMOR Anthony, LOVENKRANDS Peter Rosenkrands, LUALUA Kazenga, MATHISON George, McCALL Willie, McCURLEY John, McDONALD John, McGHEE Mark, McPHILLIPS William, MELLOR William, MILBURN John Edward Thompson, MILLS David, MITCHELL David, MOONEY Edward, O'BRIEN Alan, PHILLIPSON Tom, PINGEL Frank, QUINN Wayne, RAINNIE Alex, REID O, ROBINSON James, ROUTLEDGE Wayne Neville A., SAHA Louis Laurent, SCOTT Malcolm, SCOTT Willie, SINCLAIR John, SISSOKO Moussa, SMITH Thomas, SPINK James, TAYLOR Ernie, TAYLOR John Harold, THEAKER Clarence Alfred, THOMAS Barrie Ernest, THOMAS John, THOMPSON Henry, TUDOR John, TURNER Arthur, VAN AANHOLT Patrick, WARBURTON John, WAYMAN Charlie, WILLIAMSON Michael James, WILSON James, WRIGHT Tommy, YANGA-MBIWA Mapou, YOUNG David

February

First Meetings:
AS Roma, Aston Villa, Bayer Leverkusen, Bolton Wanderers, Brighton & Hove Albion, Bristol Rovers, Burnley, Chesterfield, Exeter City, FC Metalist Kharkiv, Grimsby Town, Hull City, Plymouth Argyle, SC Heerenveen, Southampton, SV Zulte Waregem, Tottenham Hotspur, Valerenga, Watford, West Ham United

Debut:
ANDERSSON Andreas, ASPRILLA Faustino Hernan, BARKER Michael, BEST Leon Julian, BOTTOM Arthur, BRAZIL Gary Nicholas, BRIDGES Michael, BRUCE Alex, CISSE Papiss Demba, CRAIG Albert, CROPLEY Alex, CUNNINGHAM Andrew, CUNNINGHAM Anthony Eugene, DAVIDSON David, DE JONG Luuk, DENNISON Robert, DEVINE Joeseph, FOGGON Alan, FORSTER William, FOX Ruel Adrian, FRANKS Albert, GAVILAN Diego Antonio Zarate, GRIFFIN Andy, HAIDARA Massadio, HALL Fitz Benjamin, HEWARD Harold, HEYWOOD Frederick, HINDSON Gordon, HORSFIELD Arthur, HUGHES Thomas, JENAS Jermaine Anthony, KEATING Albert, KELLY Dominic, KERRAY Jimmy, KILCLINE Brian, KNOX Tommy, KUQI Shefki, LEIGHTON William, LINDSAY William, McCOMBIE Andrew, McGRATH John Thomas, MITCHELL Kenny, MITCHELL Thomas, MORAN Paul, NICHOLSON Ben, NOLAN Kevin Anthony Jance, ONYEWU Oguchialu Chilioke, PATTISON Matthew Joseph, REILLY George, RICHARDSON Joseph, ROBLEDO Jorge Oliver, SHEEDY Kevin, SIBLEY Albert, SMITH David, SMITH William, SPEED Gary, TAYLOR Ryan Anthony David, THOMPSON Tommy, WHITE Len, WILSON Terry, WOODS Harry

March

First Meetings:
AZ Alkmaar, Bologna, Corinthians, FC Anzhi Makhachkala, Fulham, Glossop, Monaco, Olympiakos, Real Mallorca, RSC Anderlecht, Swindon Town, Vitoria Setubal, Walsall

Debut:
ADAMS George, ARMSTRONG Adam, ASKEW Billy, BARBER Stanley, BATTY David, BENSON Robert, BEST Jeremiah, BLACKHALL Raymond, BLYTH Thomas, BRITTAIN Martin, CANNELL Paul, COLE Andrew Alexander, COOPER Edward, CROWN Lawrence, DABIZAS

Nikos, DAY Billy, EDGAR Eddie, ELLIOTT Robert James, FELL Jimmy, FROST Arthur Douglas, GIBSON James, HARROWER Jimmy, HIGGINS Alexander, HOLLAND Chris, HOLLINS Dave, HUNT Andy, IMRIE William Noble, INNERD Wilfred, JONES Roger, KEEBLE Vic, KELSEY William, KENNEDY Alan, KINSELLA J, KIRKCALDY James, LIDDELL Robert, LOWRIE George, MARIC Silvio, MARSHALL Terry, McCAFFERY Aiden, McCULLOCH Alex, McDERMOTT Terence, McDONALD Thomas, McDONOUGH Darron Karl, McGOUGH Richard, McKELLAR David, METCALF Arthur, MITCHELL Robert Carmichael, MOLE George, MONCUR Robert, MOORE Craig, NATTRASS Irving, NEILSON Alan, OATES Graham, O'BRIEN Andrew James, PARKINSON Andy, PATTINSON Daniel, PEACOCK Darren, PEART John George, RAINE James, RAMAGE Peter Iain, RANDALL Charles, REID William, ROBINSON Mark, ROBSON Keith, RUTHERFORD John, SCOTT Jamie, SCOTT William, SELLARS Scott, SHINTON Robert Thomas, SINCLAIR Tom, SOULSBY John, SPENCER Charles William, TAYLOR Steven Vincent, TEMPLETON Robert Bryson, WHARTON Kenny, WOODGATE Jonathan.

April

First Meetings:

Barnsley, Blackburn Rovers, Cardiff City, Como Calcio 1907, Newton Heath, Northampton Town, Olympique de Marseille, Sport Lisboa e Benfica, Stoke City

Debut:

ALLEN Geoffrey, ANDERSON William, APPLEYARD William, ARCHIBALD John, ARENTOFT Preben, BEHARALL David Alexander, BERTRAM William, BLAKE Sidney, BRADLEY Robert, BROWN Noel, CAIRNS Thomas, CHALMERS William, CLARK Frank Albert, CLARK Robert, CRUMLEY Robert, DIATTA Lamine, DIXON Edward Stanley, DODDS John, DONALDSON Andy, DONALDSON ?, DUNCAN Scott, FAIRHURST David, FERGUSON Brian, FERGUSON Robert. GARLAND Peter, GASCOIGNE Paul, GORDON Jimmy, GREY Thomas, GRUNDY Arnold, HALL Ernest, HARKER Chris, HODGSON Gordon Henry, HUGHES William, IRELAND Stephen James, JOBEY George, JOHNSON Harry, KENNEDY Keith, KRISTENSEN Bjorn, LINDSAY James, LITTLEFAIR James, LOCKEY Jim, LOWERY Jeremiah, MACKENZIE Roderick, MAHONEY Mick, McBAIN Tom, McCLEN Jamie, McINTYRE Edward, McLEAN David, McTAVISH John, NIBLO Thomas Bruce, PEARS Billy, PENMAN William Salmond Thomson, PRIOR Ken, PUNTON William Hamilton, ROCHE David,

ROXBURGH Robert, RUTHERFORD R, SCOTT John, SRNICEK Pavel, SWAN Chris, SWEENEY Paul, TAIT Alex, THOMPSON Frank, THOMPSON George Alexander, TINNION Brian, TURNER David, WAKE Henry, WHITSON Tony, WOOLLARD Arnold James, WRIGHT Brian

May

First Meetings:
Aberdeen, Glasgow Rangers, Hibernian, Torino Calcio, Ujpesti Dozsa

Debut:
AMBROSE Darren Paul, AMEOBI Sammuel, BELL Derek, FERRIS Paul, HOPE John, HOWEY Stephen Norman, MAKEL Lee, MANNERS Peter, RUSSELL Samuel, STUBBINS Albert, THOMAS Martin Richard, WATSON John

June

First Meetings:
ACF Fiorentina

July

First Meetings:
1860 Munchen, Deportivo la Coruna, FK ZTS Dubnica, Lillestrom Sportsklubb, Lokeren

Debut:
BELLAMY Craig Douglas, BERNARD Olivier Jimmy Wilfrid

August

First Meetings:
Accrington Stanley, Atromitos Athens, Futbola Klubs Ventspils, Leyton Orient, Mansfield Town, Morecambe, NK Croatia, Troyes, Zeljeznicar Sarajevo

Debut:
AITKEN William, ALBERT Phillipe, ALLEN John, ALLEN Malcolm, AMALFITANO Romain, ANCELL Robert Francis Dudgeon, ANITA Vurnon San Benito, BA Demba, BARROWCLOUGH Stewart, BARTON Warren, BASSONG Sebastien, BEASANT David John, BELOZOGLU

Emre, BENNETT Albert, BENTLEY Roy, BERESFORD John, BIGIRIMANA Gael, BIRD John, BIRKETT Ralph, BOGIE Ian, BOWYER Lee David, BRACEWELL Paul, BRAMBLE Titus Malachi, BRENNAN Frank, BROWN Malcolm, BURNS Michael Edward, BURTON Alwyn Derek, BUTT Nicky, CABAYE Yohan, CAMPBELL Adam, CARR Franz, CARR Stephen Babeson, CARTWRIGHT Peter, CARVER Jesse, CHANDLER Albert, CHARVET Laurent, CLARKE Jeff, CLARKE Ray, CLIFTON Henry, COLOCCINI Fabricio, CONNOLLY John, COPPINGER Jamie, CORDONE Daniel, CORT Carl, CURRY Thoma, DA SILVA Claudio Roberto, DAVIES Alan, DAVIES Ian Claude, DILLON Kevin, DONALDSON Ryan, DUFF Damien Anthony, DUMAS Franck, DYER Kieron Courtney, ENRIQUE Jose Sanchez, FAIRBROTHER John, FERDINAND Leslie, FEREDAY Wayne, FERGUSON Shane, FOTSO Geremi Sorele Njitap, GALLACHER John, GARBUTT Eric, GIBB Thomas, GIBSON Colin, GINOLA David, GIVEN Seamus John James, GLASS Stephen, GOMA Alain, GOOD Curtis, GOWLING Alan, GRAHAM Doug, GUIVARCH Stephane, GUTHRIE Daniel Sean, GUTHRIE Ronald George, GUTIERREZ Jonas Manuel, HAMANN Dietmar Johann Wolfgang, HAMILTON David, HARDWICK Steve, HARRIS Neil, HENDERSON James, HENDRIE John Grattan, HIBBITT Terry, HILL Jimmy, HILLEY David, HISLOP Neil Shaka, HODGES Glyn, HOTTIGER Marc, HUTCHISON Duncan, KADAR Tamas, KARELSE John, KEEGAN Kevin, KEELEY Glenn, KETSBAIA Temuri, KLUIVERT Patrick Stephan, KOENEN Fransiscus, LEACH Thomas, LEAVER Phillip, LEEK Ken, LINDSAY Duncan Morton, LUQUE Albert, MACDONALD Malcolm Ian, MARCELINO Elena Sierra, MARSHALL Gordon, MARTINS Obafemi Akinwunmi, MARVEAUX Sylvain, McGUIGAN John, MILNER James Phillip, MURRAY John James, MUTCH Alexander, NAYLOR Jimmy, NEALE Duncan, NELSON Jimmy, OBERTAN Gabriel Antoine, PAPAVASILIOU Nicos, PARK Oswald, PARKER Scott Matthew, PATON Harry, PEARCE Stuart, PEARSON Jim, PERCH James Robert, PISTONE Alessandro, QUINN Michael, RANGER Nile, REMY Loic, ROBERT Pierre Laurent, ROBERTSON John Grant, ROBINSON Paul, ROBINSON Ray, ROGERS Ehud, ROZEHNAL David Sebastian, RUSH Ian, RYAN John, SCOTT James, SCOULAR James, SERRANT Carl, SEYMOUR Stan, SHANKLEY Robert, SHEARER Alan, SIMPSON Daniel Peter, SIMPSON Ronald Campbell, SMITH Alan, SMITH Jimmy, SOLANO Nolberto Albino, STARLING Ronald William, STEWART Ian, STIMSON Mark, SUGGETT Colin, TAYLOR Colin, THORN Andy, TOMASSON Jon Dahl, TUOHY William, VARADI Imre, VENISON Barry, VIANA Hugo Miguel Ferreira, VIDUKA Mark, VUCKIC Haris, WARD Edward, WILKINSON Jack, WILSON Carl, WILSON John, WITHE Peter,

WOOD Edmund, WOODS Charles Morgan Parkinson, WRIGHT John Douglas, WRIGHT William

September

First Meetings:
Arsenal, Ayr United, Barcelona, Bohemians, Bradford City, Brentford, Burton Swifts, Cambridge United, Chelsea, Club Sport Maritimo, CSKA Sofia, Darwen, Dundee United, Everton, FC Levadia Tallinn, Feyenoord, FK Dynamo Kyyiv, Gillingham, Halifax Town, Halmstads Bollklubb, Hapoel Bnei Sakhnin, Heart of Midlothian, Internazionale Milan, Leicester Fosse, Loughborough Town, Morton, NAC Breda FC, Norwich City, Oldham Athletic, Partizan Belgrade, Royal Antwerp, Sheffield United, Wimbledon, Wolverhampton Wanderers, Woolwich Arsenal

Debut:
ABEID Mehdi, AGNEW William, AITKEN Andrew, ALDERSON Stuart, ALLAN Ronaldm, ALLAN Stanley, ALLEN Edward, AMEOBI Foluwashola, ANDERSON Andrew, ANDERSON John, BARNES John Charles Bryan, BARR J, BEARDSLEY Peter Andrew, BELL David, BEN ARFA Hatem, BENNIE Robert, BEYE Habib, BIRNIE Edward, BLACK Neville, BLACKBURN Robert, BLANTHORNE Robert, BOAM Stuart, BOOTH Curtis, BOWMAN J, BOYD James Murray, BROWN Harry, BROWNLIE John, BURGESS Charles, CALDWELL Steven, CALLACHAN Ralph, CAMBELL T, CAMPBELL Johnny, CAMPBELL Sulzeer Jeremiah, CASEY Tommy, CHANNON Michael Roger, CLARK Lee Robert, COLLINS James, COOPER Joe, CORNWELL John, COWAN William Duncan, CRATE Thomas, CRIELLY Robert, DA SILVA [MIRANDINHA] Francisco, DALGLISH Paul Kenneth, DAVIDSON Tom, DENMARK James, DISTIN Sylvain, DODGIN Norman, DONNACHIE Joseph, DUFFY Alan, DUNCAN John, DYSON Keith, ELLIOT Robert, EVANS Reg, FAYE Abdoulaye Diagne, FIDLER Albert, FINLAY John, FLANNIGAN David, FOYERS Robert, FRASER John, GARDNER David Richmond, GATTI Ignacio Maria Gonzalez, GHEE Thomas, GOODWILL Thomas, GRAHAM William, GUY Alan, HADDOCK Peter, HALL Alexander, HALL Thomas, HANNAH George, HARDINGE Harold Thomas William, HAREWOOD Marlon Anderson, HARRIS Albert, HARVEY John, HARVEY Bryan, HAY James, HEARD Pat, HEDLEY Richard, HENDERSON John, HIGGINS William, HOOPER Michael Dudley, HOWARD Pat, HOWIE James, HUGHES Gordon, ILEY James, JACKSON James, JEFFREY Harry, KEEN James, KEITH Richard, KELLY Gary, KELLY John, KELLY William, KERR Brian, KHIZANISHVILI Zurab, KING George, KING John, KINGSLEY

Matthew, KIRKMAN Alan, LAIDLAW Jimmy, LANG Tommy, LEE Robert Martin, LITTLE John, LOGAN James, LOW Wilfred, LOWERY W, LUALUA Lomano Tresor, MATHIE Alexander, McCRACKEN William, McDONALD John, McDONALD Neil Raymond, McINTOSH Robert, McKANE Joseph, McKAY William, McKINNON Robert, McMENEMY Harry, McMICHAEL Alfred, MILLER James, MILLER William, MITCHELL Stewart, NESBITT John, NEVIN George, NOBLE Peter, N'ZOGBIA Charles, ORR Ronald, OWEN Michael, PAILOR Bob, PARK John Bluey, PYKE George, QUINN C, RAMSAY Andrew, RENDELL Thomas, RICHARDSON Edward, RICHARDSON James Robert, ROBERTS Richard, ROBINSON Bobby, ROBSON Bryan Stanley, ROGERS Joseph, ROSS William Eric, ROSSI Giuseppe, RUSSELL Tom, RYDER Isaac, RYDER Joe, SCOTT Kevin Watson, SHIEL John, SIBIERSKI Antoine, SIMPSON Neil, SMELLIE Richard, SMITH John, SMITH Jack, SORLEY Jock, SOYE Jimmy, SPEEDIE Finlay Ballantyne, STEWART James, STEWART Willie, STOBBART George, STOTT James, SWINBURNE Tom, TATE Isaac, TAVERNIER James Henry, TAYLOR Allan, TEJADA Francisco Jimenez, THOMAS Andy, THOMPSON Willie, TIOTE Cheick Ismael, TOZER Ben, URWIN Tom, WALKER Andrew, WALKER Leonard, WALKER Thomas Jackson, WALLACE Joseph, WARD W.A., WARDROPE Willie, WARE Harry, WATTS Charles, WHITE John, WHITEHEAD Robert, WHITTON David, WILLIS David, WILSON William

October

First Meetings:

Ardwick, Athletic Bilbao, Bastia, Birmingham City, Charlton Athletic, Club Brugge Koninklijke Voetbalvere, Colchester United, Dynamo Kiev, FC Girondins de Bordeaux, FC Zurich, Fenerbache Spor Kulubu, Ferencvaros, Ipswich Town, Juventus, Lincoln City, Middlesbrough, Notts County, Oxford United, Panionios Athen, Pecsi Doza, Port Vale, PSV Eindhoven, Queens Park Rangers, Shrewsbury Town, Small Heath, Sporting Lisbon, Tranmere Rovers, West Hartlepool Rangers, Willington Athletic

Debut:

ACUNA Clarence, ALLCHURCH Ivor, APPLEBY Matty, AULD John, BAILEY John, BAMLETT Thomas, BARKER John, BARTON Joseph, BATTY Ronald, BLACKLEY John, BRAYSON Paul, BROADIS Ivor, BURNS Mick, BURRIDGE John, CAIE Sandy, CLISH Colin, CONNELL John, CRAGGS John Edward, CRAIG Derek, CRAWFORD Jimmy, CROSSON David, CUMMINGS Robert Douglas, CURRY Bill, DALTON George, DAVIES Reg, DAVIES Ronald Wyn, DICKSON Charles,

EASTHAM George, ELLISON Raymond, FASHANU Justinus, FOULKES William Isiah, GALLACHER Kevin William, GIBSON Robert, GILFILLAN Robert, GILLESPY Toby, GREEN Anthony, GREENER Ron, GUPPY Stephen Andrew, GUTHRIE Chris, HALLIDAY Bruce, HAMILTON Dereck Vivian, HEDLEY George, HEDWORTH Chris, HEWISON Robert, HIBBERT William, HILL John, INGLIS John, JACKSON Darren, JACKSON Peter, JOHNSEN Ronny, KEEN Errington, KEIR M, KITSON Paul, LAWRENCE James, LUKE George, MACFARLANE Alexander, MAGUIRE Gavin, MALCOLM Walter Grant, MARKIE John, MARTIN Dennis, McCREERY David, McINROY Albert, McNEE John, McWILLIAM Peter, MOONEY Tom, O'NEILL Leslie, PATERSON Bill, PATTEN John, PAYNE Lee, PEARSON Thomas Usher, PUDAN Albert, RAFFERTY William, RAMSAY Alexander Parrott, REAY Harry, ROWLANDSON Thomas Sowerby, SANTON Davide, SHACKLETON Len, SIMM William, SLOAN Scott, SUDDICK Alan, THOMPSON John, THOMSON Robert, TILDESLEY James, TODD Kevin, VEITCH Colin Campbell McKechnie, WADDLE Chris Roland, WAUGH Ken, WILKINSON Jonathan Montgomery, WILSON Billy, WILSON James, WITHE Chris, WOODBURN Jimmy

November

First Meetings:
AS Lucchese Libertas, Ascoli, Bournemouth, Bradford Park Avenue, Bristol City, Bury, Burton Wanderers, Coventry City, Darlington, Derby County, Dinamo Tbilisi, Doncaster Rovers, Eintracht Frankfurt, FC Basel, FC Porto, FC Sochaux Montbeliard, Leeds United, Leicester City, Liverpool, Metz, Middlesbrough Ironopolis, Millwall, Northwich Victoria, Nottingham Forest, RC Celta de Vigo, Rendall, Rotherham United, Southend United, Swansea City, U.S. Città di Palermo

Debut:
ANDERSON Stanley, BASSEDAS Christian, BELL John, BOWDEN Edwin, BRADLEY George Joseph, BRADLEY William, BRADY Garry, BRANDER George, BROWN Alan, BULLOCH Hugh, BUTLER Joe, CAMERON Hugh, CARROLL Andrew, CASSIDY Tommy, CHOPRA Rocky Michael, COWAN John, CRAIG Benny, CRAIG David James, DOUGLAS Angus, DOWSEY John, FERGUSON Duncan, FLEMING John, FUMACA Jose Rodrigues Alves Antunes, GARDNER Alexander, GARDNER Andrew, GARROW Herbert, GAYLE Howard, GAYNOR Tommy, GEORGIADIS Giorgos, GIBSON William, GODDARD Paul, GOSNELL Albert Arthur, GRAHAM Samuel, HALLIDAY William, HARPER Stephen Alan, HELDER Marino Rodrigues Cristova, HESLOP

George, HOCKEY Trevor, HOPE George, HUDSON Ray, HUGHES Aaron William, JOHNSON Peter, KRUL Tim, LENNOX Malcolm, LIVINGSTONE Archie, McCOLL Robert Smyth, McDERMIDD Robert, McDONALD Rob, McFAUL William Stewart, McKAY Robert, MEGSON Gary, MITCHELL Ian, MITTEN John, MONKHOUSE Alan, MULGREW Tommy, NAPIER Christopher, NICHOLSON Gary, O'BRIEN William Francis, O'NEILL Michael, PANCRATE Fabrice, PEDDIE John Hope, PUGH Kevin John, REID Alex, RICHARDSON Ord, ROBINSON David, ROGERS Thomas, SAUNDERS Wesley, SCANLON Albert Joseph, SHEPHERD Albert, SMITH Anthony, STENHOUSE Henry, STEVENSON Jimmy, TAPKEN Norman, THOMPSON Alan, THOMPSON William, THOMSON Jimmy, WALKER Nigel, WATSON John, WATSON Peter, WATSON Stephen Craig, WEAVER Sammy, WILLIAMS Ronald, WILLS Tom,

December

First Meetings:

AC Cesena, AS Bari, Burslem Port Vale, Crewe Alexandra, Gainsborough Trinity, Manchester United, Sheffield Wednesday, Stockport County, Stockton, Sunderland, Tow Law Town, Walsall Town Swifts, West Bromwich Albion

Debut:

ALLON Joseph Ball, APPLEBY Richard, BAIRD Ian, BARTLETT Thomas, BEDFORD Henry, BELL Anthony, BODIN Paul, BOLTON Hugh, BRADSHAW Darren, , BROCK Kevin, BURKE Dick, BURLEIGH Martin, BUSBY Vivian Dennis, CAHILL Tommy, CARLTON William, CARNEY Stephen, CARR John, CARR John, CARR Kevin, CLARK Albert, CRAIG Thomas Brooks, DUFFY Chris, EDGAR David, ELLIOTT David, EVANS Thomas, FINDLAY John, FORD David, GALLACHER Hugh Kilpatrick, GARNHAM Alfred, GASKELL Alex, GORRY Martin Christopher, GOURLAY Archibald, GRAHAM John, GRAY Andrew, GUY Lewis, HAGAN Alfred, HALE Ken, HARDY Stanley, HARFORD Mick, HARRIS Joseph, HUDSPETH Francis, HUNTINGDON Paul, HYND John, JEFFREY Michael Richard, KELLY David, KELLY Peter Anthony, LACKENBY George, LARNACH Mike, LAUGHTON Denis, LAW John, LITTLE Richard, LOUGHLIN Jimmy, LOW James, LOWES Tommy, MAITLAND Alfred, MARTIN Mick, McCLARENCE Joe, McCORMACK John, McGARRY Ronald James, McKINNEY William, McNAMEE John, McNEIL Matthew, MILNE William, MORDUE Thomas, MOWATT Archie, MULGROVE Keith, NESBIT Anthony, NULTY Geoff, O'BRIEN Patrick, OSTLER John,

PATERSON Tom, PEACOCK Gavin, RANSON Ray, REDHEAD Bill, RIDLEY James, ROBINSON Stuart, ROBLEDO Eduardo Oliver, ROBSON Thomas, ROEDER Glenn Victor, SANSOM Kenneth Graham, SCOTT George, SCOTT Matt, SHOULDER Alan, SMAILES Andrew, STEPHENSON Paul, STEWART Thomas, STOKOE Bob, THAIN John, TREWICK John, WATKIN George, WAUGH Robert, WHITEHURST Billy, WILLIS Robert, WILSON George, WILSON Joe, WILSON Joseph William, WILSON William, WINSTANLEY Graham, WRIGHTSON Jeffrey Joseph

About the Author

Born and bred in Newcastle and raised on a staple diet of stories of Hughie Gallacher from my Grandfather and Jackie Milburn from my Father there was never any doubt about where my football loyalties would lay.

Going to St James's Park for the first time as a child and seeing Newcastle play a goalless draw with Everton, which if memory serves me correctly was an instantly forgettable game from a football point of view - but to me it was just amazing. I'd never seen so many people in the same place at the same time before, almost 30,000 - I was hooked straight away.

Now, after more years than I care to remember, it's all about sharing the history of, to me, the greatest football club in the world with all you good people out there.

Also available by this Author:

Newcastle United Manager Menagerie

ISBN: 978-1514256015

All the statistics for every Newcastle United Manager from 1892 to 2015. From how many games they managed, to how many games they won, drew or lost, to how many goals their teams scored and conceded - and in what competitions.

If you ever wanted to know exactly how any manager performed, or wanted to compare any manager to any other - this book has the information for you to do so.

St James's Park
...well, at least the way the author would like it to be.

Lightning Source UK Ltd.
Milton Keynes UK
UKHW021254300620
365806UK00002B/218